Connecting Children

Connecting Children focuses on children's understandings of care and their views of different family lives including lone parent households, two-parent families, step families and foster care. Based upon an exciting mix of research methods including surveys and in-depth interviews with children, the book portrays the lives of children aged 10–12 and shows how families connect children in different ways, both in the household but also in their wider kinship networks. The children studied reflect upon family life, especially upon situations where their own family lives change dramatically, such as when parents divorce or are unable to care for them. The book:

- describes the different ways in which children consider their parents, siblings, relatives and friends to be important to them
- describes the conditions under which children think it possible and desirable for adults and children to enact the ethic of care
- portrays children as contributors to family life as well as recipients of their parents' care
- illustrates how children provide support to their families in both practical *and* emotional ways.

Children's conceptions of what constitutes a family emerge as highly inclusive, while at the same time they hold strong views about the importance of being part of a loving family. These notions are matched by inclusive practices so that children identify many significant others beyond the boundaries of the household.

This book will be of interest to social scientists and those working in education, social work, child care, counselling, social policy, childhood studies and the social sciences.

Julia Brannen is Professor in The Sociology of the Family and **Ellen Heptinstall** is a Research Officer, at Thomas Coram Research Unit, Institute of Education, University of London. **Kalwant Bhopal** is Lecturer in Sociology at Middlesex University.

Connecting Children

Care and family life in later childhood

Julia Brannen, Ellen Heptinstall & Kalwant Bhopal

London and New York

First published 2000
by RoutledgeFalmer
11 New Fetter Lane, London EC4P 4EE

Simultaneously published in the USA and Canada
by RoutledgeFalmer
29 West 35th Street, New York, NY 10001

RoutledgeFalmer is an imprint of the Taylor & Francis Group

Typeset in Sabon by Wearset, Boldon, Tyne and Wear
Printed and bound in Great Britain by TJ International Ltd,
Padstow, Cornwall

British Library Cataloguing in Publication Data
A catalogue record for this book is available from the British Library

Library of Congress Cataloguing in Publication Data
Brannen, Julia.
    Connecting children: care and family life in later childhood/Julia
Brannen, Ellen
    Heptinstall & Kalwant Bhopal.
        p. cm.
        1. Children–Family relationships. 2. Family life. 3. Parent and
child.
    4. Grandparent and child. 5. Brothers and sisters. I. Heptinstall, Ellen.
II. Bhopal,
    Kalwant. III. Title.

HQ767.9 .B734 2000
305.23–dc21
                                                          00-036885

ISBN 0-415-23094-2 (hbk)
ISBN 0-415-23095-0 (pbk)

Contents

Preface

Three concerns have driven this study. The first has been a desire to focus on children's care in families through the perspectives of children. While the contexts in which parents do their parenting and the ways in which they parent are much debated, children have been portrayed rather passively in these discussions. Little research has investigated how children themselves view family life and how they experience the variety of different types of families in which they grow up. A second concern has been to locate children's family lives within a broad framework of kinship and social networks, to enable children themselves to define the boundaries around their changing family lives and those they consider important to them. A third concern has been to understand how children make sense of care in all the different meanings of the term. The concept of care as moral commitment to others, a key motif of private life, is increasingly contested in public life, by the state and by the labour market. How children view and interpret commitment in different contexts and relationships, especially in family life, is an important question, therefore, together with other aspects of care – material, social and emotional. The study has sought to consider children as active providers of different types of care as well as recipients of their parents' care.

This book is the outcome of a research project, *Children's Concepts and Experience of Care in Different Household Contexts*, which was funded by the Department of Health over three years between 1996 and 1999, at the Thomas Coram Research Unit, Institute of Education, University of London. Inevitably, books are rarely completed during the duration of the project. Given the impermanence of researchers' contracts, many move on to other research while the writing is still in progress. This book is no exception and needs to be viewed in the context of such constraints. Moreover, the book should also be viewed in another way. Insofar as it speaks to children's lives as they experienced them, the insights the book offers are shaped by the questions which we, as adults, framed and put to children and by children's relationships to us as adults. As is suggested here, children's views of their family life provide only snap shots of their current everyday life. As some children's accounts also suggest, reflecting on family change was not something that many chose to do. Rather than acting as observers and commentators of family life, children lived *in* their families. In short, while children provide rich accounts which are both public and private, their voices were often muted.

I would like to express my gratitude to the funder of this work, in the person of Dr Carolyn Davies at the Department of Health who assisted the project in a number of ways, including sitting on the Project Advisory Group and the appointments panel which recruited the project team – my colleagues and collaborators – Dr Ellen Heptinstall, who had responsibility for the everyday running of the project, and Dr Kalwant Bhopal. I wish also to acknowledge the support of a number of other people who assisted the project, each in their particular way. Thanks are due to the members of the Advisory Group: Jane Allberry, Valerie Brasse, Carolyn Davies, Barbara Fletcher, Helen Jones, Judy Juhasz, David Matthews, Margaret O'Brien, Wendy Rose, and Carol Smart. We also wish to thank Charlie Owen for help with computing and data preparation; those who transcribed the interviews, especially Dr Julie Speedie who has also helped in the final stages of copy editing; Peter Aggleton for commenting on the manuscript; Franca Allen for inputting the Questionnaire Survey data; Nicky Castle for doing the vignette sketches for us; and Helen Thomas and Sharon Lawson who also assisted us. Dr Pamela Storey generously made herself available to the project team during a period of three months when I was a Visiting Professor in Norway.

Just as no research is done without its participants, so the greatest debt is owed to those who are the focus of the book, the children themselves. It was a rare privilege to carry out research with children. Speaking for myself, the children in the study challenged many of my assumptions and gave me a fresh view of children and childhood. My colleagues and I wish to thank them for providing us with such rich resources. In transforming their words into data, we hope we have done them justice.

Lastly, thanks are due to the children's gatekeepers who provided the team with access to children: head teachers and teachers; social workers and their managers; the children's foster carers and mothers who also participated generously in the study.

Julia Brannen, Fordingbridge, November 1999

1   Themes and concepts

The central focus of the book is children and their connection to family life: both the ways they are connected to families of different kinds and the connections they make themselves in terms of meanings, intentions and actions. While children and family life are typically bracketed together in academic and popular discourse, children themselves are rarely very visible. Moreover, as the absence of a child perspective in both the study of family life and other contexts bears witness to, the notion that children have the possibilities for agency and hold views, sentiments and opinions is at most misconceived or at least contentious. This book is about the ways in which children reflect upon family life both in terms of its meaning and importance to them, but also in terms of the ways in which they consider family life 'ought' to be enacted in the context of moral or normative guidelines. Based upon children's accounts of family life, the book describes and analyses the ways in which children, as competent and reflexive actors, make family connections: how they define family and family relationships and, in the context of those meanings, how they connect themselves to others in terms of the practice of social relationships. As we shall show, inclusive notions of family may be matched by inclusive practices so that many children define family connections well beyond the boundaries of the household.

Just as children are active participants in the process of making family connections, so too families connect children, at some times and in some contexts imperfectly, while at other times and in other spaces families serve to bind children into close-knit social networks. The different types of households in which children live in the context of parents' separation, divorce, and re-partnering are of course key determinants of the structures of children's family networks but, as we shall show, they are not the whole story.

This book focuses on four different types of family setting: two-parent families, lone mother families, step families and foster care.

Household structure *per se* does not alone influence children's experiences after family change. As other research has shown, the success of post divorce relationships and arrangements between children and non-resident parents vary a great deal over time and are governed by other criteria: the quality of everyday care and relationships; the understanding and respect children receive in families; and the ease with which children are able to negotiate and renegotiate dividing time between their parents, when they continue to have contact with both mothers and fathers (Smart, Wade and Neale 1998).

While the situation of foster children, whom we included in the study, is qualitatively different in some respects from other children, most foster children have been through family change related to their parents' relationships. Moreover, this group may be considered a critical case since children's entry into foster care involves negotiating often traumatic changes in family life and attributing meaning to these experiences and relationships.

Care as a concept

The engine of family life is 'care' – care defined in terms of the practice of caring, and care as a product of caring through being cared for. Central to the concept of care are notions of relationship and connectedness and a desire to create a sense of well-being in others. As feminist sociologists first recognised, care is a form of labour and love (see, for example, Finch and Groves 1983; Waerness 1984a, b; Land and Rose 1985; Ungerson 1990; Graham 1991; Thomas 1993). Feminists explored the consequences of care responsibilities, especially its material and practical aspects (housework and the division of labour), for gender relations and gender inequalities.

As Morgan (1996) argues, the emphasis placed on the work aspect of care occurred for very good reasons at the time since there was a need to redress the 'invisibility' of carers. But the main conceptual endeavour has now been extended to a wider examination of the concept with a new focus upon the cared for, and on the relationships between carers and cared for. As Morgan went on to suggest care encompasses a wide range of skills, acts and sentiments. It cuts across the Cartesian divide of mind and body. Caring is implicated in the conduct and experience of everyday life and is a constituent of cooperation and solidarity in social relations. As Waerness (1984a, b) first argued, caring occurs between different kinds of persons – symmetrical relations as well as between subordinates and superordinates, for example between children and parents. In the latter case, caring occurs where there is a significant 'need' to be cared for which may be socially constructed in terms of a person's age. Those cared for are typically constructed as dependents since they are the recipients of others' care and are deemed to rely upon others taking care of them. In the case of foster children, caring has a particular resonance. Because of parents' failure to care sufficiently for children, children are 'looked after', that is, they are entrusted to the care of the state. Moreover, according to British social policy, the every-day care of foster children is carried out by those who are *not* invested with general responsibility for the children; this responsibility remains with the state (social services) and with their birth parents.

Much of the theoretical and empirical analysis of care has linked care with gender and has focused upon understanding the processes by which certain categories of (female) persons are expected to take responsibility for caring about and caring for others. These processes bring about the incorporation of care as a central tenet of gendered identities. Responsibility, however, puts those giving care in positions of power; care implies the exercise of control (Walkerdine and Lucey 1989). While in the eye and intention of the care giver, care is designed to produce positive consequences, from the position and perspective of the cared for, care may be experienced as constraint. For example, for a frail elderly person, care may be experienced as a feeling of dependence or loss of self identity. However, children may experience their parents' care as both constraint and liberation, as parents seek to foster in chil-dren a sense of independence but also to protect them from risk and danger. Yet resentment of care as control within family relations is likely to be offset or balanced out by the perception of care as love. Indeed, control within family relations may be understood as an expres-sion of 'caring about'. In short, care is a double-edged concept which overlaps with a variety of other concepts including power and control.

As Mason (1996) argues, drawing upon the work of Sevenhuijsen (1993) and Tronto (1993), care raises critical central questions to do with relationships and their negotiation; these implicate other concepts of dependency, responsibility, and competence in providing care. Many of these concepts have been developed in relation to care conceptualised as a practical activity and so less conceptual emphasis has been placed upon orientations to care, which is not to say, as Mason argues, that care should not be divorced from caring activity. Rather than thinking of care as either labour or love, Mason suggests that it is more useful to conceptualise the practical activity of 'caring for' someone as intrinsic to care as 'sentient activity' – 'caring about some one' and being atten-tive to the needs of others. Mason goes on to suggest sentient activity may develop into 'active sensibility' in which persons come to feel responsible for and committed to other persons.

Care is a form of ethical activity and moral thinking which, as Mason

(1996) argues, is not well captured by the dichotomous approach which has been applied to care as either love or labour. Drawing on the work of Gilligan (1982) and the writing of Benhabib (1992), Smart and Neale (1998) argue that care adds a moral dimension to the avoidance and repair of harm. In creating and maintaining committed and cooperative relations with others, care becomes a central rather than a peripheral moral question. As Finch has argued (1989) and demonstrated (Finch and Mason 1993), in modern British society family obligations are no longer defined in terms of an absolute duty to care, nor is there a normative consensus concerning the rules about kin support. Finch (1989) offers a framework for interpreting the ways in which individuals apply moral rules in everyday life concerning the 'proper thing to do'. While people endorse general principles, they make decisions in particular circumstances and with respect to a variety of claims which may also have a moral dimension. Thus, while people may agree with a principle about caring for kin in the abstract, they may disagree about the 'right thing to do' in a particular circumstance. Thus, morality in everyday life is constantly negotiated in relation to particular situations, social conditions, the specific history of social relationships and in the context of other, often competing moral claims and social norms.

Concepts of care as they apply to parent/child relations have been shaped by social constructions of motherhood and childhood – typically mothers are assumed to have responsibility for children, and children are portrayed as their passive dependants. While a main concern in the book is with parenting as care, the hope is to provide an interpretation of children as active co-participants in their parents' care, as children themselves make sense of it, and to take into account the experience and pursuit of parental care as control. A second concern is to understand the ways in which children construct care as a moral activity and the conditions under which they consider both adults and children are committed to the ethic of care and its practice. A third consideration is to add to the body of knowledge concerning children's active contribution to care. In this regard, following Mason's helpful conceptual distinctions, we are concerned not only to identify the practical contributions children make (care as work) but also to identify whether and when children engage in sentient activity – that is, they identify and understand the feelings and needs of others so that they may respond to them appropriately. In this regard, if it is the case that children engage in sentient activity, then it may be possible to detect the processes by which sentient activity turns into active sensibility. In short, we may begin to understand how children's own caring identities are constructed both through expectations concerning the enactment of the ethic of care (under their own agency) and through their experiences of others' care.

Family life and later childhood

In this book, we are principally concerned with children's perspectives of their care experiences in families and their contribution to family life. As we shall argue, these perspectives are shaped by what it means to be 'a child', in particular a child in later childhood (11–13), as well as meanings of the term 'family'. Thus childhood constitutes an important social construction which underlies both children's and parents' perspectives. The focus on childhood, as a new area of study, has challenged the long domination of theories of children's psychological and biological development in which the notion of society, insofar as it existed, was relegated to 'social and cultural factors'. In the new sociology of childhood, a conceptual shift has taken place whereby the notion of the child as 'project' and the notion of child as 'becoming' have given way to the concept of the child as 'being' (Hallden 1991). In this conceptualisation, children are considered to have abilities and competencies which make them active participants in social settings rather than 'adults in waiting' with characters which are yet to be forged.

As others have commented (for example, Frones 1994), two contradictory pictures emerge of family life and its relation to children's childhoods. The first suggests the growth in importance of institutions which organise and influence children's lives and the increasing power of experts and professionals both inside and outside family life. The second picture emphasises the importance of family life as a source of private meaning and influence. In this latter scenario, parents are depicted as economic providers of children's welfare and well-being and as stimulators and facilitators of children's social, emotional and intellectual development. As these two scenarios suggest, family life has both gained and lost importance (Frones 1994).

These two pictures of family life are underpinned by two social processes influencing childhood: individualisation and institutionalisation (Frones 1994). Individualisation turns on the process by which children are enabled and encouraged to become individual personalities in social and symbolic spheres: not only the right to a share, albeit usually a lesser share, of resources and status, but the right to an agentic voice – to occupy a space in the symbolic order of discourse. According to individualisation theory, the practice of modern family life is characterised by 'negotiation' in which, in practice, children participate to varying degrees, but are conceptualised as having the capacity to do so

(Andenaes and Haavind 1993; Andenaes 1996; Dahlberg 1996; Alanen 1998). In this model of family life, openness and rights are endorsed, on the one hand, but in the context of negotiated contracts between parents and children, on the other.

Children's childhoods are also shaped by processes of institutionalisation. Foster children, a group included in our study, are especially subject to these processes since they are looked after by the state. British social policy no longer places most 'looked after' children in institutional care. However, foster carers are no longer considered to be substitute families; indeed, foster carers (note the terminology) are not *in loco parentis* since responsibility is shared between the state (social services) and children's birth parents. In this study, all the children were experiencing a new form of institutional setting as they made the transition from primary to secondary school. The transition to secondary school is typically assumed to involve an increase in the structuring of children's lives as they approach the serious business of working for educational qualifications. But it also assumes a growth in children's autonomy, thereby implicating the process of individualisation. The move to secondary school gives children a little more responsibility for the self. Inside school, children are expected to have increased responsibility: for example, for managing their mobility between classrooms, for interpreting a differentiated school curriculum, and for negotiating new peer relationships. Outside school, they typically start to travel to school by themselves (secondary schools are usually further from home than primary schools) and take up extra-curricular activities. While some of these changes are outside the control of parents, parents are likely to encourage children to be more personally responsible and may endeavour to support them backstage. But children must negotiate school environments which are strongly bounded (schools are segregated from the outside world) and which are strongly hierarchical (by age and ability groups). Moreover, with the growth of parental involvement and home–school contracts, some of the autonomy children gain when they start secondary school may well be cancelled out as a result of the weakening of boundaries between school and home.

If, as Frones (1994) argues, the phases of childhood which have been most open to change are later childhood and early adolescence (ages 11–14), then individualisation processes are likely to be at their most intense not only during, but in the lead up to, this 'new puberty'. In later childhood, children must acquire many social competences as they traverse its life course transitions, which may require them to develop autonomy and negotiate scope for action. However, the practice of new competencies will vary according to different patterns of peer culture, parent/child relations and the institutionalisation of childhood.

Institutionalisation and individualisation often create tensions for children and push in different directions. One critical issue for children in later childhood is the negotiation of their continuing attachment to family in the context of the need to become competent in new social arenas and relationships. Related to this is learning to negotiate relationships and roles across different contexts, with their different norms and expectations, and how to negotiate the boundaries between different institutional arenas – school, home, peer groups. These things children must do in a climate in which many normative expectations prescribe that children should be autonomous or self regulating. Children today are frequently expected to identify and 'read the rules' for themselves (Bernstein 1996). For foster children, compared with community children, these processes of individualisation and institutionalisation stand in particular opposition as foster children are constrained both by their parents' actions (or inaction) and by the authority of professionals and the decisions they take on their behalf. At the same time, foster children are expected to achieve independence and to leave care at an earlier age, that is compared with most young people who now tend to remain economically dependent on parents for longer periods. While having more immediate expectations of independent living, foster children have the least social capital to prepare themselves for it.

For parents, the tension between individualisation and institutionalisation processes is different. Parents are expected to continue to regulate their children but to cede some overt control to them. Typically, in the context of their earlier protective role, parents may consider the increase in responsibility and the greater mobility of young people in their early teens, compared with their younger years, to be fraught with risks and hazards, especially in the context of the growth of the 'risk society', for example increased traffic on the streets (Hillman et al. 1991), and the weakening of community controls, for example fewer mothers and younger children in the community (with the rise in mothers' employment (Brannen et al. 1997) and in the institutional care of young children). In the context of the transition to secondary school, parents may feel a greater urge to control their children while at the same time their methods of upbringing and their expectations of children's self regulation deem otherwise.

In this context, trust relations which typically operate in relations between parents and children may need to be renegotiated when children are assumed to require or seek greater autonomy. Parents have to decide to exert less control or exert it differently. There is a balance to be struck between being overly caring and controlling – the risk of being overprotective – and encouraging and allowing children to extend their sphere of autonomous activity. A dilemma for parents is the balance between three sources of control of children: their own care and control; professional control or state control (in critical circumstances when children are 'out of control'); children's own self regulation. For foster carers, the balance is complicated by the fact that, since foster children are not their responsibility in principle except in a practical, everyday sense, foster children remain the responsibility of their biological parents and of social services.

Children's care in families: some recent policy influences

A central theme in this book concerns children's experiences of care, principally the care provided by parents. As in the past, and so on in the present, family life and parenting continue to be highly contested public issues. In its genesis and implementation, public policy has a complex relationship to public discourse but indirectly influences the views of citizens. Four recent developments which are influential in current public discourse are worth mentioning and are germane to the issues covered here.

First, there is the genderless discourse of 'parental responsibility' which springs from government's desire to shed its welfarist responsibilities in its concern to disperse responsibility and thereby encourage 'active citizenship'. This renewed emphasis on parental responsibility coincides with the state's concern to transform each and every parent into economic providers by advocating entry to the labour market, while at the same time insisting that children are parents' 'private responsibilities' and that child care is an issue of 'parental choice' (Brannen 1999). In respect of children who are placed in the care of the state, the principle of birth parents sharing responsibility has already been noted.

Second, despite the emphasis on parental responsibility, parenting continues to be problematised and subjected to the surveillance of experts, as has long been the case. This recent increase in the 'pedagogisation' of parenting means that, in many spheres of children's lives, parents are no longer simply subjected to professionals' authority; parents are made 'partners' with experts in the shaping of children's lives. Underpinned by parent education, parents are constituted, via 'parent involvement', 'parent participation' and 'parent partnership', as collaborators with professionals in schools, social services and the law. However, it is the form in which control by experts is exerted that has changed over time rather than the fact of control itself, as the history of British social policy demonstrates, for example concerning the direct and indirect surveillance to which working-class mothers have histori-cally been subject (see, for example, Davin 1978; Riley 1981). New pol-icies, for example home–school contracts, in which parents are made accountable for their children's behaviour in school and on the street, go against the spirit of other reforms which grant children a greater sense of participation and ownership such as pupil involvement and citizen education (Edwards and Alldred 1999b).

Third, the household settings in which parents care for children con-tinue to be a matter of much political and public policy debate in which the desirability of particular family forms (married, two-birth parents) is asserted, a concern underpinned by ideological certainties of what 'a proper family' should look like. One important policy development which shapes children's and parents' understandings of parenting con-cerns the ways in which the law treats parent/child relations after divorce. Policy discourses about family change – when both parents no longer live in the same household – have been subject to recent trans-formation broadly conceptualised as a move from valuing social parenthood to biological parenthood (Maclean and Eekelaar 1997).

Over the past twenty five years there has also been a significant shift in the way in which the post-divorce family is conceptualised in legal and political discourse. 'The dominant model of the lone parent/recon-stituted family, with its roots in the institution of marriage/remarriage, the bounded family unit and the clear gendering of parenthood has gradually given way to the new biological, co-parenting family, with its roots in increasingly institutionalized status of biological parenthood, cross household parenting and the blurring of gender roles (so that a newly articulated fatherhood now takes its place alongside a somewhat more muted motherhood)' (Neale, Wade and Smart 1998: 41). With this new emphasis on biological parenthood – upon separated biologi-cal parents taking shared responsibility for the child, children's ties to their birth parents are given new public significance. As increasing numbers of families in Britain experience changes in family forms over the life course, it is perhaps surprising that social policy has not pursued a different direction and emphasised the social ties of children to a variety of family members and carers, whether birth parents or not.

Fourth, under the provisions of the 1989 Children Act, and in line with the United Nations Convention on the Rights of the Child 1991, family law has granted children some rights to self expression and participation. As Neale and Smart note: 'Children may have their wishes and feelings ascertained under the welfare checklist (s. l(3)); they can institute court proceedings in their own right and be made parties to a dispute with their own legal representation' (Neale and Smart 1998: 10–11). This acknowl-edgement of children's agency following parents' divorce or, in the case of public law, children taken into the care of the state, is however heavily constrained in practice. As Roche (1996) argues, professional power and standing tend to be enhanced; for whether children's views are sought or acted on depends upon adult perceptions of whether children are competent enough to define their own needs (Neal, Wade and Smart, 1998). How far children themselves consider that children should be consulted in such matters is a matter of some considerable empirical interest.

These policy developments and debates concerning the emphasis on parental responsibility, the professionalisation of parenting, the prioritising of children's families of origin in the context of family change, and granting children some legal, albeit mainly symbolic, agency, are pervasive in public discourse and form part of the backcloth against which children make sense of family life.

Children's care in families: the study's research questions

In family research and certainly in studies of younger children, children have been typically conceptualised as passive recipients and socialised dependants of parents' and adults' care. As Hockey and James (1993) argue, such social constructions of children result in a denial of children's personhood and render them incompetent in adult spheres. In adopting a 'child perspective' in this study, we consider how children, as reflexive, moral agents themselves make sense of their experiences of parents' care and how they, as active co-contributors to care, interpret moral imperatives to care for, and to cooperate with, others. However, children's views about care are not unmediated; they should not be considered as somehow independent of adult society. They need also to be considered in the context of dominant public discourses which focus on matters about which children may also have views – debates about the structure of the family, the desirability of divorce and its effects upon children, the nature of parenthood and parenting, and what it means to be a 'child'.

Our approach recognised that caring involves exercising intra- and inter-personal competencies which are culturally shaped and enacted in different social milieux, albeit our main concern here is with family life. These milieux are structurally organised according to principles of age, generation and authority relations and by markers of power and prestige. While emphasising children's agency, a child perspective must also take account of structural influences, notably children's often unequal status *vis-à-vis* adults. In this study, we sought to examine children's views of how care should be exercised in different contexts and in particular situations, not only family life. As we suggest, the ethic of care is negotiated according to the particular situation, and the person's positioning and resources available within that situation. Many of the settings and contexts children inhabit are typically structured by children's status as recipients of care, while other settings are less adult dominated but are structured by social hierarchies among children themselves. It is also necessary to consider that the ethic of care may compete with other context-specific norms between which children will have to negotiate.

In addition, social relations within a context are influenced by the permeability of the boundaries around it (James and Prout 1996). Strong boundaries in social relations tend to provide for exclusivity, for example the 'attachment' of mothers to their young children, whereas groups which operate with weaker boundaries are likely to be more inclusive in their caring orientations and practices. Where children's family relationships cross different social settings, notably when their parents live in different households, and where children have a multiplicity of carers (biological parents, step parents and foster carers), children's experience of care and their beliefs about care will be shaped by the permeability of the boundaries between these contexts. While this study did not provide a detailed examination of children's perspectives in other contexts, it did seek to enable children to express their concerns and discuss their relationships beyond the limits of their households in their wider social networks.

In short, the study's approach was to investigate the meanings children attach to concepts of care primarily in relation to family life, including Morgan's distinctions between care as acts, intentions and sentiments (Morgan 1996).

The research design through which we chose to address these conceptual issues was a community sample of children in which we embedded sub samples of children growing up in four family settings – lone parents, step families and two-parent families and children in foster care. While we considered that the foster children were like other children, we also recognised differences: in having rather more adults in charge of them and having experienced rather more discontinuity in their lives and more traumatic family life transitions. Despite these differences, we thought it important to redress the way in which researchers have traditionally focused on these children as special and different and to include them in a study of 'normal' childhood.

The structure of the book reflects the conceptual concerns of the study. First, in Chapter 2, we seek to examine children's intentions as moral actors: how they interpret the requirement to care in a range of situations, not only in families. In this regard, using the vignette technique, we have analysed their views of children and adults as providers of care in particular contexts. Next, in Chapter 3, we examine how children gave meaning to notions of family and household structure. We also seek to identify the range of persons children considered to be the important people in their lives and, in the context of family change, their active family networks as they existed at the moment of the study. In the following chapter, Chapter 4, we consider children's perspectives and sentiments concerning family change and the ways in which they portrayed their own role in the relevant social transitions – becoming a lone parent family, becoming a step family, moving into foster care – and their current lives in these different family contexts. In accordance with our conceptual concern with children's cultural and moral understandings at a general level, we examine in Chapter 5 children's views of motherhood and fatherhood and in the same chapter, using children's maps of their significant others, we examine the particular meanings children attached to their own relationships with their parents. Similarly, drawing on material based on children's maps of their significant others, in Chapters 6 and 7 we examine the importance children placed upon their siblings in the context of different family structures and practices, together with a variety of significant others including grandparents, relatives, friends, and 'formal others'. In accordance with our desire to examine children's actions and contributions to care, in Chapter 8 we follow in the footsteps of other researchers to examine children's contribution to the domestic economy (O'Brien 1995; Morrow 1996) but are, in addition, interested in understanding children as emotional actors in taking the position of the other and responding to others' feelings and needs (including parents and other family members). In this chapter, as in other chapters, social constructions of what a child 'is' come to the fore, with implications for children's contribution to and participation in the ethic of care. Finally, but not least importantly, in Chapter 9, we address the issue of parents' power over children's lives in terms of the control they exert in caring for their children and the ways in which children understood and responded to parents' exercise of control.

The study's design and methods

Our methodological approach in the study involved the following research strategy. We sought to combine an extensive approach to understand the ways in which children's views and practices were distributed across a wide range of children in the community, with an intensive approach in which we sought to elicit the perspectives of particular groups of children. We included a range of methods which took account of children's interests and competences, while being attentive to the sensitive nature of family life and family change. We included mothers' views of children's experiences since mothers were key figures in children's family lives but also because mothers could provide important contextual material.

Broadly, the study encompassed three phases of fieldwork. In the first phase, we carried out a self completion Questionnaire Survey in schools (N = 941 pupils). We administered the questionnaire to children in their last year of primary school (10–11-year-olds) and in their first year of secondary school (11–12-year-olds). In addition to providing extensive data on children's views according to a number of key structural variables – gender, household type, social class, ethnic background, parents' employment and occupations, the Questionnaire Survey's second purpose was to help identify children for the case study interviews notably living in different family forms.

Following the school Questionnaire Survey, we conducted seven school-located focus groups in which children were invited to discuss issues concerning care and family life. Their particular purpose was to develop the interview schedule and they proved to be particularly helpful in drawing up vignette situations which we used in the case study interviews. The focus groups also directed us towards the use of family trees as children showed interest in identifying their extended kin.

In the third phase, we conducted 63 interviews with four groups of children living in the following household forms: two-parent, lone mother, step father and foster care. The interviews, which covered children's particular experiences of care and caring, were conducted separately with mothers or children's main carers. Embedded in the interviews were a number of other methods which included a family tree, a map for locating significant others, and vignettes. As James (1995) and Mauthner (1997) suggest, children have different competences, and may be especially skilled in drawing and are used to visual techniques.

The Questionnaire Survey

The Questionnaire Survey was not intended to be representative of British school children. Rather, we sought to paint a picture of children attending state schools and living in typical London neighbourhoods including children from different ethnic groups. As noted already, the Survey targeted 10–12-year-olds in their first year at secondary schools and their last year of primary school. We selected mixed-sex state schools in two Local Education Authorities in South London, recognising the possibility of a working-class bias since, in London, middle-class parents often opt for 'out of borough' selective schools or use the independent sector. The schools had sizeable proportions of minority ethnic groups. For each of the three secondary schools we chose, we selected three 'feeder' primary schools. In practice, one of the secondary schools which was grant maintained drew its intake from a wider catchment area.

In selecting the schools, we examined the small area census data for different wards within each borough which had significant proportions of Black and South Asian origin pupils and an equal spread of children of middle-class and working-class parents. School profiles, as they were advertised in published documents and on the Internet, were also examined. Through direct approaches to the head of schools and Local Education Authorities (LEAs), we gained access to three secondary schools and nine primary schools in two LEAS, although two initially selected secondary schools and one primary school declined to take part. The research team visited each of the schools to discuss access and the nature of the study. The heads agreed to our request to seek parents' permission for their children to participate. This was done by letters written by the schools to the parents and taken home by the children. If parents did not withhold their permission, the assumption was made that children were allowed to take part. Only one parent refused permission. In recompense for the schools' help, the researchers offered to provide each school with detailed analyses for their school of some of the survey questions which were of educational interest to them. This offer was accepted and the data duly provided.

Between January and March 1997, the Questionnaire Survey was administered to all Year 6 children in the primary schools and Year 7 in the secondary schools. The questionnaire consisted of mainly closed questions but some open-ended questions were also included. It was administered by the research team, who introduced the study to the children and gave instructions about completing the questionnaire, in the formal conditions of the classroom usually in a double lesson period, in secondary schools usually during Personal, Social and Health Education (PSHE) or Religious Education (RE). Among a number of issues, the researchers explained that the study was about children's views and experience of everyday life. They emphasised confidentiality, the right not to answer a question (children were not offered the right to withdraw altogether), and the purpose of the identifier codes on each child's questionnaire. Two researchers were present in each class and divided their time in helping children who had difficulties in reading or particular queries.

Children's responses

The final achieved sample consisted of 941 children – 349 in the last year of primary school and 592 in the first year of secondary school. The overall response rate of 88% was similar for secondary and primary schools. A handful of children were excluded by teachers, usually for language reasons or 'special needs', and a couple of cases because of emotional problems. A chain reaction occurred in one class when two children objected to the survey because they thought questions about parents' jobs 'too personal' which led to the withdrawal of nine other children. However, much the greater part of the non-response rate was due to children's absence (9%), while 22 questionnaires were unusable because children had not completed their personal details.

Given that children were constrained to participate in the survey, we did not expect them to be overly enthusiastic about it. One of the last questions on the questionnaire concerned their views of the survey. As our study and those of other researchers (see for example, Edwards and Alldred 1999a) suggest, few children expressed active dislike in partici- pating: in our study, just over half (52%) said they did not mind doing it, while 30% suggested they enjoyed it, 12% ticked the 'partly like/partly dislike' option and 6% ticked the dislike option. No differ- ences in response to this question were found on household form or other factors with one exception: girls were more likely to say they liked filling in the questionnaire while boys were more likely to dislike or 'not mind'. Children were also invited to make any comment they wished at the end of the questionnaire. Over half of the comments (32/50) were about the questionnaire, more than half of which were positive, while other children commented critically on the 'personal' nature of some of the questions. But on the whole the children appeared very interested in completing the questionnaire while, as we left the classroom, a few chil- dren asked, 'Will you be coming back?' and 'Can we do this again?' A few children sought advice about personal or family problems either verbally or, in one case, on the questionnaire. We endeavoured to refer them to appropriate sources of help without breaking confidentiality.

School differences and sample characteristics

We chose schools with a reasonable representation of Black children – in each school they comprised at least a fifth of the year groups. However, South Asian origin children were much less evenly distrib- uted across schools. In addition, there were school differences by gender, with significantly fewer girls in the secondary schools compared with the reverse situation in primary schools where, in seven of the nine schools, girls were in the majority. Clearly, single sex schools are preferred at secondary level. Moreover, since two thirds of the schools sample was accounted for by the three secondary schools, secondary school differences are likely to be more important, as we indeed found (Table 1.1.1 and 1.1.2, Appendix). While the secondary school samples were disproportionately male (57% versus 40% in primary schools) and contained similar proportions of Black children (around a quarter), one secondary school had a more middle-class intake (with half of fathers in professional or managerial jobs as compared to only 10–15% in the other two secondary schools) and a high proportion of South Asian origin children (27% as compared with 4–5% in the other two secondary schools). In another secondary school, there was a particularly high concentration of lone parent children (40% compared with 23% and 17%), while both this school and the third secondary school were predominantly working class, according to both mothers' and fathers' occupations (Registrar General's Socio-economic groups non-manual and below). A comparison of secondary and primary schools produces fewer systematic biases, with the exception of ethnic origin and a sex imbalance (57% of primary school pupils were girls and 40% were boys), which suggests that the primary school samples more or less match the secondary school samples (Table 1.1.2, Appendix).

Overall, our Survey sample included more boys than girls (54% versus 46%). The measure of ethnicity referred to here is based on self report, with half the sample classifying themselves as White, UK origin (49%), 25% as Black African or Black Caribbean, 17% as South Asian origin, and 10% as 'other' (for example, mixed race)[1] (Table 1.2, Appendix). Two thirds of the Survey sample were living in two-birth-parent families at the time of the Survey (66%), just under one quarter in lone parent families (24%, of whom 93% were lone mothers), 9% in step families, and 2% (15 children) were living with grandparents or in foster care (Table 1.3, Appendix). The proportion of step family children (9%) was similar to the figure of 7% reported for all households with children in the UK for 1991–2 (Haskey 1994) and to the 8% figure given by the National Child Development Study (Ferri and Smith 1998). The proportion of children in lone mother families (24%) was slightly higher than national estimates of 19% in 1996–7 (*Social Trends* 1998). Significantly more South Asian origin children lived in two-parent households (90%) compared with under half of Black children (47%), 68% white UK origin children and 61% of the 'other' ethnic group. Lone parent families were disproportionately Black, while step family children were equally likely to be Black or white (Table 1.3, Appendix).

Like mothers nationally, who have a youngest child aged between 11 and 16 (1994 figures: Brannen et al. 1997), one third of children's mothers were employed full time (33%), and a quarter part time (27%), for 7% of cases it was unclear if mothers were part or full time, and a third was non-employed (34%) (Table 1.4, Appendix). Mothers were more likely to be working if their children had no siblings or were the youngest child and similarly, if there were fewer siblings (two or less). Like mothers nationally, more white mothers and Black mothers were employed than South Asian origin and other mothers. Lone mothers were equally likely to be employed as not employed, as compared with mothers nationally who have slightly younger children (that is, in the children's age group 5 to 9 years) (Holtermann et al. 1999); in our study, 47% were employed – 25% full time and 22% part time. Compared with two-parent households, lone parent households were much more likely not to have an earner. Among fathers, under three-quarters were said to be working full time or unspecified hours (69%), 14% were said to be working part time and 14% were not in employment for a variety of reasons (Table 1.5, Appendix).

As noted, our sampling strategies had consequences for the social class composition of the sample, even though we sought a roughly equal spread. By sampling state secondary schools in London, we could not achieve this. Whether we focus on fathers' or mothers' occupations, the sample emerged as predominantly working class, with only a third of resident employed fathers and mothers reported to be in higher status jobs (professional or managerial), (36% of couple mothers and 23% of lone mothers) (Table 1.6, Appendix). There were, moreover, some problems in eliciting from children their parents' occupations. In contrast to their attitudes to the topic of the study, namely family life, children considered parents' occupations to be much more sensitive issues. Some 11% of children failed to reply to the question on fathers' occupations, and 3% gave inadequate information or said they did not know. In the case of mothers, 13% failed to answer questions about their mothers' jobs. However, the great majority of children gave sufficient information to enable the researchers to code their parents' occupations according to the Registrar General's classification.

The case study sample

As we have explained, we wanted the case study children to reflect three different household forms. We planned to obtain three equal sized groups of children via the Questionnaire Survey: two-birth-parent households, lone mother households and step father households (16 in each group, with equal numbers of boys and girls in each). Again, we returned to the schools and discussed our request for access to the relevant children. The school heads contacted parents for permission to pass on children's addresses and phone numbers. Only one parent in a primary school declined permission and seven parents from the secondary school. In order to achieve as wide a spread of children as possible by ethnicity and social class in each group, we obtained more addresses than we needed – 120 in total. It proved difficult to achieve three equally-distributed groups according to household type, ethnicity and social class for the following reasons. First, as noted, ethnicity was highly associated with household form. Second, many parents did not refuse outright but postponed their participation, making it difficult to assess the likely characteristics of the final sample. Third, in two cases, children gave different accounts of their family form from that which appeared to exist at the time of the interview (one lone mother family turned out to be a step father family at interview and vice versa) and in one case the family form had changed in the intervening period.

Following some pilot interviews (9 mothers and 7 children), access to which was obtained through other strategies (personal contacts and snowballing), fieldwork began in September 1997 and continued until February 1998. In order to seek the families' permission, the research team sent letters to the mothers and enclosed pamphlets about the study, one for the mother and one for the child. The researchers (Ellen and Kalwant) telephoned the mothers and explained the study and asked if they were willing to participate and, if so, whether they would ask the children if they wanted to take part. The researchers telephoned again to check with the mothers but felt that in many cases the mothers had made the decisions on the children's behalf. In the lone mother, step father and two-parent groups, around 69 families were approached who met the study criteria (including the balance of sexes and ethnicity as well as family type), with a response rate of 75% for the lone mother group ($n = 18$), 71% for the two-parent group (14 mothers, 15 children), and 65% for the step family group ($n = 15$). Eleven mothers said they did not wish to participate, five families had moved out of the area, two mothers declined because of family illness and trauma, one family was no longer a step family, and one mother declined for language reasons. In only two cases, it was clear that children had refused to participate. It was difficult to determine whether mothers had consulted children about participating in the research.

In order to find the foster care group, access was more complicated, with more gatekeepers and hence more difficulty in accessing the total relevant populations of children looked after by local authorities. We approached two Social Services Departments (SSD) in each Local Authority in which we carried out the Survey. We requested access to children in the age group 11–12, but because of insufficient numbers had eventually to include a couple of 13-year-olds. We also requested access to children who had been in care for at least 2 years: for comparability purposes (with the other groups in the Interview Study) and for ethical reasons since we thought that foster children to be interviewed ought to have had time to settle into their foster care placements. Since one SSD was too busy at the time to take part, we had to seek cooperation from an SSD in a third Local Authority. The processes of gaining access to foster children were quite different in the two SSDs. In one case, the researcher who took charge of this exercise had much more room to negotiate and was able to gain some assessment of the potential pool of foster children since she was given the full list and direct access to the children's social workers. This SSD eventually produced a list of 31 children's names – all the children in foster care in that authority who fulfilled the criteria we specified, while the other SSD produced only six names. However, the social workers in the first SSD eventually excluded ten of the 31 children for a range of reasons including children's disabilities. As a result of the method of access granted by the SSDs, we are able to estimate a 'true' response rate for one SSD where we obtained access to eleven of the original 31 children on the list, while in the second SSD we secured the consent of four out of six children.

The process of obtaining access to foster children was lengthy, taking several months and requiring visits to SSDs, numerous telephone calls and form chasing. Social workers rarely responded to the researchers' request to complete a form or return telephone calls. In order to comply with the 1989 Children Act, social workers said they were required to secure birth parents' permission for their children's participation in our study, although in cases where birth parents had no fixed address or were considered mentally unfit to give consent, social workers made the decision on their behalf. We had, therefore, to negotiate with three sets of gatekeepers before we were able to ask children directly whether they wanted to take part in the study: social workers, birth parents and foster carers. Out of a total of 37 original names we were given, six children refused to take part and four birth parents refused their permission. All the foster carers approached agreed to participate. Eight boys and seven girls were interviewed, including two sets of siblings (two sisters and one brother and sister). Despite these lengthy negotiations, interviews with the foster children started on time. Because of the number of gatekeepers and the difficulty of making contact with social workers and birth parents, foster children were rather more constrained in their opportunity to participate in the study as in other matters (Chapter 9).

The final sample of 63 children (31 girls and 32 boys) included: 15 two-parent children; 18 lone mother children; 15 step father children;

and 15 foster children. In aiming to include a substantial number of children of South Asian origin children and Black children, we could not ensure they would be distributed evenly across the household types. Of the 12 South Asian origin children, nine were in two-parent households and of the 17 Black children, six were in lone mother families and four in step father families (Table 1.1) The mixed race children included three children of South Asian and white UK origin and two who had one Black parent and one white parent. Four of the mixed race children were in lone mother families and one in a step family. In the two-parent group, there was one pair of siblings and, as noted, two sets of siblings in the foster care group.

Comparing the pattern of parents' socio-economic status in the Questionnaire Survey, the household case studies were rather more working class (albeit in the Questionnaire Survey some children did not wish to divulge parents' jobs). In the case study sample, of the 48 mothers in employment, only one-sixth (eight mothers) were in higher status employment (nurses, teachers and (residential) social workers). The majority of the other mothers were in manual work, which included the 13 female foster carers whose occupational status, according to the Registrar General, is coded as semi-skilled manual. Similarly, of the 45 employed resident fathers, step fathers and male foster carers, only seven were in higher status occupations while ten were not employed because of sickness, unemployment or full-time study. Twelve mothers had no current employment or very part-time work, while 22 were in full-time work (excluding the 13 foster carers) and 13 were in part-time jobs.

The case studies in context

The focus of the book concerns children's perspectives on family life, and children's interview accounts are central to this. As we have noted, mothers were also interviewed to help contextualise children's accounts. However, inevitably the character of people's lives, especially the material environment tends to disappear in a study which

Table 1.1 Children's household structure by ethnic origin

	South Asian	Black	White	Mixed race	All
Two-parent	9	3	3	–	15
Lone mother	3	6	5	4	18
Step father	–	4	10	1	15
Foster care	–	4	11	–	15
All children*	12	17	29	5	63

*This includes 3 sets of siblings.

places so much weight on participants' words. Moreover, the context of the interview encounter and the way access was negotiated are not easily integrated within an analysis of people's accounts. Moreover, as we later comment, a great deal of the data which this study generated is not presented in the book. Important insights are, however, provided in the reflections which the researchers recorded directly after completing the interviews. These commentaries covered the interview content and context, and included an account of the researcher's feelings about the conduct of the interviews. This was later transcribed with the interview. These summaries provide a rich contextual resource for the study to which it is not possible to do full justice here. In addition, a set of commentaries was provided by the person who transcribed both mother and child interviews. Re-reading these commentaries, a number of features of the study emerge which are underplayed in the body of analysis to which we would want to draw attention.

The first concerns the working-class character of the study which is borne out in comments about the families' housing and the conditions under which some of the interviews were carried out, but also in references to a wide range of health and other problems which seemed to mark the lives of many of the study families, especially those of the children. Indeed, disadvantage was not confined to the foster children in the study who had a great deal of problems related to their families of origin and their entry into care. While the intention is not to portray the children and their parents and carers as victims of poverty and adversity, it is perhaps only in a contextual review that it is possible to give some idea of the material, social and health conditions with which the study families and the children had to contend.

On several occasions, researchers' notes testify to poverty, in particular to poor-quality and rather cramped accommodation. This was particularly so for the lone mother and step father families where only 7 out of 26 received any financial support (regular or irregular) from the non-resident fathers (Chapter 3). Some interviews were conducted in entrance halls or in tiny kitchens where there was no room for a table or chairs. Other comments refer to poor sound insulation which caused the researchers concern about the confidentiality of the interviews, especially when there were other siblings in the house. Researchers were less concerned about parents overhearing children's interviews since the strategy was to interview mothers and children simultaneously in separate rooms; this ensured a measure of confidentiality but put pressure on space.

The significant problems experienced by some children may well relate to social disadvantage and to a combination of lone motherhood (past and present) and lack of financial resources (due to mothers' non-employment or fathers' failure to contribute financially). Excluding the foster children, most of whom had multiple problems including learning and behavioural problems, one fifth of the other children had a significant health, behavioural or emotional problem. All but one of these children were classified as from working-class families (parents in manual jobs or unemployed). Several children were severely overweight or had a significant health problem. A number had learning difficulties. Others had behavioural problems or reported having been victims of bullying. In addition several families, not only the foster children, had in the past experienced problems related to marital violence and abuse. The children's problems were often emphasised by the mothers rather than by the children themselves. Four families (three minority ethnic families) experienced an adverse change in their fortunes through the fathers' premature deaths. Lone mother households were particularly disadvantaged since only four mothers were working full time and only three were receiving regular financial support from the fathers.

The researchers' comments refer also to the conduct of the interviews themselves which took place in all but one case in the home and lasted between one and two hours on average. They refer to problems of interruptions, often from younger children, and to mothers exerting control over their children's interviews. For example, two mothers expressed concern about their children being interviewed alone with strangers, notably related to their fear of paedophiles. Another (middle-class) mother ordered her daughter to participate in the interview but told her to be quick and to eat her dinner while talking, so that she could get on with her homework and music practice. The children were on the whole very accommodating, offering to miss their favourite TV programmes in order to participate in the study and, in one case, the second half of a key football game. One boy was interviewed on his birthday but did not divulge this information to the interviewer until his non-resident father arrived to give him a birthday present.

We tried to ensure that children's consent to the interview was an informed choice. Before the interview, we briefly explained that the interview would be taped, described the sort of questions we would ask, discussed issues of confidentiality, and stressed that children could refuse to answer questions. We then asked children if they wanted to ask us anything; a few had questions about confidentiality and the purpose of the study. During the course of the interview, two children refused to give their mothers' occupations on the grounds that they might 'not be allowed' to do so. Three foster children declined to discuss the reason for being taken into care and three other foster children said they preferred not to talk about their birth mothers. Several children appeared to have difficulty understanding some of the questions and, as we shall describe, some of the boys and many of the foster children had difficulty expressing their feelings, preferring to talk about factual matters. Some children regularly returned to topics which engaged them such as their love of football and swimming. With a couple of exceptions, children seemed particularly to enjoy the vignettes and completing the map of significant others perhaps because they offered a different form of participation, although spelling and writing difficulties often emerged during this latter exercise. Several foster children had short attention spans which alerted us to the need to offer regular breaks during the interview. Foster children were also more uninhibited than other children, for example interrupting the interview to enquire about the workings of the tape recorder and to ask how much longer the interview would take. In practice, none of the children ended the interview prematurely although the researchers often tried to hasten the end when children looked tired, bored or distracted, as some did.

Analysis

In analysing data, it is always important to remember that data are always a product of the research process. This is no less the case in studying children's perspectives. Research participants respond differently to different methods. Adult participants prefer some methods rather than others (Brannen 1993) and children, similarly, have preferences (James 1995; Mauthner 1997). In carrying out development work for the study with children, this became clear and we chose to include a range of methods such as vignettes, family trees and maps of significant others which we also considered helpful in elucidating family relations. In line with our wide remit of research questions, we chose in the main particular methods for particular purposes but, in some cases, we have addressed the same issue using different methods. In general, we have used our different data sources to complement one another (Brannen 1992), as will become evident later in the book.

The book draws on a qualitative analysis of children's interview accounts together with quantitative data from the Questionnaire Survey. Most of the Questionnaire Survey data were pre-coded, in contrast to the less structured interview data. However, we did attempt to match some of the questions and answers in the mother interview with those of the child interview, in order to compare mothers' understandings of children's views with those of children themselves. Simple comparable codes were allocated where similar types of information were obtained from both mothers and children.

Given the design of the study, the Questionnaire Survey of 941 children (which also served as a successful means of identifying children in different family forms) and the 63 interview case studies, one of the particular tensions for the analysis concerns breadth versus depth of analysis. Another is the nature of the analysis itself and the balance to be struck between a thematic analysis across the study participants and a case study approach to the particular children and their families. We hope that we have achieved a balance although we have often erred in favour of the former. A further tension is having far too much data. Indeed we gained some very important insights into children's views of care and family life from the seven focus groups which we carried out between the Questionnaire Survey and the interviews (upon which we have drawn for some of the quotes at the start of each chapter). These data have been omitted from the analysis presented here. Finally, we want to stress that children's perspectives as they emerged in the study reflect the conceptual concerns of the person who designed it (Julia) and were mediated through the adult–child relations in the research encounter. While we have only touched on these latter issues, in presenting our analysis we have tried to contextualise children's responses, as far as space has allowed us, in particular to indicate the kinds of questions we asked children. Moreover, the interview data would lend itself to further analysis, for example a finer grained textual analysis of mothers' and children's accounts and an analysis of mothers and foster carers' perspectives on children's family lives. Rather, in this book we have addressed the central theme of the study: children's concepts of care, their experiences of and contribution to care in modern family life.

Note

1   Children were asked two questions about their ethnicity. The first question referred to their perceptions of themselves as either 'White British', 'Black British', 'Asian British' or 'Other'. The 146 children who described themselves as 'Other' were identified and their questionnaires were examined for specification of their ethnicity. A total of 60 children were re-allocated to the other three ethnic groups on the basis of their description of themselves. For example, children describing themselves as Italian, German or White English were re-allocated to the 'White' group. Children describing themselves as Black Jamaican, Black African or Somalian were placed in the Black group. Children who called themselves, for example, Kenyan Indian or Asian African were re-allocated to the South Asian group. Of the remaining 86 children in the 'Other' group, 40 (47%) described themselves as 'mixed race', 24 (28%) as 'British' without giving further details, while the remaining 22 (26%) described themselves as Turkish, Colombian, Brown British (Middle Eastern), Bolivian or Mauritian.

2 Children's beliefs about care

If everyone was caring it would be a perfect world, but a perfect world would be boring.

As we noted in Chapter 1, care has a clear moral dimension, in the sense that people often feel under an obligation to provide it. However, in practice, they do not simply act upon a sense of obligation or set of absolute principles. They negotiate 'guidelines' as they apply in particular conditions and situations (Finch 1989). Like adults, children are active participants in caring relationships both as receivers of care and givers of care. Their participation in care relations occurs moreover in public domains as well as in the private sphere of family life. In this chapter, we consider children's moral or normative expectations and beliefs about care and caring relations as they relate to different contexts, including the public domain of the school and the market place and the private sphere of family life. In this endeavour, we used the vignette method. It was developed by Finch and Mason (1993) in their study of adult family obligations, to examine in a systematic way children's beliefs about the 'right and proper thing to do' with respect to care and care relations in particular contexts and under a set of controlled conditions. In two vignettes, a focus concerned guidelines which children considered they should exercise in negotiating social relations – both with other children and with adults. Two vignettes focused on children's normative views about adults as givers of care, while one vignette suggested care may be a matter of reciprocity between adults and children.

We used the vignette approach during and at the end of the interviews with the case study children ($n = 63$). The vignettes discussed in this chapter asked children to comment on four sketches depicting different social situations which had implications for acting in a caring way. The interviewers also read out an accompanying text. Our intention was to provide a hypothetical set of situations which were distanced sufficiently from children's personal lives but which were also situations which children were likely to have encountered either in the past – the vignette on household change – or were likely to meet currently during course of transition from primary to secondary school – the vignette about inclusion/exclusion from a school peer group. The other two vignette topics related to more routine events they were likely to encounter – one related to children's increased autonomy outside the home (queuing to be served in a shop), and the other related to parents' need for children's help at home in the context of their working long hours in the workplace. Broadly speaking, the four vignettes were divided between those relating to public and private contexts.

In interpreting children's responses to the vignettes, we are not making the assumption that children would necessarily act in similar ways in negotiating their own lives. Rather, their responses should be understood as indicative of the degree of consensus which exists concerning the appropriateness of acting in a caring way in particular contexts. Their responses illuminate the conditions which make being caring possible and likely, or impossible and unlikely, and they also underline the complexity of negotiating care in the context of competing norms and expectations. Nonetheless, it is evident in children's interpretations of the vignette situations that some children, on some issues, projected their feelings about events and relationships in their own lives onto the characters and situations in the vignettes.

The public sphere

We chose two situations for the vignettes within the public sphere, the school playground and a shop. Both are ordinary, everyday settings and provided for situations which posed significant issues concerning the care of children, in the first case care between children and, in the second, between adults and children. The framing of the vignettes provided for children's active participation in care as well as children's receipt of care. (The data are presented in numerical, tabular form in the Appendix.)

Vignette set in the school playground: caring relations between children

Children were asked to consider a sketch of a girl called Jane who was portrayed as somewhat distressed and standing apart from a group of children in the school playground (Figure 2.1). The sketch was accompanied by the following description read out by the interviewer: 'Jane

Fig. 2.1

has just started secondary school. She has not yet made any friends. One day a group of children from her class see her crying in the playground.' Children were asked to consider, from the point of view of the children in the peer group, the 'right thing to do' in principle and to consider the conditions which, in practice, might influence whether the group members acted in a caring way. This vignette was especially pertinent since the study children had just started, or were on the point of starting, secondary school; making new friends was likely to be a significant issue for them. The secondary school context provided considerable challenges for children, notably a large organisation with a strong hierarchical structure in which the new children were positioned as subordinate to teachers but were also the youngest and probably, in physical terms, the smallest children in the school. Thus the vignette provided a meaningful and critical set of situations in which to examine children's beliefs about the negotiation of caring relationships.

In principle, the majority of children (53/59) agreed that 'the right and proper thing to do' within the school context was for the group to care for Jane (Table 2.1, Appendix). Some children suggested that Jane should be included in the group. '*I think they should go over and calm her down and ask her what's wrong and then they should talk to her and say, you shouldn't be shy you should go and talk to friends, talk to people you think are nice. Make sure they like you and things like that*' (Niaz, South Asian boy). '*I think they should go over and ask her if she wants to hang around with them*' (Tara, mixed race girl).

Some of the children avoided answering the normative question about what ought to happen and suggested what the group would do in practice, with three of the four such children suggesting that group might bully Jane. '*[They'll] start going up to her and calling her names*' (Sally, white girl).

Similarly, asked how the group would regard Jane, just over half the children (31/59) constructed Jane as an outsider to the group by drawing attention to her 'difference' or 'otherness' in terms of inferior dress, intellect and behaviour. While several children commented unfavourably on Jane's clothing, the illustrator had not intended to portray Jane as being different in terms of dress. '*. . . it's one of those things, she's not wearing a short skirt and they were. Or something like that, they didn't particularly like her because she had – because she wore a cardigan and they all wore jumpers*' (Amy, white girl). '*. . . she's sad, an embarrassment to our class. They should make friends, but I can see what's happening. They probably think she's not good enough to be in their gang or group or whatever*' (Anton, Black boy). '*She's stupid and um, they think that she's dumb 'cause she ain't got no, they ain't got no friends*' (Jasmine, mixed race girl).

Other children highlighted the character of the group as a consideration in Jane's treatment, typically classified dichotomously as bullying or caring. '*It depends on what they're like. They could be like, bullies and saying, let's go and pick on her. Or, they could be saying "Oh! gosh, why is that girls crying? Let's go over and talk to her"* ' (Chloe, Black girl).

Asked whether the group would in practice do something to help Jane, rather fewer children said the group would help compared with those who agreed with the principle that it ought to help (32/57 compared to 53/59). Children referred to a number of key structural features of the context which encouraged or constrained the ethic of care: the ethos of the school, the ethos of the peer group and the gender of its members. For example, Niaz, a South Asian origin boy suggested that Jane, if she had been a boy and at his school, would not have cried in the first place: '*. . . our school's not like that. I know this is very sexist, but if you're a boy you can't do things like that. So you can't cry, you've got to make friends and you can't just sit down and cry, waiting for people to come.*'

We asked children specifically about the effects of the age order. Rather more children suggested that older teenagers would exclude Jane from the group than said they would act in a caring, inclusive way (26/58 compared to 12/58). Just as some children positioned Jane as 'weak' because she cried, so younger children were in general perceived as weak compared with older children. '*I think they [teenagers] would probably just walk off and ignore her or they would either, like, not even think about it because she's younger than them'* (Lucy, mixed race girl). On the other hand, one girl suggested that because children were older they should try to help younger children. In her view, this was the way things were supposed to happen and she related an incident from her own experience which supported her contention: *'Yeh, 'cause they're older they're suppose to be trying to make friends, like that girl who helped me, she's my friend'* (Jasmine, mixed race girl).

Given the constraints mentioned against putting the ethic of care into practice in schools, it is not therefore surprising that, when we asked an additional general question at the end of this vignette – whether it was possible to be 'too kind to others' – many children agreed with the statement (33/55) but many either disagreed or expressed caveats (18/55). Some children were clearly mindful of the power imbalance which occurs when one person becomes overly indebted to another and in which there is a risk that the 'beholden' person may exploit the person who has provided the kindness (or indeed the situation in reverse). As Lee, a white boy, said: *'Well, if you're too kind, they might take advantage of you. And in that way I think it is [possible to be too kind].'*

To sum up, while a normative consensus existed among children about the importance of the ethic of care in social relations *between* children in the school playground, children framed their discussion concerning the likely practice of care in terms of the structure and culture of secondary school which are organised and enacted in a strongly hierarchical way, both between teachers and children but also between children based upon the social construction of age and size. Norms of care were negotiated in which older children were seen as likely to pick on younger, 'weaker' children which meant that younger children often sought older protectors. Children suggested strong boundaries around the peer group and identified criteria which made membership of the 'in' group possible or problematic to do with dress, cleverness, and appropriate behaviour. In accordance with their cautious approach to being at the bottom of the pile (school or peer group), many children were reluctant to agree with the principle of bestowing kindness too liberally and readily identified the power imbalance which being 'too kind' to others might set up.

Vignette set in a shop: relations between adults and children

The second vignette aimed to tap children's views of the normative guidelines which operated with respect to relations between children and adults and the extent to which adults and children were respectful of one another in a public context. The vignette sketch depicted two girls buying sweets in a newsagent's (Figure 2.2). The accompanying text, which was read out by the interviewer, described the following set of events: 'When the children get to the counter, a woman – aged about 30 – stands behind them, waving her money at the shopkeeper, clearly wanting to be served first.'

There was unanimity among children about the principle that the shopkeeper should serve the children first (59/59): 'because they were there first', as many children noted (Table 2.2, Appendix). The woman's claims to usurp the children's right to be served was clearly deemed illicit. Children considered that 'first come first served' was a clear principle which should not be breached. Cogniscent of the children's and the woman's equal status as *customers*, children thereby asserted the norm of 'fairness' over and above support for the idea that adults, *qua* adults, should have a right to be served before children. It is important to note also that none of the children suggested that the two girls should be treated as 'special' on account of their status as children.

Moreover, children complained that in practice it was commonplace for adults to assert their superiority over children in such public places. *'Adults always do that. Just because they're older than us, they think we can't stick up for ourselves'* (Latasha, Black girl); *'Most people would serve the adults, not sure why, but . . .'* (Clark, Black boy); *'Some people ignore the younger children and go off with the older people'* (Jason,

Fig. 2.2

white boy). A white girl volunteered a similar incident happening to her own younger brother: '*Like, my little brother, he was queuing up to buy some sweets and he was there in front of people and they never served him. I don't know why they do that, really*'. Asked a specific question on whether a similar situation had happened to them, the majority of the study children confirmed this (41/54) and many gave graphic accounts of their experiences. Sometimes they portrayed themselves as highly pro-active in responding to their predicament; perhaps this was wish fulfilment or perhaps it reflected what they had actually said at the time. '*It happened at a wedding. I went to get a drink and I was waiting and waiting. There was a woman behind me and the man served her instead of me. I got angry. I said "Why aren't you serving me, is it because she looks nicer?" He took no notice*' (Elliott, Black boy). A few children said they felt unable to speak up and were constrained not only by their young age but also by their small size: '*At school older children sort of push in front of you. You don't really do anything, you sort of sigh*' (Ceri, white girl). In response to a similar incident, a Black girl said: '*I kept quiet because it was a big bloke*'.

From children's viewpoint, the adage – 'children should be seen and not heard' was further extended so that children were seen to be totally invisible to adults in such public contexts. By insisting on their own preferential treatment as adults, children said adults could make children feel ignored, powerless and belittled. A white girl, Daniela, clearly identified with the vignette situation: '*It makes you feel a bit, like you're not there. You feel a bit unhappy because they're just ignoring you*'. '*[The girls in the vignette] will probably feel, like, that they weren't there, kind of thing, invisible. Because although they're children, they're still human beings and they do have equal rights*' (Rebecca, white girl). A Black girl, Chloe, stressed the girls' felt powerlessness: '*They feel small, like they don't have any power in their life.*' A South Asian origin boy, Niaz, suggested that the adults should try putting themselves in children's shoes: '*That woman should actually have experience of what it was like to be a child.*'

Given that children felt that a central principle of fairness had been breached, and given their strong feelings about children's invisibility to adults, it was not surprising that the majority of children (38/46) agreed, when asked, that the girls should speak up for their rights in the shop. By contrast, a couple of children offered a defence of the shop keeper's behaviour on the grounds that the woman might be a close friend. However, those who agreed the girls should voice objections opted for a cautious, polite approach: '*I think they should say, "Excuse me, I'm getting served first, I was in the queue before you"* ' (Sally, white girl); '*I don't think they should be rude because then the lady is going to get all upset and the shopkeeper is going to have to deal with it'* (Amy, white girl). Another girl took a bolder position and adopted a grown-up manner: *'If that was me, I would say, "Excuse me darling, would you budge over?"'*

Children were very conscious that they should not disturb the peace by causing trouble in a public place and some feared the adults might retaliate if they voiced their complaints: *'I think that them two [girls] should tell the woman that they were there first, and then, if the woman starts arguing, just step away and let the woman be served'* (Lee, white boy). *'I wouldn't bother [saying anything] I'd just wait because it's just going to start an argument. There's no point'* (Baldev, South Asian origin boy); *'I wouldn't [say anything] but I would whisper to my friend'* (Ceri, white girl).

In order to explore whether children considered old age 'a legitimate excuse' for an adult taking precedence over children in a public place, we asked whether, if the woman was elderly, she should be served first. Half the children said that she should be served first (30/58), one-third felt it should not make a difference (16/58), and the others said it would depend on the circumstances (11/58). However, children who subscribed to preferential treatment for an elderly person suggested rather more commonly the presence of additional problems connected with old age, rather than age *per se*: *'Old people have so many problems with their heart and stuff like that, I would let the old lady go in front. And I would also, like, help her carry her bags or whatever because I don't want the woman to have a heart attack in the middle of the road and people think that I didn't care'* (Latasha, Black girl). Children who disagreed with preferential treatment placed greater weight on 'fairness' based on the principle of 'first come first served': *'Not to me it doesn't [old age make a difference], I don't know why people think, just because old women are old, they need – they should get everything first. In my books everyone has to line up, so –'* (Elliott, Black boy).

We asked children a general question at the end of this vignette whether they agreed that adults ought to protect children. Two-thirds agreed (28/40) and one-third gave a mixed response (12/40) One girl said: *'They [grown-ups] have to be careful with children and they have to look after them because they are more grown-up.'* Or, as another girl put it, *'they have more experience of what happens out in the big wide world'*. A South Asian origin girl, Bibi, gave a more sophisticated explanation which referred to adults' responsibility for passing on experience to younger generations: *'Because adults are, like, adults are the generation of today, children are the generation of tomorrow, so the older generation should look after the new generation and nurture them.'* By contrast, some children regarded protection as a matter of reciprocity between adults and children: '*Grown-ups should always protect children and children should always look after adults*' (Anna, white girl). '*Everyone should look after each other*' (Niaz, South Asian origin boy).

Those coded as giving a mixed response suggested that adult protectiveness should be balanced by the need to allow children to grow up and become independent: '*They [grown-ups] should watch over them, yes, protect them, but they shouldn't, like, always be around and everything. They should let you go and have your friends on your own sometimes, and not always be next to you*' (Kevin, white boy). '*Yes, but not too much or they won't learn anything about life*' (Ceri, white girl). '*Not watch over them all the time, you know, but they should protect them. They should tell them how to protect themselves*' (Hayfa, South Asian origin girl). '*No, not all the time, they should stick up for – I think they [children] can stick up for themselves*' (Serena, Black girl).

To summarise, in the public space of a shop and in their role of customers, children felt that the principle of fairness should be applied equally to children and to adults. Children's strong identification with the situation also suggested not only the breaching of the principle but the widespread practice of adult disrespect for children. While children thought that they should assert their rights in such a situation, they saw a practical difficulty in speaking up for themselves. Keeping the peace was seen as the more feasible course of action, given adults' greater power and resources. Moreover, children did not give blanket support to the principle of respect for old age *per se* but were more inclined towards preferential treatment for old people on account of ill health and other problems. Despite these views, most children considered that adults' job was to protect children, although a significant proportion drew attention to the double-edged aspect of adult protectiveness and saw a need to balance protection with providing children with the space to develop some autonomy. A few even thought that adult protection of children should be reciprocal.

The private sphere

With respect to the private sphere of family life, we selected one extraordinary situation. Since an important focus of the study concerned the different types of household structures in which children today grow up, we selected the situation of household change in which a father was leaving the family home. Through this vignette, we sought to examine children's views of the 'proper thing to do' in terms of the care of children and also children's views of the experience of household change: the conditions under which children thought it 'right' or not for the father to leave the household; their views about who the child in question, a boy called Joe, should live with after the separation; the boy's feelings in response to the separation; and where he might turn for help in the event of his parents splitting up. In the other vignette, we selected the situation where parents were working long hours in their family business in which the children are called upon to help them after school. (The coded responses are given in Tables 2.3 and 2.5, Appendix.)

Vignette on household change: parents' care and children's feelings and participation

The household change vignette depicted an 11-year-old boy called Joe hiding behind the door witnessing his father leaving the family home in a taxi. On the wall there is a 'happy family' photograph of Joe with his younger sister, and his mother and father (Figure 2.3). The interviewer read out the accompanying text: 'Joe is 11 years old and lives with his mum, dad and younger sister. Joe's dad wants to go and live somewhere else without Joe's mum and without Joe or his sister.'

Children's consideration of the morality of Joe's father's actions, that is whether or not to leave the family home, suggested rather more disapproval (36/60), with nearly one-third in favour (17/60) and the rest favouring a trial separation (Table 2.3, Appendix). Fewer children

Fig. 2.3

in two-birth-parent families (3/15) and foster children (1/13) favoured Joe's father leaving the household compared with rather more children from lone mother children (8/18) and step parent children (5/14). These findings can be compared with responses from the Questionnaire Survey which indicates rather more resistance on children's part to parents' separation and divorce, especially among the children living with both birth parents (Table 2.4, Appendix). However, the Survey question posed a number of options which allowed children to avoid making a clear choice and also did not spell out the likely continuation of conflict if parents stayed together.

In response to this vignette, the most common reason children said the father should stay was 'for the sake of the children' (13 children). *'They shouldn't split away. They should live together because they've got children. Their children wouldn't have a father'* (Sunita, South Asian girl, two-parent family). Barry, a white boy of few words who lived in a step family, simply said: *'It's bad for the kids.'* Three children commented that a separation would be hard to come to terms with at this point in the life course. *'Because he's 11, he's just gone to secondary school. He's been living with his mum and dad for eleven years, so they shouldn't split up'* (Salome, white girl, lone mother family). Children worried about the effects on Joe's studies and on his sociability. Elliott, a Black boy who lived in a lone mother household, said: *'He's going to be thinking, I wonder if he's leaving because of me.'* Amy, a white girl living in a step family also noted: *'He'll probably think it's all his fault, he did nothing to help them and all the stuff that you always think, like that his parents don't love him any more and they're just worried about themselves.'*

Similarly, children who favoured a break-up unanimously felt that arguments between parents would be bad for the children. *'If they don't get on together, then I think they should split up because they can't just pretend that they're happy together, just for the kids'* (Emily, white girl, step family). *'It is probably better having one person, one happy person, than two people arguing all the time'* (Leila, mixed race girl, lone mother family).

Children were unanimous in saying that, at least initially, the separation would be a very negative experience for Joe. Joe was described as sad, lonely, unhappy, upset, gutted, confused, hurt, angry, guilty, torn apart. *'Joe feels upset. Horrible man, he could have stayed and it would have been a happy family'* (Claudia, mixed race girl, lone mother family). *'Joe thinks – why is my dad leaving? I've spent all this time with him and now he's leaving. It's like a piece of me is going away'* (Elliott, Black boy, lone mother family).

Several children volunteered comments on their own unhappy experience of family change, notably three children living with foster carers. '*I know how he feels: upset. He'll probably start turning against his dad for leaving him. I turned against mine for a while, but you learn to forgive him*' (white girl, foster family). '*Joe's very, very sad and angry. Like I was angry. My mum never told us the truth. She picked us up from school, went home, got some clothes and we went. She said "We're going on holiday" and she said that Daddy's waiting for us there*' (white boy, foster family).

While all but one child agreed that Joe would have a bad time when his parents separated, opinions on how he would feel a year later were more divided. Half (28/57) said Joe would feel better a year later, or get used to the situation, while rather less than half said that Joe would feel the same, worse or would have mixed feelings. To most children, feeling better did not mean that the pain Joe felt initially had gone away although there was some acceptance of the notion of time as a healer: '*He'll get used to it, but he'll still be upset*' (Lujayn, South Asian origin girl, two-parent family); '*I think he'll feel that it ain't so bad now as it was when it happened. And I bet he's feeling, like, I wish I could have done something. Like, regretting it, like*' (Claudia, mixed race girl, lone mother family); '*He would feel better but he'll still miss his dad and his family might be a bit wonky*' (Mirza, South Asian boy, widowed lone mother family). Some children saw good and bad sides: '*He might be happy that all the arguing has stopped but he might be sad that his dad hasn't been there for him when he needed him*' (Tara, mixed race girl, lone mother family).

Several children who thought Joe would still feel bad or worse a year later implied that Joe would have little or no contact with his dad. One child said that seeing other children with their fathers was a constant reminder of her loss: '*He won't feel any better. It sticks with you. Honestly, it just sticks with you, because you've got the loss there, you see other people walking down the road with their mums and dads. No, you never get over it*' (Rebecca, white girl, lone mother family). Jasmine was also unsure that Joe would ever feel better for similar reasons: '*He might have forgot about it a little bit, but if it was me I wouldn't, because you would miss your dad, like, just say you're used to playing with him. When you're walking home from school, you see through a window, like your dad, a dad tickling his little girl or boy or something like that, then it would break your heart, wouldn't it?*' (mixed race girl, step father).

If Joe maintained regular contact with his father, this could, however, mitigate negative feelings in children's view. '*Well, if he keeps in touch with his dad then he'll probably feel really bad, thinking why do they live apart and everything?*' (Hayfa, South Asian origin girl, two-parent family). Willy, a white boy living in a lone mother family, spoke from his own positive experience: *'If that were me, when I first didn't see my dad I was upset, but now I don't mind because I'm still seeing him.'* Again, the response of a girl living with foster carers may have echoed her feelings about her own situation: *'I don't think he'd really care after a bit. If he didn't get any visits from his dad, I don't think he'd give a toss or anything'* (Debbie, white girl). Liam, a white boy in foster care, feared that the parents might not be able to sort out an amicable arrangement between them whereby Joe could see his father: *'If his dad wants custody and he takes his mum to court and there's loads of rows, he might feel worse. But if the dad just wants to see him every week and when he comes to pick Joe up and the mum and dad talk, "Hello, how are you, want a cup of tea?", like some parents do, he might feel better.'*

Half of children (27/54) thought that, in principle, mothers were best qualified to care for Joe after the separation, while no child felt he ought to live with his father only. More children with an experience of separation favoured Joe living with his mother (ten in the lone mother group, seven in the step family group and seven foster children, compared with only three children in the two-parent group). Only two children said Joe should share his time with both parents, ten said it was up to Joe, while eight were not sure (the rest include other and non-responses). Mindful that Joe's father was depicted as the parent doing the leaving, there was a possible implication that the father had been the cause of the separation. While most children suggested that the father was to blame for leaving, one girl suggested that he was leaving because of the mother's affair. The portrayal of the father leaving may be one reason why so many children favoured the principle that Joe should live with his mother after the separation, while no child felt he ought to live with his father. *'I think he should live with his mum because his dad didn't have to move out because his mum didn't chuck him out, so it was his decision for moving out'* (Jasmine, mixed race girl, step family). In one child's view, Joe's father had rejected his son. *'He should live with his mum because his dad left which shows that he don't want him anymore'* (Scott, white boy, step father family).

Children's reasons for their choice of Joe's mother as the person Joe 'should' stay with also identified the history of Joe's care, in which Joe's mother was said to have provided rather more and rather special care. Several children mentioned the 'special' feelings mothers had for their children because of giving birth to them and because they did most of the caring in practice. *'Mothers understand their children more and fathers, they've got to go to work and everything'* (Rebecca, white girl, lone mother family); *'Mums have got more feelings for children than dads'* (Willy, white boy, lone mother family); *'I think it's the mother he should live with, because fathers you can't rely on. You can rely on a* mother, because mothers – *what's it called* – *they love their children, that's their flesh and blood*' (Inderpal, South Asian origin boy, lone mother family); '*After all, his mum did bring him in the world, so –*' (Elliott, Black boy, lone mother family). Liam, a white boy living in a foster family, said mothers should have 'custody' of children because they were the children's main carers: '*Not all the time, but most of the time it seems to be that the mother gets custody of the children because the mum is, like, more organised over kids than the dad. Like, they're known for the housework and cooking meals and that lot. So he should live with his mum.*' However, some did not specify which parent Joe should live with but suggested that he should live with the parent who was the 'best' person to care for him or the person who had been most 'loving'. '*It depends on who is the most loving and genuine one*' (Chloe, Black girl, step family).

The great majority of children supported the principle of children having a say in decisions concerning where they should reside following the break-up. Only three children, all from the two-parent group, said that Joe should not have a say. In children's view, Joe's happiness was paramount and Joe would know best what would make him happier. '*Joe should decide where he wants to live. He might not be happy if he is made to live with his dad and he won't be happy for the rest of his life*' (Willy, white boy, lone mother family); '*I don't think you should go to somebody you don't want to go with*' (Sally, white girl, lone mother family); '*He's big enough to make the decision; it should be Joe's opinion, no one else's, because it's his life*' (Zarina, South Asian girl, lone mother family); '*If he wanted to live with his dad, because then he could talk man to man, then it's up to him. But if he wanted to live with his mum, I think it's his choice really*' (Jasmine, mixed race girl, step parent family). Perhaps reflecting perceptions of their own situation, two foster children mentioned that professionals might limit Joe's ability to make a choice: '*He should have a say if it doesn't go to court*' (Robert, white boy, foster family); '*He can say what he wants to, but at the same time the social worker will say where they want to put him because that's what is best for him*' (Gail, Black girl, foster family).

As to finding someone Joe could turn to in the event of his parents separating, half of children (27/58) suggested a number of different people. Mention was made of Joe's parents, either his mother or both parents. However, friends topped the list, followed by Joe's parents, his sister, teachers, ChildLine, relatives, and counsellors. Only two children said Joe would have no one to talk to. A close, trusting relationship was considered important by seven children. '*Maybe he should turn to relatives, someone he's really close to*' (Baldev, South Asian boy, two-parent family); '*He could turn to one of his friends or an adult he can trust and who knows about stuff like that'* (Bibi, South Asian girl, two-parent family); *'He should talk to people who understand him'* (Leila, mixed race girl, lone mother family).

While 16 children said Joe should talk to his parents or his sister, others noted that this would be difficult: *'He can't really talk to his parents because they'll have different points of views'* (Ceri, white girl, two-parent family). *'I won't talk to my parents or my sister because if I talk to my sister then she knows and she needs to talk to someone. I won't talk to someone living in my house and not a friend because you don't want them to know about your personal life'* (Willy, white boy, lone mother family). *'He could speak to his sister about it because she's going through the same thing really'* (Tara, mixed race girl, lone mother family); *'He can't talk to his sister because she would feel just as bad'* (Jake, Black boy, two-parent family).

The fact that ChildLine posters are displayed in many schools probably contributed to children's reference to this organisation (8 children). One child had personal experience of ChildLine's support after her father left the family following incidents of domestic violence. *'It's hard to trust anyone about these things, I know that much because I know what Joe's going through. I talked to ChildLine because I needed help'* (South Asian girl, lone mother family). Another recalled a friend's use of ChildLine for a similar experience: *'When my friend's parents split up he was really sad and he phoned ChildLine then and they really helped him'* (Niaz, South Asian origin boy, two-parent family).

To summarise, children's comments on family change suggested that parents should consider children in making decisions about their relationships. More children disapproved than approved of Joe's father leaving the family home; children living with both birth parents and children living with foster carers especially represented disapproving viewpoints. Children almost unanimously painted a very negative picture of the immediate effects of the separation on Joe, although half gave a more positive account of Joe's feelings a year later. Feeling better would, children said, depend upon Joe continuing to live with his mother and having regular contact with his father. In the event of household change, most children either subscribed to Joe continuing to live with his mother or with the person who was the 'better' or more loving parent. Children's support for the mothers and the blame apportioned to the father was, however, influenced by the portrayal of the father as making the move. In accordance with children's view that family life and household change should prioritise children, almost all the children subscribed to the view that children should have a right to a say in decisions concerning which parent they live with when their parents separate.

Vignette set in a family business: children's contribution to household work

The aim of this vignette was to examine children's views about making a contribution at home and, in order that children's contribution should be seen as having 'real', that is economic, value to the household, we selected a family-run business as the vignette setting. The vignette sketch depicted a man and woman, both of whom portrayed working in a grocer's shop, and a young girl who was wearing school uniform and carrying a book and a school bag. Children were given the following information: 'Seeta is 12 years old. She comes home from school and has homework to do. Her parents own a grocery shop which is open until nine o'clock in the evening. Both her mum and dad work long hours.' We gave the girl a South Asian origin name since many corner shops in Britain's cities are run by South Asian origin families. Moreover, a family-run business typically depends upon the contribution of all its members. We also thought that portraying parents working late in the shop would have wider significance, given the lengthening hours of working mothers and the long hours of fathers in Britain (Brannen et al. 1997), and might provoke some comment from children, in particular the problem in reconciling the demands of paid work with those of family life.

With respect to the central normative principle as to whether Seeta ought to help her parents in the shop after school, most children considered that she ought to help (48/58) (Table 2.5, Appendix). However, most also suggested that the help she should give should be modest. *'But she could help, like when she comes home from school, . . . sit down for a while and ask her parents, do you want any help or something, or just help for a little while. And then go and that's it really, just help a bit?'* (Harinder, South Asian origin boy). In fact, three-quarters of children who said Seeta should give some help (37/48) qualified their responses and suggested that Seeta should only help if other conditions were first fulfilled, namely that Seeta should do her homework first; those who said Seeta should not help at all (8/58) also gave her education as the reason. Given that Seeta was portrayed in her school uniform and carrying a book and school bag, and also given the current emphasis in schools on homework, this view was hardly surprising. As a Black girl (Serena, lone mother family) noted: *'If she's got homework to do, I think she should do her homework first and then help them.'*

By contrast, four children, two of whom were of South Asian origin, said Seeta should give help *because* it was a family business. *'Yes, definitely, I think if we had a family business I would be doing as much as I could to help. I think it's important for everyone to play their part in the business'* (Jahangir, South Asian origin boy). One girl whose father

Fig. 2.4

owned a printing business suggested Seeta should help, albeit only 'a bit': '*I think she should help them a bit, because that's kind of, like . . . where the parents get all the money from, where she gets everything from. She should help them a bit from what she's getting*' (Tara, mixed race girl).

In this vignette, the normative concerns about the importance of helping parents collide with competing and more salient normative guidelines governing children's lives, namely the expectations of being a pupil and the requirement to do homework. (Children's own contributions to care are discussed in Chapter 8.) When some of the children were asked whether they would help if they were in Seeta's position, they testified to conflicting priorities – between fulfilling the obligations of school and expectations to help at home. Some children described feeling 'confused' by these different demands. A South Asian origin girl: '*I'd feel like I really want to get my homework done, but I think I should help my parents. I'd be quite confused*' (Hayfa, South Asian origin girl). '*I would feel – I hope they don't make me do the work, 'cos I want to do my homework*' (Niaz, South Asian origin boy). Niaz further suggested that Seeta's parents ought to want the best for their children and should make sure that Seeta succeeded at school in order to gain a good job. Accordingly, in his view this would mean *not* working in a shop. '*No I do not [think she should help]. Because unless her parents want her to be successful, they should let her do her homework. Doing grocery people, what sort of job's that? . . . We have the chance to make somebody clever, let's not ruin it.'*

Moreover, given that parents are now expected to be responsible for ensuring children do their homework, it is also not surprising that some children emphasised the parental role rather than their responsibilities as material providers or breadwinners for the family. Children considered that at least one parent's responsibility should be to help their children with homework rather than working in the shop. Salome, a white girl living in a lone mother family, said: *'No, I think her mum and dad should help her with – one should look after the store and the other should help her with her homework. I don't think both of them should look after the shop at the same time, because if the child is really stuck she can't go to her parents if there's customers and say "Hey can you help me with my homework please? I'm really stuck and it has to be in by tomorrow."* ' Another girl similarly noted: *'I don't think – I think there should be just one person looking after the shop . . . I'd feel really lonely. Not really lonely, but um, um I wouldn't feel helped with my homework. I mean I would really be stuck and my mum and dad wouldn't be able to help me, because they would be looking after the shop.'* As we argue in Chapter 5, children's normative views concerning the proper role of parents were generally non-gendered in that they did not consider a clear division of labour should exist between mothers and fathers. Similarly, in this vignette, children suggested that parenting should be equally the job of mothers and fathers.

Accordingly, children were concerned that the demands of the family business on their parents would impact on the time their parents would have for *them. 'Well, I'd feel sad really because like it's like no one, like you're in a prison. You walk in – walk in, no one says hello, nothing and then you – you do your work and you sleep and you eat and you go out'* (Inderpal, South Asian origin boy). Several children from lone mother families suggested that Seeta would be adversely affected by her parents' long working hours in the shop. *'I suppose yes, because she won't – she'll be lonely as well, because she'll –, if she's the only child she's not going to have that much company is she, with her parents working down the stairs all the time?'* (Tara, mixed race girl). *'I think they wouldn't be around much, a lot of the time, because they would get off to work, go to bed, get up, go to work, get back, go to bed . . . I think it would be a bit kind of split up. Not split up as in moved away, but a bit kind of, not a family group . . . I'd feel quite lonely, because if they were always working and then by the time they're off work, they'd be tired and they'd want to go to bed. So I think I'd be quite lonely'* (Leila, mixed race girl). In this last case, Leila may have been reflecting that long working hours might threaten her close relationship with her own mother; her father, to whom she was also close but whom she described as 'a bit of a workaholic', lived in another part of the country.

Children were also asked the specific question whether the long working hours of Seeta's parents would affect Seeta's family life. The great majority (53/57) said there would be adverse effects for Seeta, while rather few children noted the effects upon parents. Again, children testified to the importance of parents' time for their children. '*Yes because she'd like to see her mum in the morning and when she comes home, her mum's working 'till nine and it's a bit upsetting, because she don't get to spend hardly no time, except on – what was the shop? – spending at the weekends as well*' (Melanie, white girl). '*Yes, I think because the bond between the child and the parents should be strong and the only way that can be done is by time being spent with each other*' (Jahangir, South Asian origin boy). For girls especially, time with their mothers meant time to talk about personal matters: '. . . *she won't have no time to talk about it to her mum. Just say, just say she starts her first period, something like that*' (Jasmine, mixed race girl).

Long hours could mean parents not having time to support children. Inderpal, a South Asian origin boy, said that parents being unavailable meant being unable to help if their child was being bullied at school. He then went on to suggest that the parents might blame Seeta for having to work the long hours in the first place which in turn could turn her into a 'naughty child'. '*Yes, I think they could affect, like the child could be getting racial or being bullied and they might know so – and that's when, where problems, like the family. And they might say "Oh, it's your fault we had to work long hours – what's it called? We work so long hours and you've made her . . . into a naughty child".*'

At a number of points in the interviews, children living in foster care referred to their own feelings of anger – originating probably in anger at own parents and at being in care. When asked whether working long hours affected Seeta's family life, a white boy, Jason, who lived with foster carers, said: '*I would feel quite annoyed.*' Another boy in foster care, Liam, mentioned the parents being 'grumpy' because of having to work long hours with similar repercussions for Seeta's own mood: '*It might affect them because they might be grumpy after a long hard day's work, because they might have had someone in the shop come up to them and like, give them a hard time, and they might be so grumpy. If you look at them, they don't look so happy. And they might be grumpy and when they get home – when Seeta gets home they might be in a bad mood and they might put Seeta in a bad mood. It might affect her.*'

In order to examine whether the expectation to help parents was gendered, children were asked whether it would be different if Seeta was a boy. The majority of children (44/60) said that gender would make no difference to whether the child in the vignette would help the parents: '*No it wouldn't make a difference because boys and girls are just the same*' (Willy, white boy). The rest were split between those who thought boys and those who thought girls would do more. Interestingly, given there were some differences in girls' and boys' own household contribution (Chapter 8), children's normative beliefs here were not influenced by their own gender.

To summarise, children's normative views concerning helping parents were linked to their views about what it means to be a child in Britain today. Children gave only qualified support for helping their parents in the family business although a few said that the fact it was a family business meant children's help was important. The great majority considered Seeta should help only after she had done her homework and only give a small amount of help, while some thought she should not help at all. Rather, children endorsed a different principle which they considered to be their priority, namely to fulfil obligations as school children by doing their homework. For children the 'proper' sphere of work was school work.

Children's views of what it means to be 'a proper parent' were also evident. Children considered the condition of parents who worked long hours in the shop according to the prerequisites of the child/parent relationship rather than those of provider or bread winning roles. Children considered that parents ought, first and foremost, to 'be there for their children' – to care for their emotional needs, to support them with their problems, and to help with their homework; in short they should spend their time with their children. Such findings are not surprising given that children had only recently started secondary school, an event which is accompanied by increased homework demands. Several children talked about parents' long working hours in emotive terms, especially foster children and some who lived with lone mothers. Moreover, children's beliefs were not influenced by gender, neither the gender of the children commenting on the vignette nor of the child depicted in the vignette.

Conclusions

The four vignettes constituted a device for enabling children to indicate the principles which children thought ought to guide caring behaviour and how these principles might play out in practice in a range of public and private settings. All the situations, with the exception of the family business, were likely to have been experienced by many children in the study: making friends in the school playground, competing with adults for service in a shop, and experiencing fathers leaving the family home.

The first vignette was set in the public domain of the school playground and focused on care relations between children, notably concerning the inclusion of a child who was isolated from the peer group. While generally subscribing to the principle of being caring and acting inclusively towards the isolated girl, many children had doubts about this happening in practice especially in their own schools. Children constructed the isolated child as an outsider and emphasised her 'otherness'. As children's own accounts suggest, the hierarchical context and culture of the school and norms pertaining to social hierarchies of age and body size which shape the negotiation of children's relations to one another, mitigated against the principle of acting in a caring manner. As new entrants to secondary school, both the child in the vignette and the children in the study were positioned at the 'bottom of the pile' which constituted a significant constraint upon children feeling that it was possible to act in a caring and solidaristic way, together with the sense of imbalance which can be created between givers and receivers of care.

The second vignette, set in the public space of a shop, focused on normative guidelines governing child/adult social relations. Children subscribed to the principle of fairness based on 'first come first served' with respect to their equal status as customers. In their view, children considered that this principle should over-ride other normative guidelines concerning respect for age – old age or young age. From children's perspective, ill health and need constituted 'legitimate excuses' for giving care rather than old age alone. Where adults infringed the principle of fairness and ignored children in such settings, which many children maintained from their own experience was very common, children considered such adult actions as constituting disrespect for and injustice to children. Moreover, children's assertion of their rights to complain about injustice was generally muted. Rather, children sought to uphold norms concerning the public order by not disturbing the peace; in not speaking up for themselves, they were mindful of their relative powerlessness when confronted by stronger, better resourced adults. On the other hand, most children were adamant that adults ought to protect children. Some were, however, ambivalent and suggested that a balance needed to be struck between the need to protect and the need to help children develop autonomy.

The last two vignettes were set in the private sphere of family life. The first focused on parents separating. Here children subscribed to normative guidelines pertaining to parenthood and family life, namely that family life should be centrally about children and that parents ought to consider children when making decisions about their relationships and household arrangements. Because the father was depicted as leaving the family household, children were censorious of the father.

On the other hand, children subscribed to the norm that the child should live with the 'parent' who had provided most of the care or had proved to be the more loving parent – usually seen as the mother. Moreover, children subscribed to the view that the child in these situations should have a say in decisions concerning which parent he or she should reside with.

The last vignette was set in a family business and sought to explore children's normative views about helping parents, for which children offered only qualified support. Here the beliefs about offering help to the family-run business clashed with their allegiance to norms governing children's expected obligation to do their homework in their status as school workers. Children's views were therefore indicative of what it means to be a child in Britain today. Their normative views of 'proper parenthood' were also evident in this vignette in that children interpreted parents' responsibility to work long hours in their family business as contravening the norms of 'proper parenthood'. Children have clearly understood the policy messages about 'good' parenting practice. First and foremost, children considered parents should 'be there for their children' and should spend time with them, especially in providing support for homework. From children's perspective, family life ought to be centrally about children.

In addition to providing an insight into the moral or normative guidelines which children considered ought to govern parents' and children's social relations, the vignettes also provided a context for children to reflect on their own experiences of these commonly experienced events. Children's reflections in the vignettes offer insights into the status of children in society, particularly children's perceptions of how adults view and treat them: that they often ignore their presence in public places and forget that children have feelings and wishes related to parents' divorce. They offer insights into children's relationships with one another: children's difficulty in transcending social hierarchies of age and in negotiating group norms operating in institutional contexts which sustain hierarchies' power and exploitation. In some instances, children identified with the characters and situations portrayed in the vignettes. Contingent upon whether children chose to make the connections and upon the depth of their feelings about their own experiences, some children projected their feelings on to the characters in the vignette and the vignette situations. This was particularly the case for some of the foster children and a few of the lone parent children who sometimes used emotive language. That they should do so is not surprising given the disruptions they had experienced in their family lives and their many unresolved problems and feelings.

3 Children's families and social ties

Meanings and structures

[Family] is the people you are related to and the people you care about.

Representations of what constitutes a 'proper family' are everywhere in the mass media and form powerful images in children's literature and in the minds and discourses of the adults who teach, care and take responsibility for children. However, children's understandings of what family means to them in their own lives are often broad and inclusive (Levin 1995; Moore et al. 1996; Morrow 1998). As Levin's study showed, children and young people include within the rubric of the term family their parents, siblings, grandparents, step parents and step siblings, and their uncles and aunts but they also include pets and people not usually considered as kin. Morrow's study of 8 to 11-year-olds suggested that children's definitions of what counts as family become more complex as they grow older. Nonetheless, as the study by O'Brien and her colleagues suggests, ideological representations of what families 'ought' to look like remain powerful influences upon children. (O'Brien, Aldred and Jones 1996).

This chapter provides a context for later discussions. First, it presents evidence concerning children's representations and normative views of what makes a family and family life. Drawing on the responses of the case study children selected on the basis of four type of household settings in which they were currently living (two-parent, lone mother, step father and foster care), we examine whether children's own experiences of particular living arrangements were influential in shaping their views of the notion of 'a proper family' – both in terms of what families 'are' in practice, and what families 'ought to' look like. Second, this chapter examines those persons children include as being significant to them, a theme which is taken up in detail in Chapters 5, 6 and 7. Here we describe the method by which we elicited children's accounts and as the analysis in this and subsequent chapters indicates, children's ties extend well beyond their households and kin.

Third, the chapter then changes tack to look at the family networks of children as they experience family change: their potential for family ties and the ties they have access to at the time of the interviews. We have done this to provide a context for the later discussion of children's accounts of family change, and their reports of the importance of different family members and of people who are not kin. Selecting children on the basis of their current living arrangements risks reifying household structure and distracts attention from the fluidity of household boundaries, both over time and at any moment in time, and underplays the existence or absence of other family members in the family network. Moreover, the significance of household structure *for* children is premised on the importance of parents while, as other studies have shown (Morrow 1998), siblings may be of equal consequence *to* children themselves. At the end of the chapter, we illustrate the variation in family networks *within* a particular family type. Through a consideration of children's perspectives of meanings of family and through an examination of children's broader family networks as they are lived in practice, we will begin to address the key question to which we return in later chapters: how far children's lives are lived according to narrow, exclusive notions of household structure and family relations and how far, in the context of family change, they work with broad, inclusive notions of kinship.

Children's views of family structure

'There's no such thing as a "proper" family'

In the interview study, we asked children whether they thought there was such a thing as a 'proper' family, without suggesting what kind of family that might be. An analysis of their responses suggests that nearly two-thirds did not agree with the notion of a *'proper'* family (40/63) (Table 3.1). Many interpreted the notion in terms of a 'happy family' or a 'perfect family' and distanced themselves from these notions, although one (South Asian origin) girl interpreted the term to mean 'prim and proper'. Very few referred to the nuclear stereotype of two parents and their children. *'No, it's impossible to have a perfect family'* (Latasha, Black girl, two-parent family). *'That's something like in fairy-tale land when they show the happy couple walking and they're going with their children and their dog to this place. But I don't think there's any such thing as a happy family – or a perfect family. There is happy*

Table 3.1 What counts as a family?

	Agree	Disagree	Agree/ Disagree	Don't know	No answer	Total N
Notion of 'proper' family	14	40	2	6	1	63
Two adults and no children	14	46	1	0	2	63
Mother and two children	36	21	1	0	5	63
Mother and her daughter, father and his son by earlier marriage	44	15	0	3	1	63

families, but not perfect families . . .' (Inderpal, South Asian origin boy, lone mother family).

A few children spontaneously referred to household structure in referring to a 'proper family'. For example, a South Asian girl, Bibi, living with both birth parents, clearly rejected the conflation of the two-parent norm with normality. *'No, it's like saying here's a normal family, two parents, two children. If you're not that, you're weird, you're dysfunctional. It's just like saying, this is the perfect family, you're not perfect and they are. It's just not fair.'* Tara, a mixed race girl living with a lone mother, asserted that families are 'not like that': *'No, you can't have a proper family. I don't know what a proper family is. There isn't a right way to have a family. Like people say, a mum, a dad, daughter and a baby. But there are very few people who have families like that.'* By contrast, another mixed race girl, Leila, living with her lone mother was somewhat ambivalent, subscribing to the nuclear stereotype while trying at the same time to assert its similarity to a family where parents live apart: *'What, like a mum, dad together in a house and everything? Well, yes I suppose so. If a family's like all together, the mum, the dad, the brothers and sisters and everything then that's a proper family. But it's the same – well it's not the same, but you still have a family if they're apart.'*

In response to other questions about the meaning of the term family, children's replies suggest that their ideas were strongly grounded in their own family experiences, and that their idea of which persons 'make a family' was not restricted to the household and often included non-resident parents and siblings, aunts and uncles and other relatives. Asked 'the most important thing about being part of a family', the great majority talked in terms of parents' love, emotional security and affective support. Asked the converse question of what they would miss most in not being part of a family, children talked about the absence of parents' love and attention.

'Children make a family'

We also asked children whether they thought particular household structures counted as families, by using short vignettes which the interviewer read out in the course of the interview. The first vignette consisted of a household of two adults and no children. From most of the children's point of view, a family without children was not considered a 'proper' family but a family in the making (46/63) (Table 3.1). *'The child makes the family. It's like a triangle. Without a child there's no triangle'* (Baldev, South Asian origin boy, two-parent family). *'Two people together doesn't make a family really. You've got to have something else, like a child or something to make it a family. Because they've got to have something together.'* (Leila, mixed race girl, lone mother family). One girl reflected on the fact that the couple was part of a bigger family: *'Because they still have the people's mums and their sisters, if they've got any, and the rest of their relatives'* (Claudia, mixed race girl, lone mother family).

'Love makes a family'

By contrast, in relation to the second scenario of household structure – a lone mother and her two children – most children (36/63) agreed that this was a family while one-third disagreed (21/63) (Table 3.1). The critical issue for those who agreed was the existence of love and care. *'Yes, yes I think that's a family, because you've still got a parent and you still – you still get love . . . all a family needs is love. . . . Say you're on your own and one parent, you still get love, that's still a family. Because family's all about love. If you get love, then you're a family. But if you get nothing what's the point of having a mother and a father? Or a father or a mother?'* (Inderpal, South Asian origin boy, lone mother family).

   For those who disagreed that a lone mother household constituted a family, many gave a structural reason – the absence of the father from the household. However, these children were disproportionately of South Asian origin (9/21). *'No. Because you always need a father to have a family. So that's not a family. I don't think'* (Harinder, South Asian origin boy, two-parent household). As Morrow's research has also shown (Morrow 1998), children of Pakistani origin were also less likely to perceive a lone mother household as a family compared with children from white families.

Children's responses to this question were influenced, not surprisingly, by family type. Only five of the fifteen children living in two-birth-parent families and four out of fourteen foster children who answered the question suggested a lone mother household was a family, compared with most children in lone mother or step family types (16/18 in lone parent families and 11/15 children in step parent families).

'Step families need working at'

Despite the greater diversity among step family forms than among other household types, rather more children agreed that it was a family (44/63) than disagreed (15/63) (Table 3.1). Moreover, there was slightly more agreement that this family form was a family – containing, in the scenario, a mother and daughter and her new partner and his son – compared with those who agreed that a lone mother family was a family (Table 3.1). However, among those children who agreed, several qualified their answers by suggesting that a step family could only become a family if certain conditions were met. As several comments implied, there could be problems in this type of family and the conditions for being a 'family' could not be left to chance. In short, some children seemed to suggest that step families need 'working at', as one child commented referring to her birth father's new step family: '*If they kind of got on together and kind of worked together, it could become a family. Because my dad's got a girlfriend and a child and they don't want to get married but kind of live together and that. And they're kind of like a family and they care for each other and that. So!*' Two children, one of whom was currently living in a lone mother family and the other in a step family made points about the importance of love and respect in step families: '*Yes. Because they might say it's a family in their own way. So I can't really say it ain't a family. Because there's always a – like to treat each other with respect and love each other is still a family*' (Claudia, mixed race girl, lone mother family). '*If you're happy really. It's still family because you're living together*' (Chloe, Black girl, step father).

Among those who did not define this arrangement as a family, the fact of the father's son not being 'blood related' to the mother and daughter was seen as particularly problematic (comments by six children): '*It's not. I wouldn't call it a family – because family's like your own flesh and blood isn't it?*' (Liam, white boy, foster care). A South Asian origin girl living with two-birth parents identified with the daughter and blamed the mother for bringing the step father and his son into the household. She clearly felt that the children were being coerced into becoming a family: '*Because your stepfather's son doesn't have anything to do with you. It's just because your mum married him and you're just having to be with him because your mum wants you to'* (Sunita, South Asian origin girl, two-parent family).

It is undoubtedly significant that all the children from step families who were asked the question and all but two children from the lone mother families (16/18) defined this arrangement as a family, compared with only half of the children from two-birth parent and foster care families (8/15 and 7/14 respectively).

To sum up, just as research by Morrow (1998) has also indicated, most children held an inclusive view of what counts as a family. They rejected unitary notions of a 'proper family', attributed inclusive definitions to the term family, and generally agreed that different family forms constituted families. Children identified clear criteria which turned a group of people into a family, namely: the presence of children, the presence of at least one parent (not necessarily two) in the household, and, most important of all, the provision of love and care (see also Chapter 5). However, we also found that children's own current living arrangements and/or their past experience of living arrangements affected their definitions of family life to some extent. Children living in lone mother households and in step families had rather more inclusive views about household structure, compared with children living in two-birth-parent families (who were disproportionately of South Asian origin) and children in foster care who lived with neither of their birth parents. But more significant to children was the issue of how family life is lived than what families ought to look like. While being open-minded about what families 'are', children have specific ideas about what parents are 'for', namely providing children with commitment through unconditional love and care (Chapter 5).

Children's significant others

We also examined, again in the interviews, the importance children placed upon their social ties including wider kin and persons who were not kin. In order to do this, we used visual–spatial techniques. The method for establishing which significant others children considered important to them was adapted from the 'Five Field' map of Samuelson et al. (1996) originally designed for clinical work with children who had experienced social and family difficulties. In our study, children were given a large sheet of paper upon which were drawn three concentric circles and divided into four segments which cut across the three circles (Figure 3.1). Each segment represented a different domain of social relationships in children's lives: the household, relatives and kin, friends and 'formal others', for example teachers, social workers and family doctors. Children were asked to write in the names of people in the relevant domains (household, kin, friends and formal others). They were also asked to bear in mind while locating their significant others that the three concentric circles signified different degrees of 'importance' – with people considered to be 'very important' to be located in the inner circle, those less important in the middle circle, and those least important in the outer circle of the map. The term 'close' was avoided since, in the pilot interviews, some children confused closeness with proximity. In any case, we did not wish to define the criteria of importance on children's behalf. An example of a child's map of significant others will be given in the context of the case study discussion.

After the children had completed the map, the interviewer went through each domain and asked them to clarify the identities of the persons they had mentioned and their connections to them. The interviewer noted these on a sheet of paper and the social context in which

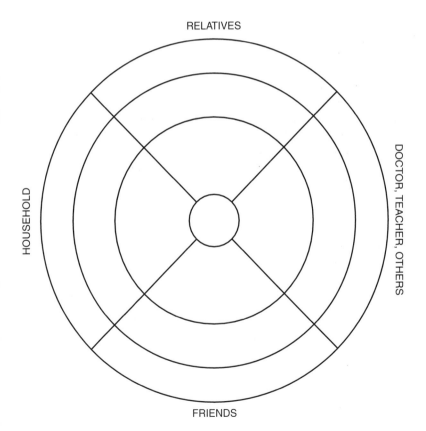

Fig. 3.1

the child knew the persons concerned, for example if friends were made at secondary or primary school, or if they lived in children's neighbourhoods. This exercise provided a basis for discussing with children their relationships with their parents and significant others later in the interview (See Chapters 5, 6, 7).

An overview of these maps indicates that children were inclusive in their approach to their social ties. Ties which children identified as significant were not limited to household members but included a wide variety of people – non-resident parents and kin but also persons who were not kin. Moreover, children did not restrict close ties to their nuclear families or households. Most children placed the greater proportion of their significant others in the inner rather than in the other two circles; the average number of significant others placed in the inner circle was 19.3 compared with 5.0 in the middle circle and 3.5 in the outer circle (Table 3.2). In the inner circle which indicated greatest importance, children tended to place those who lived with them in the same household, including their siblings and pets, but also a range of other people – their non-resident parents and siblings, their grandparents, and other blood relatives, particularly aunts and uncles (who were mothers' and fathers' siblings) (See also Chapters 6 and 7, including Table 7.1). Some children included friends and formal others such as their teachers and some also placed these persons in the inner circle (Chapter 7). By contrast with kin relations, children tended to differentiate the importance of friends by distributing them across the three circles. Of the 63 children, 11 placed everyone in their inner circles.

As household structure is associated with household size, it is not surprising that the average number of persons children placed in the household segment of their maps differed significantly by household type, with lone mother children placing the smallest number of persons in household segment (Table 3.2). Lone mother children also placed fewer people overall in the three circles and also in the inner and middle circles. Lone mother children included on average the fewest friends and formal others. Such findings have been noted in other studies; for example Cochran and Riley (1990) found that the networks of 6-year-olds living with their Black lone mothers contained fewer non-kin compared with Black two-parent families.

Children's family networks

It is important to distinguish those whom children said were important to them from those who were available to them in a practical sense. In addition to examining the ties children defined as important, we also identified children's family members and differentiated between those

Table 3.2 Mean number of persons in different circles and in the household segment (based on children's circles of significant others) by household type

Persons placed in circles/household	Two-parent	One-parent	Step parent	Foster	All children	Sig.
All persons in 3 circles	31.2	21.5	33	27.7	28.1	not sig.
Persons in inner circle	23.7	12.9	22.2	19.3	19.3	not sig.
Persons in middle circle	5.1	3.1	7.6	4.4	5.0	not sig.
Persons in outer circle	2.4	4.4	3.4	3.8	3.5	not sig.
Persons in household segment – 3 circles	4.7	3.2	4.3	4.5	4.1	0.05

that existed and those with whom children had regular contact. Since the study focused on children living in different family forms, our main concern was the actual shape and composition of the family networks of children who had experienced family change. We were not able within the constraints of the study to examine children's social networks more generally. We kept in mind three issues. First, we included contact not only with non-resident parents but with siblings who in some cases were distributed across different households. Second, households and family networks are not static entities, they go on changing. Third, children may themselves be agents activating or blocking contact with family network members. With increased policy emphasis on joint parenting after divorce, the onus is increasingly upon children themselves to negotiate the links between their parents' different households (Neale and Smart 1998; Neale et al. 1998).

We used a variety of methods to help children articulate and identify their family ties. As in the identification of children's significant others, we used visual, participatory techniques (family trees). While some reasons for choosing such techniques relate to our presumptions about children – notably our view that children seemed to enjoy these methods, similar rationales could be made for studying adults. First, we were conscious that the topic of family change is sensitive and thought that asking too many direct questions might increase its sensitivity and make children feel they were different because of their particular family form. Second, we were aware of the considerable power imbalance of adult as questioner and child as respondent and therefore sought to break-up this mode of participation with other modes. We also thought that children might be sensitive to adults questioning them about 'private matters'. Third, family networks are often complex and may be difficult to explain concisely and coherently, especially given the lack of clear terms to convey different types of kinship or 'kin-like' relationships. Fourth, we sought to offer variety in methods of research participation.

At the start of the interviews, we asked children with whom they lived. Because we had observed during the focus groups conducted earlier in schools that some children were very interested in talking about their family links and family histories, we decided to include an inter-generational focus. We asked children to assist the interviewer in constructing a family tree comprising three generations: their siblings, their parents and parents' partners, and their grandparents. This exercise was very helpful in clarifying the sequencing of parents' partners, children's relationships to parents and their parents' respective partners, together with establishing different sets of grandparents and whether they were still alive. It was also 'natural' for the interviewer to ask children during the course of this exercise whether they had known the persons concerned and whether they were currently in touch with them.

However, in practice, we found that describing the complexities of family networks was not necessarily a problem for the children concerned. Children were quite articulate and often readily supplied the current household structures when asked to do so at the beginning of the interview, while it was more often than not the researcher who was struggling to make sense of the child's family circumstances.

Contact with birth parents

We mapped out children's family networks on the basis of their reported contact with their birth parents, parents' new partners, other key carers and their siblings including full, half and step siblings. The majority of the lone mother children and step father children whose birth fathers were still alive had maintained contact with them either 'monthly' or 'less often' (11/14 and 13/15 respectively) (Table 3.3). These proportions broadly compare with results from the Questionnaire Survey in which around four-fifths of these two groups were in contact with their non-resident fathers.

Among the case study children, contact with non-resident fathers was more frequent among the step father children than among the lone mother children (Table 3.3). None of the children in the study experienced a shared parenting situation. Three children, two with lone mothers and one with a step father, had fathers who lived far away and whom they usually saw in the holidays. Five among the lone mother and

Table 3.3   Children's contact with non-resident parents by family type: Interview Study responses and Survey responses (in brackets)

	Monthly	Less than monthly/ holidays only	No contact	Total
Lone parent children	6 (58%)	5 (25%)	3 (17%)	14* (222)
Step family children	11 (62%)	2 (14%)	2 (24%)	15 (74)
Foster children				
Mother	5	9	1	15
Father	2	4	8	14**
Other carers	(44%)	(38%)	(19%)	(16)

*The fathers of the 4 other children in the group were dead;
**The father of the other child in the group was dead.

step father children had no contact with their birth fathers; the fathers of two children had been banned by court order from seeing them; while three children did not want any contact. Only two foster children were in regular (at least monthly) contact with their birth fathers and over half either had no current contact, while four had never known their fathers. The amount of regular contact of the case study children very broadly reflects contact among the Questionnaire Survey sample which also indicated rather more, but not statistically significantly more, regular contact among the step father children compared with the lone mother children (Table 3.3).

Active family network size, network boundaries and contact with siblings

In mapping children's family networks, we drew a linkage signified by an unbroken line where contact was currently maintained with a family network member (that is on at least a monthly basis), noted irregular ties by a broken line, and drew no line where there was no current contact. We then quantified the number of active contacts and allocated children's family networks to three groups in terms of size: small (less than five active ties,) medium-sized (five to seven ties) and large (eight ties and over) (Table 3.4). Some children's active family networks were the same as their households, while others included non-resident parents and sets of siblings. In the case of foster children, most of whose parents had separated and gained new partners, and with children born to different partnerships, family networks sometimes spanned several households. As the Questionnaire Survey evidence indicates, those reporting the largest number of resident siblings were those living with their grandparents or foster carers (but numbers were very small in this group $n = 15$).

Not surprisingly, children in lone mother families had the smallest active family networks, with more step father children in the middle category, and the foster children divided between small- and medium-sized family networks. Two-birth-parent families were roughly equally divided between the small and medium-sized groups.

The boundaries of family networks were not set in stone but were

Table 3.4   Children's household type by family network size

	Small <5	Medium 5–7	Large 8+	Total
Single-parent	13	4		17
Step family	2	10	3	15
Foster children	5	10	–	15
Two-parent children	7	8	–	15

Table 3.5   Children with siblings (full, half and step) and other children in the household by family type

	No other children in household	Blood-related children in household	Other children (non blood-related) in household	Siblings in other households	no. of children
One parent	1	16	–	8	17
Two-parent	–	15	–	–	15
Foster care	1	8	11	13	15
Step family	–	15	–	15	15

N.B. These contacts include active and inactive ties; children could have more than one type of sibling, etc.

subject to continuing change. Foster children, by definition, had lost daily contact with their birth parents when they were taken into care. Even before this, because of parental separation and divorce, many had already lost contact with their birth fathers, and several had had more than one step father. (At the time of the interviews only one set of foster children's birth parents was still living together.) Lone parent and step family children had, by definition, experienced their birth fathers leaving the family home.

One of the main family network changes children experienced, in addition to those relating to birth parents, concerned sibling ties. Some children had experienced the arrival of half siblings in their own or in other households. The arrival of a step father created the potential for new step sibling relations (none in this study shared the same household with step siblings on a full-time basis at the time of the study). Some children had lost daily contact with siblings who lived elsewhere. Those with older, grown-up full siblings, typically experienced siblings leaving home in order to work away, to study and/or to live independently (four children). The extent to which children's family networks consisted in the potential for ties with other siblings and also with other children in the household is indicated in Table 3.5.

In contrast to children living with two birth parents and also lone mother children, most foster care and step family children had the potential for a web of different sets and types of sibling relationships which spanned two or more households. With the re-partnering of their birth fathers and the acquisition of step fathers, they gained new siblings. Most step family children at the time of the interviews had more than one set of siblings; just over half had experienced the arrival of new half siblings in their households, most of whom were very much younger than themselves (8/15). Over half of the step family children (8/15) had step siblings, either through their current step fathers or through their birth fathers' new partners' previous relationships (a few had both). However, none of the step family children lived permanently with step siblings, although one child lived with her step father's own children at weekends and another child once lived with her step father's children for a short, fraught period when the step father first joined the household.

In the case of lone mother and step father children, contact with non-resident siblings was not necessarily active. Of the eight lone mother children with siblings in other households, five had no contact and three regular contact. All 15 step father children had siblings in other households; eleven had regular contact, seven had no contact and three had contact with some and not others.

Foster children's networks had even greater potential for ties with other children. When they were first looked after, they typically joined households where there were already other children. In six out of fourteen foster care situations in the study (this means 8/15 children because two sets of siblings (four children) were interviewed), siblings were placed with the same foster carers. In eight of the foster care families, children joined foster carers' own biological children (in one case this was a grown up child). In addition, four foster children were living with non-blood-related children who were fostered with them. Seven foster care placements involved living both with the foster carers' children and with other foster children, while five placements involved only one of these categories. Only one foster child in the study joined a household where there were no other children and two foster children who were siblings lived with their carers and no other children.

Foster children typically experienced separation from at least some of their siblings when they were looked after (two foster children in the study had no siblings). Many had siblings who were fostered or adopted in other families. There were no cases where all the siblings were placed together. Only three foster children had siblings still living with their birth mothers and one pair of sisters had a sibling living with their birth father. Compared with the step family and lone mother children, foster children's contact with their non-resident siblings was considerably lower and more spasmodic: of the 13 children with siblings in other households, 12 had little or no regular current contact with at least one sibling, and four had regular contact with all siblings. Irregular contact typically involved the occasional birthday card, telephone call or visit. Yet many children lived in the hope of making contact with their siblings in the future but few had the resources to do so (Chapter 6). Instead, they were largely dependent upon their social workers and their siblings' foster carers who acted as gatekeepers. Foster children who had siblings who were living independently did not seem to fare any better in terms of contact however.

Contrasting family networks within the same household type

Considerable variety exists in children's family networks in terms of family members with whom children had contact. This variety occurs within as well as between different family forms. In order to illustrate the variety of active ties with resident and non-resident parents and siblings, we will describe some contrasting networks from the case studies. First, we present two very different networks of step family children and then two contrasting networks of foster children. We will also indicate the importance children placed upon significant others and show how their maps of significant others sometimes reflect their family networks and sometimes not.

Two step family networks

Jasmine was a mixed race, working-class girl who lived with her non-employed mother, her step father who worked as a postman, her brother aged eight and her new half brother aged one. Her active family network was simple in structure: her step father had no children from his former relationship. Jasmine and her brother had had no contact with their birth father since they were very young. While completing the family tree, Jasmine noted that her birth father had two other children from another marriage but she did not know their whereabouts, names or ages. In any case, because of the history of violence towards her mother, she said she did not want to see him. In contrast to her small family network and unlike the maps of many lone parent children, Jasmine's map of significant others was large. Jasmine placed all the members of her household in the inner circle together with other kin, friends and teachers. In the two other circles she distributed pets, cousins, friends and teachers. She excluded her birth father.

By contrast, Chloe's step family network was even larger and also complex, and Chloe had frequent contact with its many members. Chloe was from an Afro-Caribbean family and her parents worked in semi-skilled manual jobs. She lived with her mother, one older half sister aged 16 (from a relationship which preceded her mothers' relationship with her own birth father), her new half brother and her step father. Within a year of Chloe's birth father leaving when Chloe was very young, her mother found a new partner, but the relationship broke up when Chloe was 10. Her mother has no children from this partner

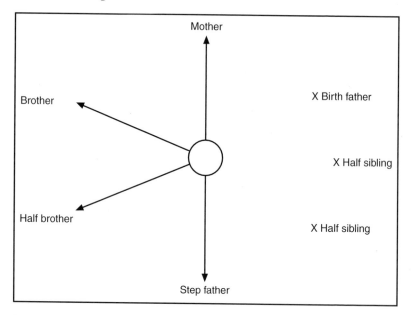

Fig. 3.2   Jasmine's step family network

and the family has lost contact with him. Chloe's mother's new partner moved into the household a year ago. He has two teenage children from a former relationship who live elsewhere but come to stay at weekends. Chloe sees her birth father regularly and also her three young half siblings from her birth father's new relationship. As a consequence, Chloe has four sets of siblings all of whom she sees regularly and with whom she has good relations.

   This network is interesting not only because of its changing composition and complexity but because it illustrates the ways in which Chloe actively negotiated her different sets of kin relations. Chloe's approach to family relations was highly inclusive; she did not distinguish between her full, half, and step siblings. While completing her map of significant others, which was very large and concentrated in the inner circle, she referred to them all as her 'brothers and sisters' and placed them in the inner circle thereby signifying their importance to her. Chloe's siblings constituted a significant source of peer group relations. As Chloe noted: *'I've got all of those people I mentioned, my oldest sister, and [step father's] children, we all go out together.'*

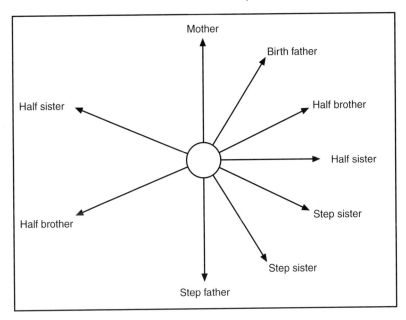

Fig. 3.3   Chloe's step family network

When sibling relations were adversely affected by rivalries, as happened from time to time, Chloe's mother said she insisted the children sort out the problems between themselves. But when discussing the importance of friends, Chloe noted significantly: '*I put my family before my friends.*' Chloe's inclusive approach to social relationships was also evident towards her friends whom she identified according to the settings in which she came to make their acquaintance, namely through school but also the two neighbourhoods where she regularly visited her birth father and her grandmother respectively. She also included as being important her 30 cousins in the UK, her numerous uncles, and other cousins living in the USA and the Caribbean. Chloe placed almost all her extended kin and family ties in the inner circle of her large map of significant others, with the exception of a handful of friends, cousins and teachers whom she placed in the middle circle. Chloe's family network has some similarities with two other Black families in the step family group. All three families had very strong ties with grandparents as well as extensive, active ties with siblings and with non-resident fathers.

Two foster children's networks

Jason had a potentially large family network but, in practice, his network was small. He lived with a working-class foster family and a non-related foster child, a girl of 14. The eldest of five children, he had one full brother and three half siblings. He said his birth parents separated when he was three years old and that he lived with his father until he was six, when his father died very suddenly. He was then placed in care and had a number of foster placements. His half brothers and sisters stayed with their father while the mother moved to live with another man; the couple have a young child, Jason's new half brother. At one point, Jason was sent to another part of the country to live with some relatives of his deceased father. However, this situation did not work out, and for a very short difficult time, he returned to live with his birth mother and new partner and half brother. This did not work out either and he was again put into care although some of his relatives with whom he had some contact have made efforts to keep in touch with him. Talking about his different foster placements he said: '*I lived with my first foster carer for one week, and I changed . . . changed, changed, changed. . . . But now I've got a more permanent – I've got a permanent*

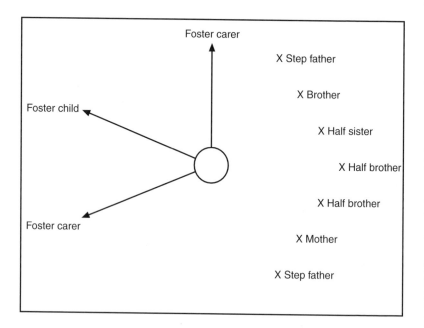

Fig. 3.4 Jason's family and foster network

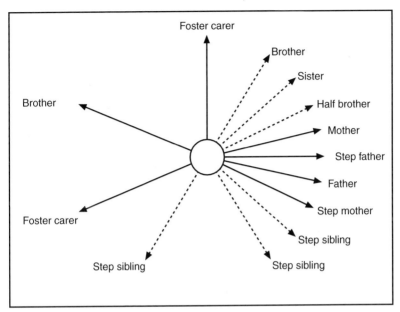

Fig. 3.5 Melanie's family and foster network

home here.' (Are you going to stay here?) *'Mm.'* (Are you happy about that?) *Mmm* . . . (Mmm? You're quite happy to stay here?) *'Yes.'* (Or do you think you would still prefer to go back and live with your mum, or not? And all your other brothers and sisters?) *'I'd like to live with my mum and all my brothers and sisters, et cetera.'*

At the time of the interview, Jason had no active ties with his birth family and he had not seen his mother for two years. He said he would very much like to see his siblings but did not know where they were living. He was not in a position to seek them out himself. In completing his map of significant others, he mentioned a lot of people, many of whom he rarely or never saw: his birth family, relatives (whom he rarely sees), the foster care family, friends from his last school, teachers, a social worker and a Guardian *ad litem*. Moreover, he placed everyone in the inner circle.

Finally, we include the family network of Melanie, an example of a large active network consisting of her biological family and her foster family. This was the first foster placement for Melanie and her brother (who was near in age). They had been in care for two years because of their mother's illness and were in regular contact with both their birth parents and their new partners. They had very irregular contact with their four step siblings (from their parents' new partners) and with their three older siblings who had been separately fostered elsewhere. The parents separately made frequent visits to Melanie and her brother, but the number of visits had been cut down because of insufficient time in the children's lives. Their family networks were further complicated by the fact that their foster carers had a large grown-up family, who had children themselves; these families lived nearby and were heavily involved in the daily lives of Melanie and her brother. Both children were now very attached to their foster carers and their foster family's extended family. Yet, the children appeared to feel quite emotionally torn between their own biological families and the extended kin network of their working-class foster family. Indeed, in completing the maps of significant others which was almost exclusively composed of her birth family and her foster family and their extended kin, Melanie insisted in putting the foster carers' grown up children and the grand-children in the relatives section of her map. Her brother had a similar dilemma when filling in his own map. He said: *'I've just remembered them.'* (Who?) *'It's [foster carers'] relatives, but I treat them as my own.'* (OK.) *'Would you mind if I write them in there?'* (No, no, no. Please do.) *'Because they're not really that family, I'll put them in here* (the relatives section), *but they're half-way.'* (Yes.) *'Borderline.'* Melanie included almost everyone in her inner circle including her birth family and she put members of her foster carers' extended family under friends. She reserved the middle circle for her mother's boyfriend and one of her step brothers.

Conclusions

In this chapter, we have sought to provide a context for the analysis of the material presented in the rest of the book. First, we examined chil-dren's understandings and representations of what counts as a family. We found that children considered family structure *per se* to be less important than the conditions under which family life is created and lived. As children suggested, in order to 'be a family', families should have children, at least one parent, and there should be love and mutual respect. The provision of love and social and emotional care was the critical factor which children considered produced feelings of closeness, a sense of security and a place to belong. While children's living arrangements and past experiences affected children's views of what constitutes an acceptable definition of what families 'ought' to look like, they did not affect their view of what families 'are' in practice.

Second, in order to set in context later discussion concerning the particular significance to children of their own parents, siblings, relatives, friends and others, we described the methods we used. We have also provided an overview of children's maps of their significant others and shown that children identified a very wide range of persons whom they considered important to them which extended well beyond the bounds of households and kin. Moreover, children's inclusive approach did not differentiate a great deal in terms of relative importance, with most children placing most persons in their inner circles which signified the highest degree of importance. We also noted that children living in lone mother families noted, on average, fewer significant others which reflected their smaller networks of active family ties.

Third, we examined the nature of children's family networks in practice. The case studies provided a powerful opportunity to do this since they were selected precisely to represent different types of family form. In practice, children's family networks varied greatly both in terms of potential ties and active ties. For some children experiencing family change, the household *de facto* constituted the child's active family network while, for others, the active family network extended across several households. From the vantage point of children, family networks not only provided children with parents' care, they also provided children with the possibility of ties with other children, namely siblings. Following family change, children may acquire half siblings and step siblings who may join them in the same household or they may live in other households. In the case of foster children, they may gain new 'sibling-like' relationships within their foster families. Foster children typically experienced their siblings being scattered across several households because of family change as well as care orders. Moreover, they had in many cases irregular or no contact with them. Just as active ties between parents and children may fluctuate over time, so too relations with siblings are subject to flux and change in terms of contact but not in terms of emotional importance, as we discuss later. Moreover, in practice, family networks vary *within* family forms. Family change and family structure are not always the main forces shaping children's contact with their kin.

4 Children's accounts of family change

Well, if you didn't live with your parents, you'd sort of feel sad. You'd miss them and you might want to meet them, want to know what they're like.

In public and practitioner discourse and in the research literature, separation and divorce are generally presented as distressing and damaging, especially for children. Numerous studies have looked at the effects of household change upon children focusing upon the economic effects, the relational aspects and the psychological (dis)stress (Maclean and Eekelaar 1997). Much of this research has been on the long-term effects and has focused upon behavioural outcomes rather than upon the perceptions and interpretations of the experience (see Richards 1996; Maclean and Eekelaar 1997 for an overview of the research). Children's own accounts of their experiences of household change are much less well documented.

Some studies have focused on children's feelings after divorce (Walczak and Burns 1984). For example, Mitchell (1985) found that children reported feelings of anger against parents some years later. More recently, Neale et al. (1998) have focused on children's experiences following their parents' separation and divorce including children living in 'shared parenting' arrangements. Their conceptualisation of the divorce process and its impact on children differs from the traditional picture, where children are portrayed as bearing the *stigmata* of divorce and as only reacting to negative events. Instead, starting from the conceptual position which accords children reflexivity and agency, children are here allowed to emerge as active negotiators of parental separation and divorce. In this way, separation and divorce are conceptualised as social processes which children must make sense of, and in which children are implicated as social actors. Moreover, instead of a unitary conceptualisation of parental separation and family reordering,

Neale et al. stress the variety and fluidity of family arrangements follow-ing separation and divorce which children play an active part in struc-turing and restructuring (Neale et al. 1998: 18).

There is very little evidence on the experience of being and becoming a step family from children's perspectives. Like much of the divorce research, much of the literature on step families has taken a 'problem approach' and examined the adverse outcomes of this family form, for example for children's behaviour (Brady et al. 1986; Amato and Ochiltree 1987; Dawson 1991), early sexual activity (Flewelling and Bauman 1990), early home leaving, drop-out from formal education (Aquilino 1991) and greater involvement in criminal activity (Mednick et al. 1990).

Children's experiences of foster care have received some attention, although studies have focused rather narrowly on the service aspects conceptualising children's experiences in terms of their 'satisfaction' with particular types of care – foster care and residential care (Colton 1989; Triseliotis et al. 1995). By contrast, little is known about how 'looked after' children negotiate the different settings and sets of family relationships following entry into care which include both the foster family and their often fragmented birth families including siblings.

In this chapter, we will examine children's accounts of family change which had occurred at different points of their life course. Four aspects of family change are discussed: the departure of a birth father from the family home; becoming a step (father) family; entering foster care; and adapting to a foster family. The accounts of household change reflect the experience of the three case study groups: those living with their lone mother; those living with their mother and step father; those living with foster carers (Table 4.1). The number of changes children experience is closely associated with their current household structure: for the lone mother group – one household change, (parents' separa-tion); for the step family group – two changes (parents' separation and a step father moving in); and for many of the foster group – multiple changes (parental separation, a step father moving in, being taken into care and joining a foster family).

Half of children in both the lone mother and step father groups were under the age of five when their parents separated. Step children had been members of step father families for lengths of time varying from eight years to just over one year. Foster children also varied in terms of the length of time they had been in care. The 15 foster children were not questioned about their parents' separations and re-partnering, but only about their care events and foster care experiences. However, some foster children spontaneously referred to their parents' separation when discussing the divorce vignette. Most foster children (11/15) had been

Table 4.1   Number of children experiencing household change events by children's household group

	Lone mother	Step father	Foster care
Parents' separation	12*	14**	9***
Becoming a step family	–	15	9
Being taken into care	–	–	15

*In addition, 2 children had never lived with their fathers and 4 fathers were dead.
**1 further child had never lived with her birth father.
***6 further children had either never lived with their birth fathers or had never known them.

with current carers for between two and five years, while two children had been with their current carers for eight to ten years and at the other extreme, two had been moved to their current carers in the past three months. Table 4.2 shows children's ages at the time of parental separation, family reconstitution and being looked after.

Interviewing children about family change

While only some children claimed to be 'old enough' to remember these events, some clearly did remember and presented graphic accounts, while others were more reticent: they were either reluctant to talk about what had happened or could not express their feelings about relationships. At the start of the interview, children were asked about their household composition. Later, children were invited to help the interviewer draw up a 'family tree' (siblings, parents and partners, and grandparents). This was followed by an exercise in which children filled out maps of significant others (see Chapter 3). On the basis of this latter exercise, children were then asked about the importance of each person mentioned and, in respect

Table 4.2   Number of children who experienced different family changes by age group at first change

Age groups at first family change	No. of children whose parents separated	No. of children whose step father moved into household	No. of children who entered foster care
Under 5 yrs.	13	2	3
5–7	7	3	4
8–9	5	5	6
10–11	1	5	2
n	26*	15	15

*This refers to children living with a lone mother and children living with a step father. It excludes four children whose fathers had died and three children who never lived with their fathers. Foster children were not asked about their experience of parental separation and are not therefore included here.

of parents, to recall and comment on associated household change events: parents' separation, keeping in touch with non-resident fathers, acquiring step fathers, moving into care. Opportunities for children to talk about family change arose also in other parts of the interview, for example in response to questions about the meaning of the term 'family' or when discussing their normative views of divorce (Chapters 2 and 3).

From the perspective of the interviewer, it was often a matter of picking up clues from the children as to whether and when children might be willing to pursue these sensitive matters. The interviewers sought to maintain a careful balance between probing and not pushing so hard that the child disengaged or became upset (Amato and Ochiltree 1987). In fact, three foster children became visibly upset when they were asked about contact with their birth mothers, which the interviewer made a point of acknowledging and then offered to change the subject if the child wished. All three children accepted this offer but two of them spontaneously mentioned their mothers at a later point in the interview. Some foster children referred indirectly to their family histories in discussing the vignette about divorce (Chapter 2). In fact, as we shall show, all the foster children were keen to include their birth families in their maps of significant others and to emphasise their importance to them, even though they had little contact with them (Chapters 5 and 6).

At the start of the interviews, the interviewers made it clear to children that they had the right to refuse to answer questions. Two children refused to give their mothers' occupations while three foster children declined to say why they were being looked after. When it came to discussing their parents' separation, no child refused to answer, but sometimes their responses were significantly brief, especially when asked about non-resident birth fathers, which suggested that they did not wish to talk about them. Perhaps they still wanted to believe in their fathers even though they felt a sense of disappointment in them. Moreover, as we shall show, in general children were anxious to be fair to both their parents and did not want to be seen to differentiate between them (Chapters 5 and 9).

Particular children clearly found it difficult to express their opinions and feelings. For example, Steve, a friendly and cooperative white boy living in a step family, was quite happy to discuss his progress in school or his contribution to housework, but became uneasy and self-conscious when asked to comment on the meaning of the term family or the importance of mothers and fathers – either in general or specifically. He seemed to need reassurance from the interviewer as well as prompting, which the interviewer tried to provide during the drawing of his family tree. At this point in the interview, Steve became visibly more relaxed and his responses, although brief, were to the point:

I: *And how long ago did [stepfather] move in?*

S: *Oh, about three years ago.*

I: *And how did you feel about that?*

S: *I didn't mind, because [step father] was mostly at work, and I didn't know him a lot.*
      We went round to see him sometimes [before moving in], we went out to places. I didn't mind.

I: *And did your mum sort of explain to you when he moved in here? Did you know he was going to move in?*

S: *Yes, she [mother] told me that he was going to move in, and so . . .*

I: *And how do you feel about him being here now?*

S: *It's OK because he's got me quite a few things for my birthday.*

Steve was typical of a number of children, mostly boys, who were happy to talk about themselves, but not family change or relationships. In contrast, three girls (two lone mother children and one from the step father group) who had been very distressed when their parents' relationships broke up were much more forthcoming. Rebecca, a white girl living in a lone mother household, lived in the North of England with her parents and younger sister until she was five when her mother decided to return to London, taking the children with her. When asked about her memories of the separation she remembered the event clearly:

I: *Now, you said your mum and dad split up when you were 6. Did you understand what was going on?*

R: *What, the actual argument?*

I: *Yes.*

R: *Yes, I did.*

I: *Did they explain it to you?*

R: *Not from my point of view. My mum just wouldn't speak about it, my dad thinks it's got nothing to do with me. But I was actually awake upstairs listening to the argument.*

R: *[Describes parents' argument].*
      And a few weeks after that, they were just, like, not talking to each other and then mum decided actually to pack up and leave. So Dad took us down here [to London].

I: *I see, and how did you feel about that at the time?*

R: *It was very upsetting.*

I: *Did you have a chance to talk to anyone about it at the time?*

R: *No, not really, because my mum – from my point of view, Mum just thought it would be alright. She was taking us down there [to London] and just leaving us there. But half our family was up there [in the North] and it was quite hard for us [children], but she never quite understood that view. Although she says she does, but she doesn't really.*

Rebecca related how two years previously, the family unit (Rebecca, her younger sister and her mother) had been referred to what she described as a 'problem solver' because of her sister's disruptive behaviour at school. Rebecca said she would have liked to speak to the 'problem solver' on her own: *'I prefer to speak to a stranger who doesn't know me and who can't judge me, kind of thing.'* However, she was not given the opportunity and confessed to feeling unable to express her feelings about the family situation in her mother's presence which may explain why Rebecca was so forthcoming in the interview.

Children's mothers and, in the case of foster children, children's female carers, were also interviewed. Their accounts of family change helped to fill in gaps – either where children said they could not remember family change or where they gave little information of a factual kind about their family reordering. However, mothers concentrated more on their own role in providing support to their children than on children's own responses to and ways of dealing with these events. They also tended to emphasise their own agency in making sure children maintained contact with their fathers.

Fathers moving out

Parental conflict which usually precedes household change and persists before parents separate appears to contribute to children's problems as much as the divorce itself (Elliott and Richards 1991; Cherlin et al. 1991). While many children claimed not to remember the time before their parents separated or the separation itself because they were 'too young', some mentioned arguments as a forewarning of things to come. Claudia, a mixed race girl living in a lone mother household, was eight at the time of her parents' separation. She remarks on her own sensitivity to what was happening between her parents so that she claimed not to perceive the final separation as a shock: *'I knew what was happening, because ... because they kept on arguing all the time and I thought "One of these days he's going to walk out" and he did'.* Another girl living in a lone mother family recalled how she was told that her parents were going to separate and suggests her own vulnerability in the process:

> *What happened was like, my dad was going out to the pub and my mum was shouting at him, saying – I mean – my sister [4 at time of separation] doesn't know this, but, like, they were about, like, my*

mum was shouting things like, 'You always go out to the pub and you never look after the kids' and that, and they had, like, an argument about this. And she come up – my dad slammed the door – my mum come running upstairs crying and cuddled me and said, 'We're going home to London.'

Liam, a white boy in foster care, described the day his father left the family home when he was six with great vividness. Although Liam described a situation in which he had no control over events, he portrays himself as an active agent:

My mum and dad was arguing together. It was really dark in the house. And we [3 children] was coming down the stairs and I burst into the kitchen, because we was playing upstairs and I couldn't hear them. And my mum was crying . . . and my dad, my dad would never hit her [mother], he would never hit a lady. And he walked out. He got his jacket and walked out in the middle of the day. I was crying and shouting 'Where are you going?' He were looking back to look at us and he was just going like that with his hand, like, as if to [say] 'go back in'.

His sister, who was five at the time, also remembered that day although her recollection had a different emphasis in which she transfers her anger from her father to her mother: *'My mum went a bit greedy with the money and my dad threw all his money on the washing machine and walked out and I ran after him . . . I didn't speak to my mum for about two days'.*

In contrast, other children may have repressed their memories of or refused to talk about these events. Anna, a white girl living in a step family, who had been eight when her parents separated, claimed she could not remember her father leaving the family home, but said that her parents told her several years afterwards how she screamed and cried.

On the other hand, parental separation is but one event in children's lives. Other events had taken over and assumed importance in current lives, notably the current transition to secondary school. While parental discord and separation may well have long-term effects on children's lives, children did not necessarily perceive them as important in the 'here and now'. Of the ten children with 'a current concern', a question which we asked children at the start of the interview as a way of trying to key into children's agendas, three mentioned family change: Willy, whose father left when he was six, said he would like his father to return to the family; Amy said she was worried about problems with her stepfather's children; while Wayne, a foster boy, worried about his mother's plans to remarry because he believed she was still married to his father. The other seven children who expressed a concern talked about other matters: finding a place at secondary school, conflicts with her mother, the onset of periods, bullying in school, girlfriend trouble and a sibling's health problems.

Incorporating non-resident birth fathers

The following four case studies, which draw on material both from the children and their mothers, highlight the different ways in which children incorporated their birth fathers into their lives when they did not live with them on a permanent basis and their feelings about them. The first two children seemed to have strong and very warm relationships with their fathers, while in the third and fourth cases two boys hinted that their relationships with their fathers were not as they would like them to have been. The evidence for this often came from their mothers, as in the first case study of Daniel where the mother, rather than Daniel, emphasised the non-resident father's importance to the child. In contrast, in the second case, Leila herself expressed satisfaction with her non-resident father. In other cases, the children suggested that their fathers were not so involved in their lives. In the third case study, Ben was proactive in introducing his father into the conversation, perhaps reflecting his own strong desire to see more of his father. In the fourth case, Andrew was clearly reluctant to talk about his father and what he did not say is perhaps more significant than what he did say. But, as his mother's account suggested, his reticence may have been hiding considerable disappointment in his father.

Daniel: making the most of a father

Daniel, a Black boy, had just started to attend secondary school when interviewed. Daniel's parents, both of Afro-Caribbean origin, had separated when he was seven and his twin brothers were three. His mother, who worked full time as a bank clerk, stayed in the family home with the three children while his father, a carpenter, moved in with Daniel's paternal grandmother and aunt who lived nearby. When Daniel was nine his mother acquired a new resident partner who worked as a bus inspector and they had a child, now aged one. According to Daniel's mother, his father, whom she described as 'not an absent father', continued to take a close interest in his children, sharing the responsibility for their welfare with her, including contributing financially on a regular basis. Most days after school, Daniel said he went to his grandmother's house where he met his father, going home when his mother would have returned from work. Daniel commented that he 'liked' the arrangement because it gave him an opportunity to do his homework in peace, without the presence of his younger brothers. However it was Daniel's mother who said that Daniel was very happy with the amount of contact he had, not only with his father, but also with his grandmother and aunt. She considered that Daniel's close contact with his father and other relatives provided him with a sense of security that was beneficial to him. Moreover, while Daniel said he liked his step father, describing his relationship with him as 'OK', according to Daniel's mother, Daniel regarded his step father as important for *her* but not for himself, since his father played a much greater role in his life.

Leila: happy to be shared

Leila, a mixed race girl, used to live with both parents in the rural part of North West England where her father worked as a freelance journalist. Her mother (as the only Black person in the community) felt isolated there and decided to return to London when Leila was seven. After a family conference which included the children, it was agreed that Leila should live with her mother while her older brother (now 14) remained with his father in the North West. Leila and her mother exchanged their roomy house in the country for a small flat in the inner city. Her mother found part-time work as an administrator, a higher clerical position. When Leila was eight, her mother acquired a new resident partner and they had a child, now aged two. Leila's mother said that because Leila was so resentful of her step father, she decided he should leave: *'At the end of the day I was quite clear that she [Leila] had to be my priority, you know, because she was my daughter and, if push comes to shove, he would [have to go], it would just have to be that way, there was no other way it could be.'* By contrast, Leila gave the impression that, as one adult might advise another, she had encouraged her mother to drop her partner because he 'wasn't good for her'.

Supported by her mother, Leila visited her father during the school holidays but felt she could telephone him whenever she wanted. Leila said she was happy with this arrangement because it gave her the opportunity for a holiday in the country on her own with her father whereas her brother could spend time with his mother in London. Leila described a close relationship with both parents; she was happy to 'be shared'. She explained the benefits of the arrangement for her parents as well as herself: *'I like it actually, because we get the best of two worlds now. We get double presents and everything and I think my mum and dad are happier without each other because they argued a lot when they were together.'* Thus, apart from the fact that the family did not live together, from Leila's point of view her relations with her parents were unchanged.

Ben: the adoring son

Ben, a white boy, lived in a small council flat with his mother, a part-time canteen assistant, and with his stepfather, who worked as a lorry driver. Ben's older sister (17) had just moved into her own flat and his brother (aged 20) also lived independently. Ben's parents separated when he was three and his step father moved in when he was four. Ben's father, a bricklayer, remarried and had a two-year-old son with his new wife who was expecting another child at the time of the interview. Ben had lived with his step father for eight years but, when he filled in the questionnaire in school for the Survey, he had indicated that he lived only with his mother, thereby diminishing the importance of his step father.

Throughout the interview, Ben had a knack of introducing his birth father into the conversation. Asked about the people living in his house-hold, Ben explained that he lived with his mother and his 'mum's boyfriend' because *'my mum is divorced from my dad'*. Asked about things he liked to do, Ben said he regularly went to football matches with his father and that he had been on holidays with his father and his 'step mum'. In response to the divorce vignette, Ben said he would like his mother and father to be together again. Although Ben said he stayed with his father 'every other weekend' he wanted to see him every weekend but his father appeared to be unwilling for this to happen: *'I've asked, but he [father] works a lot on the weekdays and sometimes he works on weekends, so then I can't go down there.'*

Although Ben's mother confirmed that Ben felt very close to his father, her account of Ben's level of contact with his father was some-what different from Ben's report. She noted that Ben had not seen his father for three weeks, while Ben claimed he stayed with his father every other weekend. Ben's mother also said Ben's father had never been very interested in any of his three children from his first marriage, and that sometimes she had to ask him to have Ben: *'I'd be ringing up, not telling Ben that I'd be ringing, "Can he come down there the weekend? He'd love to see you" and that.'* Nor did Ben's mother mention that his father took Ben to football matches and on holidays. It is possible that some of Ben's account of his relationship with his birth father was wishful think-ing.

Andrew: the disillusioned son

Andrew celebrated his thirteenth birthday on the day of the interview. Andrew's parents separated when he was five, leaving the mother, a playgroup supervisor, and their five children in a small inner city flat. Apart from Andrew, there were three older girls in their teens and one younger daughter aged 10. Andrew's father, who was unemployed, moved to a house in the same neighbourhood with his new partner with whom he had three daughters. Andrew appeared reluctant to talk about his relationship with his father, saying merely that his father was 'important to him', but 'not as important as his mother'. He was also rather vague about the frequency of contact with his father, saying initially that he stayed at his father's house 'for a couple of weekends sometimes'. When prompted, he added that he did not stay with his father as much as he used to because there were no boys of his age where his father lived and he got 'bored'. He suggested that he would stay with his father at weekends when he had 'more time' but that playing football on Sunday for a local team currently took precedence. The last time he spent a weekend with his father was two months previously.

Again, it was the mother who threw light on her child's rather bland and brief comments about his relationship with his non-resident father. Andrew's mother confirmed that her son saw his father irregularly and, unlike Andrew, explained this in terms of his father's 'unreliability'. She stressed that she had always insisted that Andrew's father should have unlimited access to his children but that he had frequently failed to collect Andrew and his younger sister when it had been arranged. He had also repeatedly broken promises to do things for Andrew who, she said, felt let down by him. Moreover, Andrew's mother also indicated that his father neglected him in favour of his new family, Andrew's half sisters. She suggested that Andrew was badly hurt by his father's uncaring attitude but that Andrew would not openly admit it: *'Andrew will tell you he doesn't care, and Andrew is a liar. He does care, he cares very much.'*

Step fathers moving in

Compared with birth fathers moving out, step fathers moving in was a less memorable event in children's minds. It is arguable moreover that this was an event at all. For most children, a step father joining the existing household had been a gradual process, with children in the step father group saying that they had known their step father for some time. Very few children said they resented their step father moving in, the majority claiming not to 'mind'. Several children, all girls, said they felt happy on their mothers' behalf. Daniela, a white girl whose step father had lived with the family for three years, said: *'I didn't mind [stepfather moving in] because it made my mum happy and I didn't really mind because he is very kind.'* Jasmine, a mixed race girl, was also happy on her mother's behalf and pleased to have a man around the house after living with her mother and grandmother for nine years: *'My mum seemed happier and my brother [seven at the time] did. I'm glad my mum is happy and he [stepfather] can fix plugs and everything like, everything really.'*

In contrast, a few children were not so pleased. Emily, a white girl, felt somewhat confused about the basis of the new relationship and the permanency of the arrangement: *'I thought he [stepfather] was just a friend.'* As we note later in discussing the case of Anna, Anna felt she had never quite come to terms with her step father joining the family although, in another part of the interview, she said that she liked him. Amy, a white girl, also discussed later, had taken an active dislike to her step father and saw him as a threat to the happy little family group of her mother and brother which had been together for seven years with no contact from her birth father:

> *To be perfectly honest, as soon as I knew him, the first night that I saw him, I didn't like him. And I know that sounds really horrible because I didn't know him. You can't say you hate someone when you don't know them, but I did.*

Most children called their step father by their first name, while only three children called their step fathers 'dad'. One of these children had lived with his step father for eight years, while the other two children had been with their step fathers for less than three years, suggesting that length of time was not always a deciding factor. Only one child regarded her step father as her 'real father'. Jasmine, who had never lived with her birth father and had not had contact with him since the age of three, said of her step father of two years: *'He's the only dad I've ever known.'*

With two exceptions referred to above (Anna and Amy), all the step family group had accepted their step fathers as part of the family at the time of the interview. As we will describe in the next chapter (Chapter 5) children's accounts suggest that step fathers had to 'earn' their place in the family by finding ways of taking an active part in children's lives. (See also Chapter 3 for children's accounts of the step father vignette). For Chloe and Daniela, the step father was considered to be another person to turn to for support and advice. Ben and Scott, both white boys, mostly appreciated their step fathers for taking them on outings.

Steve, a white boy who had lived with his step father for three years, was unusual in suggesting that his step father's presence was acceptable *precisely* because he had little involvement in his life: '*I don't mind him being there because I hardly speak to him. He spends most of his time in his bedroom.*' With the exception of one girl, Amy, none of the children and mothers in this group mentioned serious clashes with step fathers, although Emily and Scott admitted to having 'silly arguments' sometimes.

Including a step father

The following four case studies demonstrate the different ways in which children included step fathers in their lives. The first two case studies focus on two children who had positive relationships with their step fathers, but showed, in their own ways, a certain loyalty towards their birth fathers. The first girl, Marsha, made it clear that her step father was more important to her than her birth father. Although she was reluctant to say much about her birth father, she hinted at certain reasons why she preferred her step father. Her mother's account suggested more clearly that for this girl her step father represented a 'better' father. However, the girl's reluctance to discuss her birth father's 'shortcomings' suggests that she was unwilling to put him in a bad light. The second girl, Daniela, while admitting to getting on better with her step father, was anxious not to be disloyal to her birth father. The third case study concerns Anna who, after two years, still had difficulty coming to terms with living with her step father. She hankered after her birth father and made considerable efforts to keep in touch with him although, according to her mother, he showed little interest in her. Nevertheless, Anna confessed to liking her step father and showed some appreciation of him, especially his understanding of her feelings for her birth father. The fourth case study is about Amy, who actively resented her step father entering her tight-knit, lone mother family. Amy portrayed herself as acting as the 'sensible' adult to her step father's sulky response to her active rejection of him. As some of the children's accounts suggest, step fathers are not assessed in their own right but are incorporated into children's lives in relation to birth fathers regardless of whether they play strong or shadowy roles.

Marsha: finding a 'better' father

Marsha, of Afro-Caribbean origin, lived in a council house with her mother, her 14-year-old half sister and her step father. Her parents had separated when she was nine and her step father had moved into the family home when she was ten. Her mother had recently finished a course in business and was due to start a new job. Marsha placed her step father (a traffic warden) in the inner circle of her map of significant others (Chapter 5) but omitted her birth father and showed considerable reluctance to explain why, although she was generally communicative and articulate throughout the interview:

I: *Now, what about your dad, because he is sort of a relative, isn't he?*
M: *Yes.*
I: *You haven't put him . . . you don't want to put him there?* [in relatives' section]
M: *No.*
I: *So he's not that important to you, is that right?*
M: *No.*

Marsha's communicative side returned when she was asked about her relationship with her step father. She said she had known her step father for some time and she had regarded his presence in the family home positively, especially since they 'get on well' and he helps her out:

M: *It was different, because I had someone new in. My mum would have someone new in her life. But we get on well, and there's no arguments and, like, you spend more time with him than you spend time with. . . . There's no arguments like that, because we always spend all the time together.*
I: *Is he important to you? Do you feel as close to him as you would to your sister and your mum?*
M: *Yes, I talk to him as well and he helps me out as well. And gives us money, like, he'll just come into our rooms and gives us money and say 'This is for you and you can go to the cinema tomorrow.'*
I: *So do you feel he is sort of like a dad to you?*
M: *Yes.*
I: *Or just a friend?*
M: *A dad really.*
I: *Would you talk to him about problems and things?*
M: *Yes, I talk to him all the time.*

When asked whether she would like her birth father to move back with the family, Marsha said: *I'm happy with my mum and my step dad.'* This was confirmed by Marsha's mother who described Marsha's birth father as 'irresponsible' and 'selfish' towards his children, and as 'unable to show love and affection'. In contrast, she considered her new partner able to provide Marsha with the affection and commitment that she had missed from her birth father. She also said that Marsha's father had recently refused to allow Marsha to visit him and he had not seen her for four months. Marsha had given a different impression – that she saw her father fortnightly as had initially been agreed between them.

Daniela: gaining a second father

Daniela, a white girl, lived in a council house with her mother, step father and two full brothers, aged 13 and 14. Her parents separated when she was six and she lived with her mother and brothers until her step father moved in two years later when she was eight. Daniela's mother had recently left her part-time job as a care assistant and her step father had been unemployed for a number of years. Daniela said she had welcomed her mother's new partner into their home because it made her mother happy and her mother was 'in love' with him. Daniela said she got on well with him from the start, had called him 'Dad' almost immediately, and was 'happy' living with her step father on a day-to-day basis while visiting her birth father regularly. To avoid confusion, she said she had taken to referring to her birth father as 'Dad Number One'. However, when asked whether this meant her step father was 'Dad Number Two', Daniela said: *'He ain't Dad Number Two, it's just so we don't get confused.'*

She described her step father as 'very nice', noting that she got on better with him than with her birth father. However, she then followed this up quickly with the assertion that her birth father was also 'nice' and that they were 'both the same', adding that she was not able to assess her relationship with her father since she did not spend much time with him: *'I get on with my step dad better than my real dad. But then, my real dad is nice. They [step father and birth father] are like, really, both the same, but I don't really spend a lot of time with my real dad so I can't really tell.'*

Daniela's mother confirmed that Daniela had readily accepted her step father who, according to her mother, took a greater interest in her compared with her birth father who, she said, had always been uninvolved in the care of the children.

Anna: the dilemma of a daddy's girl

Anna, a white girl, lived in a small terraced house on a large council estate with her mother, step father, her sister aged nine, and her brother aged eight. Her father, a store keeper, lived in the same neighbourhood with a new partner and their young son. Her step father, a toolmaker, had two children from a previous relationship, who lived with their mother. Anna's parents separated when she was eight and her step father moved into the family home two years later. Anna said she had never really come to terms with her step father's presence in the family home: *'Well, I did mind [step father moving in]. I thought it could change, but it never [did].'* Anna said she felt very close to her birth father whom she visited 'officially' once a fortnight. On her own initiative, she sometimes also called on him unannounced during the week after school and often talked to him on the telephone. Despite resenting his presence in the home, Anna said she liked her step father. When asked whether she would still prefer to live with her father rather than her step father, she explained her dilemma: wanting to be with her birth father but appreciating her step father for understanding her feelings for her birth father: *'That's hard to say because . . . sometimes I say to [step-father] "I hate you, I wish my dad was here." But then, at the end of the day he understands how I feel inside because his mum died when he was 6, so . . . with my dad not being here, he knows how I feel with his mum not being there.'*

Anna's mother's account confirmed this picture, describing her as a 'daddy's girl' and suggesting that Anna had reacted badly to the separation and had wanted to live with her father. She also said that Anna developed severe behaviour problems after her father left and that she had found this so exasperating and difficult to deal with that she had asked Anna's father to let Anna live with him for a while in the hope that this would help her. Instead, the father had suggested that Anna should be placed in care, a suggestion her mother had rejected and deeply resented. In this context, Anna's mother found it very difficult to accept Anna's emotional attachment to her birth father who, she said, paid no maintenance and showed no interest in the children, other than having them for a visit once a fortnight. By contrast, she described her partner, Anna's step father, as making considerable efforts to help Anna adjust to his presence in the household, so much so that she considered him to be more of a father to Anna than her own father. In contrast, Anna herself gave no indication of being aware of her birth father's lack of interest in her.

Amy: the resentful step daughter

Amy, a white girl, lived with her mother, 13-year-old brother, step father and 1-year-old half brother in a large house in a middle class area. Amy's parents had separated when she was three, leaving the mother to live alone in a small flat with Amy and her brother. They had remained a threesome for six years, with no contact with the birth father. During this time, Amy's mother worked part time in a playgroup and also did cleaning jobs to make ends meet. When Amy was nine, her mother married a widower with several children. Amy had resented the break-up of their 'little family' and took an instant dislike to her stepfather. Amy blamed her step father for their difficult relationship and complained bitterly about her step father's behaviour which she described as 'unreasonable' and 'immature'. She said he had imposed strict rules which Amy and her brother had not previously been used to. When she broke the rules, as she said she was inclined to do, her step father was given to angry outbursts and, even worse, long periods of sulky silence. Amy said that, in order to make peace, it was she rather than her step father who had to make reparation; in this process she portrayed herself as the sensible adult and her step father as the resisting child: *'You just imagine him like a little baby and you treat him like one, and that is the way we get on really. Saying "Hello, did you have a nice day?" Things like that, not how you would really treat an adult. I mean, they would be the ones saying to you "Did you have a nice day?" You have to do that to him. You have to tell him that you're the adult and he's the child. . . . And it's like he's stealing my childhood away from me.'* Amy had other cause for resentment, namely the fact that two older step sisters had also come to live with them for a time and none of them had got on well together.

Amy's mother confirmed the story and explained Amy's resentment in terms of their past history as a close, self-contained 'little family'. Moreover she said that, as a lone mother, she had relied heavily on her children, and in particular Amy, for emotional support. As a result, she said Amy had become very possessive of her and would have disapproved of any new man in her life. The problems she said had been confounded by her new husband's daughters who had lived with them unsuccessfully for a while. However, in contrast to Amy, Amy's mother regarded both Amy and her stepfather as equally to blame for the poor relationship. She felt torn between loyalty to her new husband and to her daughter but unable to do anything to improve the situation and was anxious not to be seen to be taking sides.

Going into foster care

Asked about their experience of entering foster care and how they felt about it, two-thirds of foster children (10/15) described the experience, while two children who had been very young at the time (under three years of age), said they could not remember the event. Not all children were willing to talk about it. Moreover, children's accounts did not usually explain the wider context of the family situation, nor did they suggest any awareness of there having been any prior negotiation between birth parents and social workers before being taken into foster care.

Children portrayed going into care as a traumatic event for which they received little forewarning and which thereby rendered them feeling powerless. Keith, a white boy who was eight when he entered foster care, indicated his feeling of bewilderment in response to hearing fortuitously about the impending event but gave no account of the event itself: *'They said that she [mother] was ill or something and I just heard that a man was going to pick me up and I came here [foster home].'* Similarly, Mandy, a girl of Afro-Caribbean origin who was six at the time, was also not quite sure what was happening: *'First [social worker] and this other man came and speak to my mum. Me and my sisters were in our room. And then [social worker] come up and said we've got to move. So me and my sisters packed our bags. He [social worker] never told us where we were going and why. I felt sad but I didn't cry.'*

A brother and sister, Liam and Melanie, both white children, also described a sense of powerlessness in being torn from their families without warning, and claimed that their mother misled them by telling them that they were going on a holiday to give her a break from looking after them. *'She [mother] lied actually. She said she wanted to have a break. She went, "You and Melanie are going to go with someone else for two weeks." And I was crying and everything. And then Melanie started crying. And then in the morning I was really happy about going to meet some new people. Two weeks later I packed all my bags again thinking I was going home. And [carer] said, "What are you doing?" I said, "We're going home today, it's been two weeks." Because I was counting. And she [carer] said, "You're not." I sat in my room crying and then I was punching my arm and I had yellow bruising all over it because I just kept laying into my arm like that.'* His sister, Melanie, also remembered being told that they were going to stay somewhere for a few weeks so that their mother could *'get herself sorted'*.

By contrast, Debbie, a white girl, attributed to herself a degree of self determination absent in most foster children's accounts. She described how she initially put up some resistance to going into foster care but later agreed to comply with the social worker's request. Debbie described how, on the particular night the social worker arrived, it happened how the house was 'in a tip', how her mother had arrived home drunk, and how she and her mother had had an argument, presumably related to this. Although she suggests a degree of agency in going into foster care, the theme of resistance to the authorities returns at the end of her account, as Debbie suggests she was misled about the type of care: *'A social worker come round and she just come in and said, "Pack your stuff." And I was, like "Who are you and what are you telling me to pack my stuff for?" And then my mum come in and she was drunk that night and, like, the place was in a tip and that. There were cans everywhere.*

*And she [social worker] said that this wasn't a fit place for me to be. And
I had an argument with my mum that night, so I felt, yes, I'm going
away from this house. So I packed my stuff straight away and I went
into a car and I was brought here [to foster home]. And I thought I was
being put in a children's home, like, loads of children and that.'*

Adapting to a foster family

As we will later discuss in Chapter 5, few foster children considered
their foster carers as 'parents', with the large majority of foster children
simply suggesting that establishing positive rather than negative relations with foster carers constituted a significant achievement. The
following four case studies provide accounts of some of the foster children's experiences of adapting to life in a foster family and the ways in
which they regarded their birth parents. The first case study focuses on a
girl called Claire who felt very much part of the foster family and
wanted to stay with them on a long-term basis. However Claire's
account indicates no sense of the developing processes in achieving a
happy relationship, while the foster carer suggests it had been a long
haul. The other two case studies concern children who felt unsettled in
their foster families but for different reasons. The first child, Debbie,
was pressing for greater freedom while her foster carers were under-
standably anxious to protect her from further abuse and unhappiness.
Not surprisingly, Debbie was somewhat ambivalent about her relationship with her foster carers. The third case concerns Wayne, who was in
a short-term foster placement lasting two years. From Wayne's perspective, the world was either black or white: people in his life were classified as either 'nice' or 'not nice'. Wayne clearly placed his foster carers in
the 'not nice' category.

Claire: a permanent home at last

Claire, a white girl, had experienced her parents' separation at an early,
unspecified age, and had no contact since with her father. According to
Claire's current carer, Stella, while Claire and her younger brother were
with their mother, they experienced numerous changes of residence and
a succession of step fathers, some of whom had been very violent
towards their mother. When Claire was eight, the children were taken
into care 'on an emergency rota' (Claire's words) because of their
mother's alcoholism. According to Stella, the final straw came when the
mother had left the children alone for two days while she went on a
drinking spree. Over the period of a year, Claire and her younger
brother, aged nine at interview, were cared for by three different foster

families. They then joined their current foster family containing the foster carers' daughter and another foster child, and through the foster family joined a large extended kin network. The two children had been there for three years. Claire used her birthday as a benchmark for the different placement changes: *'We stayed with one family and from there I went to another where I had my ninth birthday and from there I went to this woman called X and then from there I went here, where I had my tenth and my eleventh and my twelfth [birthdays].'*

Asked about her relationship with her foster carers, Claire simply said she got on 'very well' with them and regarded them as a 'mum' and 'dad'. She added that she was happy to have a sister in her carers' daughter and stressed that her carers treated them 'all the same'. She wanted to stay with the family 'for ever'. In contrast, the foster carer's account was rather different. She portrayed Claire's adjustment to foster care as a long, painful process in which she had had to put up with a great deal of bad behaviour from Claire who often took out the anger she felt towards her birth mother on her foster carer. Stella saw Claire's childish behaviour as a reaction against the premature responsibility for herself and her younger brother which was forced upon her by her mother when she was incapacitated through drink. Stella also mentioned how, when Claire first joined the family, she refused to speak to Stella's husband because she distrusted all men and initially refused to believe that he was not a wife-beater. Unable to trust a male psychologist to whom Claire was referred, Claire eventually began to be able to talk to Stella about her feelings and anxieties. Stella also said Claire was sometimes jealous of her daughter even though she did her utmost to treat them the same.

Claire and her brother still felt some attachment to their mother and especially to their two new siblings whom Claire had never seen but wanted to see. Her ambivalence towards her mother, whom she omitted from her map of significant others (Chapter 5), and whom she had not seen for a year, is evident in her response to a question about whether she would like to see her mother more often: *'It's not my fault, not my problem. She didn't come and contact us.'* Yet, according to her foster carer, Claire worried about her mother and wondered whether the fact she had failed to make contact meant that she might be ill or dying. At Claire's instigation, the social worker had tried to trace her mother but without success.

Debbie: different families, different values

Debbie, a white girl, was taken into care at the age of ten. Before that, she had lived alone with her mother who had been an alcoholic since before Debbie's birth. Debbie did not know the identity of her father and did not think her father knew of her existence. Her mother had fallen out with all her relatives apart from her grandmother who often looked after Debbie when her mother was neglecting her. Although Debbie said she 'could' have lived with her grandmother, there was no evidence to suggest that the grandmother wanted her to. Nonetheless, Debbie visited her grandmother once a week. Her mother came once a month to the foster home and spoke to her on the telephone twice a week. Debbie expressed a 'motherly' concern for her mother noting that she was 'coping much better' now that she did not have the respons- ibility for looking after Debbie. '*It's better for her and me [being in care] because since I've been here [with foster family] she is, she is a qualified engineer now, she got her grades . . . if I was with her, she wouldn't have been able to do that.*'

Debbie had lived for three years with her carers and their eight-year- old son. Debbie did not get on with the boy and thought that he was a spy and a sneak. Elizabeth, her foster carer, had taken up fostering four years previously after hearing about child abuse. She confessed to being '. . . *very old-fashioned and out of date to a lot of things*' and disap- proved strongly of Debbie's penchant for short skirts and wearing make-up. Elizabeth acknowledged that Debbie frequently found her standards unreasonable. But she considered her main task was to protect Debbie from getting into 'bad company', which meant restrict- ing her movements. Elizabeth thought it important that Debbie had little contact with boys, because she feared that Debbie was the 'sort of girl' who would become pregnant as a teenager. For this reason, and against Debbie's own wishes, she had chosen a girls' secondary school for Debbie. As Debbie's account suggested, Elizabeth was not as suc- cessful in restricting Debbie's movements as she thought.

Yet, Elizabeth felt that, underneath her bravado and air of defiance, Debbie regarded her carers as an important source of stability. In turn, Debbie indicated an ambivalent attitude to her foster carers: on the one hand placing them among her 'very important people' on her map (Chapter 5), alongside her mother and grandmother (together with six boy friends and two girl friends), and on the other hand, she com- plained bitterly about them. She complained that she had no privacy in the house, specifically about the fact that the upper half of her bedroom door was glass covered by a bamboo screen. She complained that her carer kept her clothes in a wardrobe in her room, that she was only allowed to put up 'a few posters', and that she did not have her own tele- vision set. She said she was only allowed to talk to friends on the tele- phone for about ten minutes before her carers unplugged it in the middle of a conversation. She had wanted to go to a mixed secondary school but she was forced to attend a girls school because her carers thought she liked '... *anything wearing trousers*'. While her friends went to clubs and had boyfriends, she was not allowed any of this. She also considered her social worker as over-protective and intrusive since she vetted her friends before she was allowed to stay with them overnight.

With such a long list of complaints, Debbie said she was going to take action: she was going to tell her social worker that she wanted more privacy and more freedom and that, otherwise, she would demand to be moved to another foster home. Yet at the same time, she also said she appreciated her foster carer for being understanding and acting as an 'agony aunt'. However, she was also quite clear that she did not think of her as a 'mum' and did not want her carers to love her. In contrast to her view of her foster carers, Debbie reconstructed her life with her mother in a rather positive light, placing her in the inner circle of her map. From her new status as a teenager, Debbie dwelt on her former 'freedoms' and opportunities when she lived with her mother – to go out a lot, to bring friends home and to have boyfriends.

Wayne: the importance of 'nice' foster carers

Wayne, a white boy, had lived with his birth parents and four siblings until his mother left the family home when he was five, taking the children with her. Wayne remembered moving 'all over the place', staying in a succession of hostels. Wayne, his ten-year-old sister and his half brother (now 14) were placed with the current carers on a short-term basis, but their stay had lasted for two years. His half brother had just moved to a long-term foster home and Wayne was due to join him there, while his sister was to remain with his current carers until she could be adopted by another family. Two other brothers (now aged five and seven) had been placed with two separate foster families. Wayne's mother had given birth to two more children, now aged three and four, by two different fathers, both also in care. Wayne's mother visited him and his sister rather irregularly and Wayne had no contact with his father.

In Wayne's view, the world was divided into two camps: the people in his life who were 'nice' to him and those who were 'nasty'. He was angry with his mother because she was 'not very nice', neglecting and hitting the children and, more importantly, because she had broken up the family by leaving his father. Wayne said his mother had lied to the children when leaving the family home, telling them that they were going on a holiday. Wayne's foster carer's account was a little different in that she mentioned that Wayne's mother had left his father because of his violence towards her as well as the children. The father had since disappeared and could not be traced, although, at Wayne's request, the social worker had tried to make contact. For Wayne, the loss of his father was a great sadness in his life and he said he felt 'like crying' whenever he thought about him.

Just as Wayne spoke of his birth mother as 'not very nice', so he also spoke of his carers and the rest of the household in similar terms as 'not nice' to him. He complained about Sally telling him off, about her husband for being 'always grumpy', about his sister for constantly 'annoying' him, and about his carers' two children (21 and 19) who still lived at home, for ordering him about. Wayne complained about having to do 'lots of housework' which, according to his account, consisted mainly in running up and down the stairs carrying washing or passing on messages to the different household members. Wayne's most serious complaint was that he was allowed very little freedom outside the house. He was not allowed to go anywhere on his own, he said, not even to the shop round the corner, but had to stay in the road where he lived. Wayne's complaint about lack of freedom came to a head when he went fishing one day with a friend. They had met two seemingly 'nice men' who wanted to know the way to the lake, but when he told his carer about this, he was no longer allowed to go anywhere by himself or with his friend. Sally, his foster carer, also mentioned the same episode as an example of Wayne's irresponsible behaviour and the way in which he ignored the many warnings he had been given about 'not talking to strangers'.

By contrast, Wayne defined his older brother as one of the few people who was 'nice' to him although there was some evidence that they had not got on well when they had both lived with Wayne's current carers. Yet Wayne said he looked forward to moving in with his older half brother because he 'got on well' with him. He also idealised his future foster carers and said that because they were both teachers they could help him with his homework at secondary school.

Conclusions

Children's accounts of family change were located in the 'here and now' in which other events and issues were of more current importance to children than the past. While some children were unable or preferred not to recall these events, others gave graphic accounts.

Several children gave vivid accounts of the departure of their birth fathers from the family home. As children's responses to the vignette on parental separation discussed in Chapter 2 indicated, all children considered this a very painful experience for the children concerned. Children who no longer lived with their fathers suggested that they responded to these events and incorporated their fathers into their current lives in different ways. Some children adjusted well to having a non-resident father, remaining in frequent contact and maintaining a warm and close relationship notwithstanding. For other children, the relationship was less happy. Two such cases were presented: while Andrew became resentful of his birth father, Ben continued to idolise his father. The issue for children was not simply one of frequency or ease of contact with their fathers, but reflected the fathers' ways of showing interest in their children (or not). However, children themselves provided only small clues to their relationships with their birth fathers, exhibiting a strong reluctance to be critical of them which was reflected in their reticence. For a fuller understanding of the ways in which children experience family change, especially relations with birth fathers, it was necessary to turn to the accounts of the children's mothers.

By contrast, a step father moving into the family home was described as a less memorable event than a birth father moving out. For most children in this study, the transition to step family status had happened some years before which may account for the relative lack of problematic relationships. Moreover, where the transition was more recent, it seemed to have been gradual in that children suggested that they had known their step father for some time before he moved into the family home. A step father moving in, often in popular discourse portrayed as a problematic event, was for some children in fact a positive experience. Marsha and Daniela suggested they enjoyed a much closer relationship with their step fathers than they did with their birth fathers. For other children, the transition to being a step family had created some difficulties, but only one child still had a very negative relationship with her step father. Between the lines, children seemed to be suggesting that step fathers were under some pressure to justify or 'earn' their place in their lives by becoming interested in them and involved in their activities. However, children's accounts only provide glimpses into these relationships which, as some children suggested, were played out against the backcloth of children's relationships with others, notably with their birth fathers.

Asked about their experience of being 'looked after', foster children suggested being abruptly and traumatically removed from their homes with no forewarning and no prior discussion with them. They did not attempt to 'explain' why they were taken into care nor did they set the context in which social workers became involved before their removal. Underlying these accounts is a sense of betrayal and strong feelings of powerlessness. However, the account given by Debbie suggested she offered spirited resistance both to the social workers but also to her alcoholic mother. Foster children reported responding to foster care differently and varied in their desire to be part of a foster family. However, while foster carers described a long and painful process of adjustment, foster children themselves gave a rather static account in which they suggested that they were either settled or not. While Claire felt she had a permanent home at last, Debbie was ambivalent towards her carers and Wayne rejected his carers. Crucial to understanding children's relations with foster carers is their relationship to their birth parents about whom children felt considerable ambivalence – loving them on the one hand, while feeling disappointed and rejected by them on the other.

5 The importance of mothers and fathers
Children's views and experiences

[Parents are] people that never ever don't care about you.

From a British policy perspective, children and their care are constructed as largely the business of parents, that is, as a private matter for families. In recent years, there has been much contemporary political concern about parents' ability to care for their children in response to changes taking place in household form, notably divorce, lone parenthood and re-partnering. This political concern seeks to reinforce the ideological representation of the private nature of family life, with renewed emphasis being placed upon parental responsibility, while at the same time subjecting parents' care to the surveillance of experts. Of course, parenting, or rather *mothering*, has long been targeted for intervention by the state. However, it is the form in which the state exerts control over parenting that is changing rather than the fact of control itself. One current trend is to construct parents as 'partners' with institutions and experts so that together they may exert influence upon children. Policies on parental involvement and participation are promoted through schools, the social services and the law. In the case of the new policies on home/school relations, the extension of pedagogy to include parents in children's education alongside teachers can be seen, as Edwards and Alldred (1999b) suggest, as an attempt to extend children's family life into their school life. As Edwards and Alldred conceptualise it, the process of children's familialisation interacts with the process of institutionalisation so that children are subjected in schools to a double surveillance. Moreover, paradoxically, this may work against other policies and processes, namely to give children greater autonomy and self responsibility as they move up the educational system. While our study did not aim to address these issues, they constitute an important development in the theoretical conceptualisation of the significance of parents in children's lives.

Children's own views about the care they receive at the hands of parents and professionals are only now beginning to be studied. The importance children attach to parents and to family life more generally is underlined by a number of recent studies, most notably those by O'Brien, Alldred and Jones (1996) and Morrow (1998). These and other studies have examined children's family life perceptions in relation to children's age. For example, according to one study, younger children viewed families as synonymous with their households, while older children defined family more in terms of emotionally significant relationships rather than co-residence (Newman et al. 1993). Children in both early and middle childhood considered parents and close family to be central to their lives and expressed a strong wish to be cared for (Borland et al. 1997), while in another study, similar aged children mentioned the importance of love and security, and the need for material care (Hill et al. 1995). As already demonstrated, and as Morrow (1998) suggests, children consider the practice rather than the form of family life to be more important. However, few studies have commented on the impact of family form on children's perceptions.

In this chapter, we draw upon both the Questionnaire Survey evidence and the case study material in order to examine children's views and experience of the activity of parenting and of motherhood and fatherhood as roles and relationships. In the context of dominant public discourses about parenting and parenthood, we thought it important to examine children's own perspectives, in particular their ideas about the goal of gender equality and the emphasis on genderless parenting, rather than mothering or fathering. First, we examine children's general normative views of parenting and parenthood. Next, we go on to examine children's accounts of their own particular experiences of parenting in practice and their views of the ways in which they consider their own mothers and fathers to be important in their own lives. Because we designed the study to focus on children living in different parental situations, we are therefore able to assess how household context affects children's perceptions of parenting in principle and practice and whether children defined the importance of their resident and non-resident parents differently.

Children's normative views of parenting: what mothers and fathers ought to do

In some respects, children's views of parenting reflect dominant discourses about how family life 'ought' to be. Just as public discourses currently define parenting as genderless, rather than differentiating between mothering and fathering, for example in the discourse of 'parental responsibility', so we might also expect children to hold such views. With this possibility in mind, we asked children in the Questionnaire Survey to consider whether they thought mothers, fathers or both parents 'ought' to do particular parenting tasks. In respect of some tasks, children adopted an equalitarian view of gender relations as the ideal: both parents, they said, ought to care for children. With respect to the expressive aspects of parents' care – we asked children which parent should 'comfort children when they are upset' and who 'should play with them'; the great majority of children said these were the jobs of both parents (82% and 86%). Similarly, children considered that disciplining children was a job for both parents (84%) rather than one for fathers, the more traditional assumption. With respect to housework, again the majority of children, albeit rather fewer, thought that both parents should do the cleaning (67% compared with 28% who said it was the job of mothers and 5% the job of fathers). However, over half (58%) considered household repairs to be a father's job, as compared with 2% who said it was the mother's job and 30% who said it was both parents' job.

If such genderless views of parenting reflect dominant or consensual discourses, we would not expect children's views to be influenced by their household living arrangements and, indeed, this is roughly what we found. Table 5.1 indicates children's normative views on parenting tasks in relation to household type. Around four-fifths of children across the different household groups indicated that both mothers and fathers should comfort children, play with children and do the cleaning. However, significantly more children living with lone parents (together with the 'other' group of only 16 children living with grandparents and foster carers) thought that parental control should be the prerogative of the mother (15%) compared with two-birth-parent households (5%) and step family children (9%). Yet the great majority within each household type proclaimed this to be the task of both parents. Significantly fewer lone parent children mentioned that both parents should carry out household repairs, albeit the percentages who said it should be mother's job were very small (only 4%).

However, children's normative views of parents' participation in the labour market were less gender free. Moreover, there was no overall consensus. Children's responses in the Questionnaire Survey concerning which parent should go out to work suggest a roughly equal split between those favouring an egalitarian model of both mothers and fathers working and those favouring a traditional gender model, with fathers as providers and mothers at home. Surprisingly, girls' views were no different from boys' views (Oakley 1996): just under half of children agreed that both parents should go out to work (43%) while

Table 5.1   Children's views of which parent should do parenting tasks by household type

Comfort children N = 916	Mothers (%)	Fathers (%)	Both parents (%)	Someone else (%)
Two-birth parent	15	2	82	1
Lone parent	17	1	80	2
Step family	14	3	81	3
Other	6	6	88	–

Play with children N = 920

Two-birth parent	6	4	86	5
Lone parent	7	3	87	4
Step family	10	–	83	7
Other	–	13	75	13

Tell children off N = 909*

Two-birth parent	5	8	86	1
Lone parent	15	3	81	1
Step family	9	11	79	1
Other	27	–	73	–

Do cleaning N = 904

Two-birth parent	28	4	63	5
Lone parent	25	7	66	3
Step family	40	4	59	6
Other	57	14	21	7

Household repairs N = 905 *

Two-birth parent	2	58	31	9
Lone parent	4	58	26	13
Step family	1	54	38	6
Other	–	80	–	17

*Differences are statistically significant.

over half said that fathers should go out to work (51%), with only 2% mentioning mothers only.

In response to a second question which related to the period of parenthood when children are very young, both boys and girls expressed concern about the employment of both fathers and mothers: 59% of children thought that both parents should be at home at this time, while 38% agreed that only the mother should be. (Less than 1% of children said the father should be at home.) Such views reflect adult attitudes to mothers' employment when children are young: according to the Eurobarometer survey, over four-fifths of parents and more than two-thirds of men and women under 40 across the European Union were opposed to mothers remaining in the workforce (cited in Deven et al. 1998). Moreover, children's views of how they themselves might behave in the future when they have children under school age provide a different picture. On the one hand, their views suggest a residual, traditional gender model. More girls than boys said they would not work (34% compared to 9%) and more boys said they would work full time (27% compared to 8%). On the other hand, both boys and girls showed a strong preference for part-time employment in this situation – 52% of boys and 42% of girls thought they would work part time when their children were young. This could indicate that employment expectations of younger generations are changing as some evidence suggests (Scott et al. 1996). Young people may be opposed to the current 'long hours workplace culture' which govern the lives of many of their parents, especially fathers (Lewis et al. 1998). Alternatively, reflecting gender equality ideas, they may consider that the traditional female employment option of part-time work ought to be equally available to both men and women.

Household structure made no statistically significant difference to children's normative views on parents' employment despite the continuing high non-employment rates among lone mothers (Holtermann et al. 1999). Rather, they were influenced by whether their own mothers actually worked and, even more significantly, by ethnic background. Children of South Asian origin were more traditional in their views compared with other groups in respect of agreeing that fathers should go to work and that mothers should be at home. However, ethnic background did not appear to shape children's views about whether they would work when they had their own under school age children.

The importance of motherhood and fatherhood

Asked the open-ended question in the interviews about the importance of mothers and fathers in general, most children suggested that both were equally important, with only seven children suggesting that mothers were more important than fathers. As many of their comments concerning their own parents suggested, children were reluctant to draw distinctions between their mothers and fathers and were clearly anxious to be 'fair' to each parent. However, asked a subsequent specific question which involved making an explicit comparison between mothers and fathers, again in general, under half than said they were similar in importance (20/46 responses). Those who emphasised similarity talked about the *potential* of both mothers and fathers to parent children.

'*I think both parents are important, really, because they both have an equal job to guide you and to keep you on the right track and make sure you have a good start in life*' (Bibi, South Asian girl, two-parent family). '*Mothers are no different to fathers because the father can easily be a mother to a child . . . if you had to live with your father, your father can easily be as responsible for you as a mother can be*' (Marsha, Black girl, step family). '*Well, [mothers] teach you, same as the father, they teach you, they help you, they feed you. When they're little they feed you. They give you things and they help you – give you love and care*' (Baldev, South Asian origin boy, two-parent household).

But most children, while starting their comments with an assertion of parents' equal importance, usually went on to describe differences in practice. For example, a white boy in foster care, Keith, started off by suggesting no difference in the importance of mothers and fathers: '*I would say they [fathers] are probably important not less or more [than mothers], they are just average important.*' Asked in what ways fathers were important, Keith suggests difference through an association of fathers with a provider role and the 'doing' aspects of fathering, while not actually saying that mothers and fathers differ. '*I would say they are the same because fathers help their children, they find a home for them and see what they can do.*'

Children emphasised the importance of mothers giving children a sense of ontological security, signified in the language of 'being there for them', together with a range of support of an expressive kind – someone to turn to, someone who understands, someone who cheers you up. Several children specified mothers' biological link to their children. In addition, as several children pointed out, mothers were considered to be more likely to be practically available to children in practice, that is compared with fathers (again an implicit comparison was often made).

'*Love and security and everything, caring. Because mostly it's mothers that are more – you see them a lot more than dads, normally. So I think mothers are very important, the most important out of everybody*' (Leila, mixed race girl, lone mother). '*[Mothers are important] in every way. Because they're always there for the children and mostly, like, they look after the children more. They're always there*' (Daniel, Black boy, step family). '*[Mothers provide] support. If you're upset, then it's usually your mother who cheers you up*' (Emily, white girl, step family).

A South Asian origin girl, Zarina, living with her lone mother, whose contact with her birth father was forbidden by a court order, identified her mother as 'the main thing in my life – my mum and my brother'. In contrast to mothers, she portrayed fathers as 'strict', but also thought that fathers often took their cue from mothers. '*Mothers are the ones who give courage a lot of the time. . . . Fathers are strict. Mothers are not that strict. . . . Fathers have strict rules that you must learn. Mothers say, "Do whatever you like. Be brave." Mothers are the ones who understand because fathers they don't understand that much. They're not the best for understanding, loving. Mothers, they know how to nourish and love. They know what's best for children. Fathers, they just go on with what the mother's doing. It was the same with my dad. He just goes with what my mum's doing. So there's no point in it. That's just how it is.'*

Children also described the importance of gender matching by which boys turned to fathers for support and girls to their mothers (see also O'Brien and Jones 1995; Ghate and Daniels 1997). One boy described a gendered pattern of communication, albeit he first asserted there was no difference in the importance of mothers and fathers: *'About the same [importance of mothers and fathers]. Because most people like their dad a lot because they're like the people who can – if you're a boy the people they can chat to about boys' stuff. It's the same for a girl – like you chat to your mum more'* (Scott, white boy, step family).

As to the specificity of a father's role, several boys mentioned that fathers were there to help their children manage in the public world outside the family. For example, two boys described fathers' importance in taking sons to football matches, while one boy talked about fathers being important in helping children 'to make the right decisions'. A few children, mainly foster children, portrayed parenthood in stereotypical terms: fathers in a public role as breadwinner, and mothers in a private role as carer: *'Mothers always change babies, look after them when they are little . . . [Fathers] go to work most of the time. They earn money so they [children] can have a house and food, pay for lunches, [things] like that. Fathers take them out for trips, play football, take [children] to football matches and stuff like that'* (David, white boy, foster care).

Several children, notably some of those no longer living with their birth fathers, gave responses which downplayed fathers' importance on the grounds of their lesser availability to children and their lack of involvement in their lives, probably because of their own experiences. Some children were highly critical of fathers and levied complaints about fathers' laziness, violent temper, authoritarianism and unreliability.

'A bit different to mums because they like to watch telly most of the time' (Sally, white girl, lone mother household). *'The mother's more responsible, the mother stays there'* (Gail, Black girl, foster care). *'Because they [fathers] don't do nothing. . . . Some fathers do but most fathers just – don't really, like doing what a mum does'* (Debbie, white girl, foster care).

A white girl living with her lone mother, whose father was no longer allowed to visit because of violence to the family, depicted fathers as angry, violent and authoritarian: *'With a man, he's more like violent. He gets more angry ... he's like.... "Up to your room – into your bedroom before I smack you hard!" I mean with mothers they'll count up to three.... With fathers, they say "Up now!" They don't give you a chance!'*

To sum up, while children in their initial response to the question about the importance of motherhood and fatherhood asserted both were equally important to children, they usually went on to describe differences in terms of roles and relationships. Mothers were seen as important because they were 'there for children', and as especially able to offer expressive forms of support. Fathers, by contrast, were described in terms of an important link to the outside public world or in terms of gender specific roles (for sons), while several children were highly critical of fathers or suggested they did not measure up to mothers, probably reflecting their own poor experiences of fathering.

Children's reports of mothering and fathering in practice

Children's experience of the care that their parents actually provide is unlikely to reflect their general normative views of parenting since their experience is affected by the availability of parents to give care. By definition, those children who did not live on a day-to-day basis with both their parents should be less likely to report parents performing everyday care. This is indeed what we found. In the Questionnaire Survey, we asked children to write down the main persons who provided a whole range of expressive, instrumental and educational support (Table 5.2). In all cases, lone parent children (together with the 'other' group who did not live with either parent) were less likely to report that both their mothers and fathers 'usually' performed these activities compared with those living with both birth parents and step family children (Table 5.2). Conversely, more lone parent children, the great majority of whom lived with their birth mothers, reported that their mothers gave them expressive support, that is compared with children living with birth-parents and step family children. This is similarly the case with respect to instrumental aspects of parenting – taking them on trips, giving them pocket money, where more children living with both birth-parents reported both parents doing this compared with lone parent children. Lone parent children were also significantly more likely than the other three groups to report that their mothers provided them with educational support (Table 5.2).

Table 5.2   Children who said *both* parents 'usually' performed the following tasks for them

	All one parent children (children who see other parent at least monthly) (%)	Two-parent (%)	Step parent (%)	Other (%)	Total N
Gives you hugs	24 (31)	49	39	0	376
Helps with homework	17 (23)	46	41	13	347
Plays games with you	17 (22)	31	25	6	243
Cheers you up	20 (30)*	47	33	13	359
Praises you	30 (43)	68	44	19	510
Takes you on trips	28 (41)*	58	49	19	452
Says nice things to you	27 (40)*	56	39	19	427
Gives you money	30 (46)*	50	51	19	409
Explains things	30 (35)*	50	51	19	409
Makes you laugh	25 (37)*	42	40	14	335
Tells you off	28 (36)*	68	57	15	508

All of the above are significant at 0.000 level.
*Differences by household type are statistically significant between children who see non-resident parents more regularly, that is, figures in brackets, and those less regularly or not at all.

While we are not suggesting any direct causal connection here, it is significant that lone parent children who saw their non-resident parent on a regular basis (defined as at least monthly) were still *less* likely to report that both parents performed these parenting tasks compared with those living with two parents (see percentages in brackets for one parent households in Table 5.2), and were *more* likely to report both parents doing these tasks compared with those who rarely saw their non-resident parents. Thus, for example, if we take the last item on Table 5.2 concerning discipline (telling children off), over a quarter of all lone parent children said that both parents usually told them off (28%), while over a third of those who saw their other parent regularly said so (36%). These figures contrast with over two-thirds of children in two-parent birth families (68%) and over half of children in step families (57%) who said both parents usually told them off.

To sum up, in respect of parents' actual practices, children's experience of parenting not surprisingly reflected their parents' availability to provide everyday care to them. In this practical sense, household structure makes a difference to children's lives. Moreover, especially since fathers are much more likely than mothers to be non-resident parents, this reinforces children's experience of parenting as being gender specific. By contrast, children's normative understandings of what parents 'ought to do' for children and their importance in children's lives to some extent reflect dominant adult discourses concerning gender equality and parenting as a 'genderless' practice. Indeed, children seemed reluctant to make distinctions between their mothers and fathers and felt a need to be fair to both, yet simultaneously suggested ways in which they acted differently. By contrast, children reported less normative consensus on parents' labour market participation, expressing traditional attitudes on the one hand, stressing mothers' place in the home, and a less gendered approach, on the other. However, they also suggested that, when they became mothers and fathers, they would work part time when their children were small. In the last part of the chapter, we examine whether children placed the same importance on their own mothers and fathers and whether they differentiated between their parents according to whether they were resident in the household.

The importance of children's own mothers and fathers

As we described in Chapter 3, we asked children to position the persons important to them on a large sheet of paper which was subdivided into four domains: the household, relatives and kin, friends, and 'formal others' (for example teachers, social workers and family doctors). Children were also asked to place people within three concentric circles: those they considered to be 'very important' to them in the inner circle of the map, those less important in the middle circle, and those least important in the outer circle. This exercise provided a basis for discussing with children their relationships with significant others later in the interview. As described in Chapter 3, children tended to put the greater proportion of their significant others in the inner circle.

When we consider children's positioning of their resident birth parents, the great majority placed them in the inner circle, whatever children's family form. This was also the case for most of the foster children who placed their female foster carers (13/15), and male foster carers (11/15) in the inner circle. Similarly, most step family children placed their step fathers in the inner circle (11/15). Most non-resident fathers were also located in the inner circle (9/13 in lone mother families, 12/15 in step father families, 6/11 foster children) (see Table 5.3).

Table 5.3 Children's placement of parents (resident and non-resident) and foster carers in the inner circle by household type

Family types	Resident mothers/ female carers	Resident fathers/ male carers	Step fathers	Non-resident mothers	Non-resident fathers
Two-parent	15/15	15/15	–	–	–
One parent	17/17	–	–	–	9/13*
Step father	15/15	–	11/15	–	12/15
Foster carers	13/15	11/15	–	10/15	6/11**

Some children have been excluded from this analysis.
*An additional 4 children whose fathers had died were not included in the map.
**An additional 4 children did not know father's identity.

The importance of children's birth mothers

Children explained their placement of their birth mothers in the inner circle of their maps of significant others in various ways. In much the same way as children described the importance of mothers in general, children talked about their own mother: as providing security and stability; as a mainspring of love, understanding and support; as a shoulder to cry on; as a source of guidance and material care. Some children said they had a special bond with their mothers because they gave birth to them. A few girls also emphasised their mothers' helpfulness with respect to personal matters. As previous research has shown, children are more likely to confide in their mothers than their fathers (Brannen et al. 1994; Ribbens 1994; O'Brien and Jones 1995; Morrow 1998). Mothers' care was also described in terms of combining several different types of care – instrumental and expressive: *'She cares for me, like, she teaches me things, you know, she stands by me, sticks with me, things like that'* (Harinder, South Asian origin boy, two-parent household). *'She loves me, she buys me things, she takes me places'* (Lee, white boy, two-parent household).

Instrumental forms of care can also have expressive meaning (Borland et al. 1997). Thus children's mention of mothers' material provision of care may be seen as demonstrating 'caring about' children as well as 'caring for' them: *'She gave me a home, she buys clothes for me, she feeds me, she loves me and she cares for me'* (Serena, Black girl, widowed lone mother family).

As children's accounts of the importance of mothers in general suggested, children said their own mothers were important because they were 'there for them'. 'Being there for them' has a variety of meanings, such as providing stability and security in the long term: *'She is there for me when I am not happy and she has been there all my life . . .'* (Kevin, white boy, two-parent family). Being 'there' also refers to the security of everyday care and availability. Some of the lone parent children clearly described the importance they placed upon their mothers' *everyday care*. Resident mothers, they suggested, have the edge on non-resident birth fathers because they were the principal providers of care. A mixed race, middle-class girl, Leila, who lived with her lone mother placed both parents in the inner circle. Although she said her non-resident father was *'really important'* to her, she highlighted her mother's every-day care: *'She [mother] is really, really important because she is the one that is always around. She is the one that takes care of me . . . '* Kevin, a white boy who lived with both parents and placed them both in his inner circle of important others, said of his mother: *'She is always around me and everything and she is always talking to me.'*

Children were more equivocal about the importance of their mothers as confidants. Asked a direct question, over a third of children (23/54 children who were asked the question) said that they usually confided in their mothers, while a similar proportion (25/54) said they did so sometimes and ten children said they never did so. On particular issues which emerged in the course of the interviews, children sometimes volunteered that they would prefer to talk to friends, including about the experience of starting secondary school. Children moreover made distinctions between their parents, for example daughters preferred their mothers for 'girl talk'. *'I'll say my mum is important to me because if I wanted to tell her something personal, I can't go and say it to my [step] dad. Well, he's a man. But I could say it to my mum because I can explain it and she knows how I feel because she's come through it and things like that. She plays a role in my life, I'll never know how much. I'll never know what I'd be like without her'* (Daniela, white girl, step family). A Black girl, Chloe, also in a step father family, noted: *'Because my mum, I can talk to about – I can't talk to my dad about periods but I can talk to my mum where babies come from.'* As we found in another study of this age group (Brannen and Storey 1996), boys and girls in lone mother families were particularly disposed to talk about personal matters with their mothers compared with children in other household forms. A Black boy, Elliott, living in a lone mother household, described how he could talk to his mother in an adult fashion but when he talked to his father: *'I just go all silly. I don't know what happens to me, I just get this baby voice. But if I'm talking to my mum, I have to make sure I have my attitude . . . I can talk to my mum. She's my friend.'*

Resident birth fathers

Not surprisingly, as already noted, children were often reluctant to make explicit comparisons between mothering and motherhood, and fathering and fatherhood. Some children suggested that their own resident fathers, like their mothers, were important sources of both expressive and instrumental care. Some children gave very specific justifications for putting their resident fathers in the inner circles of their maps of significant others. Children talked about their fathers helping them with homework and taking them to football. A white boy, Kevin, referred to his birth father's shared interest in football which, to his puzzlement, his mother clearly did not share: '*My mum, she doesn't like football much. She'll only take me if there's no one else to take me. She doesn't want to take me to see any matches this season. She finds it a bit boring.*' When asked how he felt about that, he said: '*Well, I can't really understand it, because she doesn't watch it or anything, so I don't know how she can know that she doesn't like it and it's boring. So I think it's a bit weird.*'

Resident fathers were valued for special qualities, skills and activities, in contrast to mothers who were valued for their everyday care: '*He is cleverer than some of the teachers at my school,*' one South Asian origin boy, Niaz, said proudly about his father, whereas of his mother he said: '*Without her I wouldn't be alive.*' A South Asian origin girl, Hayfa, said: '*Sometimes he teaches me maths – he's good at maths,*' while she noted that her mother '. . . *[she] feeds me, she looks after me.*' Two boys talked about their fathers helping them and taking them out: '*It's mainly him helping me to build and make things and him helping me with computers and stuff, because he's experienced with computers*' (Jahangir, South Asian origin boy). '*He'll take us out, he'll take us swimming, or to the park, funfair and things. He makes . . . Fun*' (Lujahn, South Asian origin girl). Fathers were also seen as the ones to implement ideas while mothers were given the credit for having the ideas in the first place. '*My mum is the person who thinks of places to go and my dad is the one who takes us there!*' (Bibi, South Asian girl, two-parent family)

In contrast to mothers, few fathers were seen as confidants by their children. Only three said they usually confided in their birth fathers, all of whom were two-parent children, while the rest were split between those who sometimes confided in their birth fathers (and male foster carers) and those who never did so.

Non-resident birth fathers

All but seven of the twenty-eight children with non-resident fathers placed them in the inner circle. Children's descriptions of the importance of their non-resident birth fathers were both similar to and different from the accounts of children living in two-parent households. Most of the children who were in contact with their birth fathers remained emotionally attached to them and mentioned similar ways of being important as those living with their birth fathers. Claudia, a mixed race girl living with her lone mother said of her non-resident father: *'He loves me, he looks after me, he cares for me.'* Another girl, Anna, said: *'To me my mum and dad and all the rest of the family are just the same as each other'* (white girl, step family). Clark, a Black boy living with a lone mother and in regular contact with his birth father, emphasised his feelings for his father and the material aspects of his father's care: *'I care about him a lot. Sometimes I talk to him and he gives me money when I need it and buys me things that I want and lets me stay at weekends.'* Chloe, a Black girl, also in regular contact with her non-resident father, emphasised her father's permanent presence in her life, contrasting him with her new step father with whom she got on well: *'My dad's more important to me [than step father]. He's, like, been there before [step father] was there for me. He's been there for me from when I was small, really, really small.'*

For several children who were not living with their birth fathers, however, either their non-resident fathers' importance had diminished since their departure from the household, or they had always been less important to children compared with mothers. We are not able to say which was the case . A white, middle-class girl, Emily, who lived with her mother and step father saw her birth father every week since he left the household when she was two years old. She placed him in the inner circle and, when discussing why she had placed him there, Emily suggested that her birth father, in contrast to her mother, was less available to provide emotional support on a daily basis: *'My dad is not as important [as my mother] because we don't see him as much. So he's not usually there if I get home crying, sort of thing. But he's pretty important, I think.'* A white boy who had frequent contact with his lone father placed him in the inner circle but said: *'He ain't as important as my mum and sisters, but he is quite important to me. I feel closer to my mum than to my dad because she is there more.'*

Non-resident birth fathers were not seen as regular confidants although children did not focus on this issue. Rebecca (white girl, lone mother family) was unusual in even mentioning that she could not talk to her birth father about her 'problems' *'because he is a man sort of thing'*.

However, she had clearly tried to talk to him about her feelings related to her parents splitting up and described writing him lots of letters to which he responded in a disappointing way. '*But he just says that it's how life has turned out really. . . . He just takes it as everyday life.*'

Significantly, none of the children with non-resident fathers commented on their fathers' failure to contribute financially to their care (only nine of the twenty-six mothers reported that the non-resident fathers made a financial contribution to their children's upkeep).

By contrast, another mixed race girl, Tara, who lived with her lone mother, omitted her birth father from her map even though he visited the household regularly. Tara explained this exclusion in terms of his being unavailable to 'spend time' with her which she considered was the 'proper' way to be a father. '*He is kind of, like, just someone who is there to do stuff for us that, like, any other person would do really. Because he doesn't spend time with us that much. He comes to see us and he comes to give us a lift somewhere or to take us somewhere but he is not really acting like a dad.*'

Three out of four children who had no contact with their birth fathers for a long time made it clear they did not want contact and omitted them from their maps. Salome, a white girl who had had no contact with her father for eight years, said, using rather paradoxical language: '*I forget him all the time. I'm just focusing on everything else, like my homework and everything, so I really forget about him.*' Amy, a white step family girl who had not heard from her father since she was three, still hankered after him but omitted him from her map: '*I haven't seen my dad for so long and I really want to . . . I would like to see my dad again . . . I sometimes feel like I really miss him.*'

In contrast, a South Asian origin girl placed her non-resident birth father in the inner circle even though he had acted violently towards herself and her mother and had, as a consequence, been banned from seeing them. Perhaps the fact that her father had only recently moved out of the house may explain why she included him, an interpretation which is supported by the 'worry' the girl expressed about her father: '*I do worry about him. No matter how bad he is or how ugly he is, he's still my father.*'

Step fathers

As is indicated in Table 5.3, the majority of children living with their step fathers (11/15) placed them in the inner circle of their maps. As other research on step families has found, a third of step children did not identify step fathers as family (Furstenberg 1987). In our study, four children did not place them in the inner circle and made it clear that they were less important than their mothers and birth fathers. Daniel, a Black boy who had almost daily contact with his non-resident birth father, placed his step father of three years in the centre circle: '*I like him and everything, but I don't think he is as important as my mum and dad.*' Steve, a white boy, left his step father out of his map altogether while placing both his birth parents in the inner circle. He explained that his step father was not important because: '*I hardly ever talk to him. He spends most of his time in his bedroom.*' Of the 15 children in the step father group, only Amy declared that she actively disliked her step father and had a largely negative relationship with him.

Unlike children's accounts of the importance of their birth fathers, only three step family children described their step fathers as providing love and emotional support. Jasmine, a mixed race girl who put her step father in the inner circle, had not seen her birth father since she was three and had never lived with him. She said of her step father: '*He is the only dad I have ever known*'. The important thing for Jasmine was that her step father treated her and her brother no differently from their half brother, the step father's biological child. '*I think he loves us the same as [half brother] because he treats us the same.*'

From children's point of view, step fathers' care could not be taken for granted; it had to be worked at. In this sense, therefore, step father-hood is 'achieved' rather than 'ascribed'. (There is also a suggestion of this in children's normative responses to the vignette on step family form, see Chapter 3.) In their accounts of their step fathers' importance to them, children sought to justify their step fathers' role in the family and in their own lives. They supplied evidence of the ways that step fathers had become involved in their lives, thereby suggesting that step fathers' care was not necessarily expected or desired. For some, it was seen as something of a 'bonus'. Tracy, a white working class girl who had regular contact with her birth father, put both her birth father and step father in the inner circle; she said her step father was important to her because '*He is still part of my family*', thereby suggesting that he might not be. Tracy went on to give evidence of her step father's involvement; as she said, he does '*loads of things*' including cooking meals for the family and buying her things. Chloe, a Black girl, said that she got on 'fine' with her step father and supplied a small example of his involvement: '*Say, I'm sitting down in my room, bored. And he'll come up to me and say: "What's wrong"? And then he'll take me out some-where to stop me from being bored.*'

Thus, while most children placed their step fathers in the inner circle, they valued them for playing a part in their everyday lives. Those who did not place their step fathers in the inner circle failed to mention any evidence of their involvement. Only one child, however, owned up to an active dislike for her step father and had a largely negative relationship with him.

Foster children's carers

By definition, foster children were different from the other children (who lived with one or both parents). Their relationships with their carers were relatively short-term. In being taken into foster care, they had been removed from their families, usually without their explicit consent. Yet, almost all foster children (13/15) placed their female carers in the inner circle, while slightly fewer children (11/15) placed their male carers in the inner circle. In a few cases there were some significant differences of perspective between the foster carers' views and the children's views of their relationships, with some carers having a more rosy view while the children were ambivalent. As is the case for other children, carers' daily involvement in foster children's lives was important, albeit it might refer to basic forms of care. As three foster children said, their carers were important to them simply because *'they look after me'*.

Foster children seemed to emphasise their female rather than their male foster carers. Given professional concerns about child abuse in the foster care context as well as in the children's own families of origin, it would not be surprising if girls were cautious about male carers. Gail, a Black girl who called her foster carer 'Nan', even though they were not related, placed Nan in the inner circle even though she felt some ambivalence towards her and put her male carer in the middle circle. She explained the greater importance of Nan thus: *'Because he can't really look after me because he's a man and mans don't look after children. It's really your mother or your nan who is looking after you.'*

Foster children were informative in their interviews and they often expressed strong feelings. However, some appeared to have difficulty in articulating the ways in which people were important to them; they did not readily speak in terms of 'relationships'. This was not surprising since foster children had experienced poor care at the hands of their parents and, as a consequence, had highly problematic relationships with them which had caused children significant emotional damage. The following response of Jason, a white foster boy, to a question about the importance of his foster carer is typical:

I: *How do you get on with (foster carer)?*
J: *Fine.*
I: *Is she important to you?*
J: *Mmm.*

I: *In what way is she important to you?*
J: *Every way.*

No children compared their foster carers with their birth parents. Of the 15 foster children, only three said their carers were important to them because they acted 'like parents'. These children had very good relationships with their carers. Claire, a white girl who had lived with the foster family for two years, together with her younger brother, described her female carer as 'like a mum really' and her male carer 'like a dad'. As the accounts of the carers also suggested, the two children had indeed become part of the family. At the time of interview, the children (and the foster carers) were awaiting the decision of the local authority which would allow the children to stay with the family on a permanent basis. A second child, Elaine, a Black girl, had a particular reason; ten years ago, she had been fostered by her maternal grandmother while having some contact with her birth mother. When asked why her grandmother was important to her, she distinguished between 'a mum' and her real mum: *'Because she is like, not Mum, but she is like a mum and grandad is like a dad.'* A third child, Melanie, had developed a very close relationship with her female carer: *'Because she cares for me, she loves me and gives me cuddles.'* By contrast, her brother who lived in the same foster family, noted that he 'got on well' with his carers and significantly commented on the unfriendly foster care terminology – *'foster sounds like a stranger'*.

Several who placed them in the inner circle of their maps explained that they 'got on well' with their foster carers, thereby suggesting that *positive* rather than negative interaction represented a significant achievement. Debbie, who placed her two foster carers in the inner circle but was often in conflict with them, put the case clearly: *'I get on fine but sometimes I have arguments with them because I don't get my own way, because I like to get my own way.'*

Two children who did not position their carers in the inner circle simply said they did not like them. Such judgements are not surprising since children had often been placed with more than one foster family when former care placements had not worked. Children were also clearly aware that they had 'rights' in respect of decisions concerning their care (as laid down in the Children Act 1989). A white boy, Robert, who had been moved to several different foster homes, but said that he could stay with his current carers *'however long I want'*. Debbie, who complained about the lack of freedom and privacy given her by her carers, said: *'I'm having a word with [social worker] tomorrow because I'm not taking it. I'll just leave them [foster carers]. Go somewhere else where I can have a bit more freedom, a bit more privacy.'*

Some foster children for whom moving was a current issue suggested that they had little say about changes of placement. Kayley, a white girl, described how she had been moved from her previous foster home against her wishes. She felt she had been given no say in the decision and had made it clear she wanted to return. As a result, her current relationship with her female foster carer was cool (although she placed her in the inner circle). By contrast, two children described having a say. Wayne, a white boy, did not get on with his current short-term foster carers and wanted to join his half brother in his foster home while his sister was to remain with his current carer. David (also white) was going to be adopted but asked to be fostered by his aunt and uncle instead; his request was granted.

Foster children's non-resident birth parents

As for foster children's birth parents, it is perhaps much more surprising that so many children included them in the inner circle (10/15 birth mothers and 6/15 birth fathers) since, in most cases, they were taken away from their parents because of poor care. Moreover contact with parents was very variable. All but one child (14/15) had at least some, albeit irregular, contact with their birth mothers, but more than half (9/15) had no contact with their birth fathers, including four children who did not know their fathers' identities. Yet several foster children placed their birth fathers in their maps even though they had not seen them for many years. In contrast, most of the lone mother and step family children who had no contact with their birth fathers for a long time, did not include them in their maps. Jason, a white foster boy, whose father died when he was six, still placed him in the inner circle together with his mother, whom he had not seen for over two years. He also included all his brothers and sisters with whom he had no current contact, including two half-siblings he had never met. Yet he was unable to express exactly why he placed his birth parents and others in the inner circle. Similarly, Wayne placed his father in the inner circle despite not having seen him since he was five.

A brother and sister living with the same foster family were the only two children in this group openly to express their affection for their parents. They were unusual in that they saw their divorced birth parents separately on a weekly basis and, while they both said they loved their mother, they both made it clear that their father was more important to them. Melanie said, *'I love my dad, my dad is my best family,'* while her brother Liam said, *'My dad is very important because I just love him so much.'* Both children said their mother had been the one who put them in care after their birth father had left and because of ill health. They recalled how she had deceived them by telling them that they were going for a holiday. This may explain why they differentiated between their parents, favouring their father over their mother, although there may well have been other undisclosed problematic aspects of their family lives.

Just as foster children's accounts of their carers' importance were not elaborated upon, so few of these children elaborated on the importance of their birth parents. Two girls and a boy, none of whom knew the identity of their fathers, all said their mothers were important to them, *'Because she is my mum.'* Given the fact that they had been very poorly treated by their birth parents, foster children were caught in a dilemma. While continuing to love their parents, which clearly some did, judging from the affectionate way in which some children talked about them, they also had to come to terms with very negative feelings about them and their care. How then to admit that parents were important while also acknowledging that they had failed them?

Not surprisingly, some foster children expressed this contradiction by positioning their birth parents in the inner circle of their maps, while giving a different account verbally. Some preferred not to speak about their parents at all. David had not seen his father since the age of seven and he said he preferred not to see his mother because her irregular visits upset him a lot. Nevertheless, David placed both his mother and his father in the inner circle because, he said: *'they're just family and family is important to me.'* By contrast, Wayne's two accounts of his parents' importance to him were more consistent. He put his mother in the outer circle blaming her for splitting up the family when she left his violent father, taking the children with her. He also commented that when they lived with their mother she would hit him and his siblings. So Wayne placed his father, with whom he had no contact since the age of five, in the inner circle, commenting: *'I would rather stay with my dad than my mum because my dad never even hit me once.'*

Yet several children showed considerable concern for their parents' loss of their children and understanding of their mothers' inability to care for them. Some put blame on themselves. Gail, a Black girl, described feeling 'terrible' about not living with her mother: *'She tried to look after me but I understand that she can't cope with me that much.'* Debbie, a white girl, claimed that her alcoholic mother coped much better now that she did not have responsibility for looking after her.

Claire, who had not heard from her mother for over a year, and whose father had lost contact when she was five, was more able to express her ambivalent feelings in words as well, omitting her birth parents from her map: *'Sometimes I do [want to live with her again] when I miss her. But sometimes I'm angry and I don't want to.'* But even she said that her mother was 'sort of' important to her but declined to say more. Perhaps as compensation for not placing her birth parents in her map, she included a large number of friends and teachers, her foster family and the dog, together with seven aunts and uncles and their children – most of whom she never saw. The only family member she had contact with was her brother who was in the same foster home. She said of him: *'He's the only person out of my life I live with.'*

As we will discuss later (Chapter 6) with reference to foster children's positioning of their siblings, the foster children's families of origin provided meaning to their disrupted lives. Their families of origin represented the existence of a family that once existed, albeit an unhappy one, which was unlikely to be recovered and which constituted, in their view, their only chance of a 'proper family'.

Conclusions

Children's normative understandings of what parents 'ought to do' for children and how they should act out their parental roles to some extent reflect public (adult) discourses of gender equality, in particular a portrayal of parenting as 'gender free'. Children reported less normative consensus on parents' labour market participation however, expressing conservative attitudes on the one hand, for example stressing mothers' place in the home, and a less gendered approach on the other, suggesting that both mothers and fathers should work part time when children are small. In respect of parents' practices, children's experience of parenting not surprisingly reflected parents' availability notably to provide everyday care to children. In a very real sense, household structure makes a difference to children's lives and, since it was mainly fathers who were non-resident rather than mothers, for lone mother children and some step family children, parenting and parenthood were largely practiced by their mothers.

Children's accounts of the importance of parents – both in general and in a specific sense – suggest that they differentiated between mothers and fathers. However, they were also reluctant to make explicit comparisons which might suggest that they favoured one parent over the other. They felt a need to be 'fair' to both parents. Again, whether both parents were resident in the household and the history of children's relationships with their fathers influenced children's accounts of parenting in practice. On the other hand, no matter what type of household form children lived in, children considered both their birth parents to be very important to them. Children suggested that parents and carers were important to them in a wide variety of ways both in terms of expressive and instrumental dimensions of care. There was, however, considerable variation in whether they sought to confide in parents, even in their mothers. Children highlighted the importance of parents' availability to them so that non-resident birth fathers while, in many cases, being of considerable importance to children, were seen to be wanting in this respect by comparison with resident mothers. Moreover, children did not presume that step fathers, by virtue of their presence in the household, would assume importance in their worlds; from children's perspectives, care and its reciprocity had to be worked at. Yet even when parents failed children and when children had little or irregular contact with parents as was the case with the foster children in the study, in most cases children continued to love their birth parents.

As Smart and Neale (1998) and Sevenhuijsen (1998) have argued, the past history of parents' care of children is one crucial criterion by which children's residence following divorce is, and should be, decided. The fact that mothers have typically been awarded the main responsibility for children following divorce should be understood not in terms of rights based on biological motherhood but in terms of responsibilities, and the history of connectedness to children in relation to their everyday care. Children's accounts of the meaning of their ties with parents are testimony to this. As Morgan (1996) suggests with respect to adult perspectives, for children also, family life is, and should be, about 'doing' family life rather than being concerned about what a family 'is' or looks like on the surface.

6   The importance of siblings

Ideally I do hate my brother and sister sometimes but I do love them.

The small literature which addresses the significance of siblings to children has largely viewed the issue through the paradigm of developmentalism (see Kosonen 1994 for a review). Psychological studies have focused for example on children's like and dislike for their siblings and the implications of sibling relations for peer relations and later psychological adjustment (Dunn and McGuire 1992). Much less attention has been paid to the ways in which children themselves perceive sibling relations and the importance they place on them during the course of their childhoods. More recently, sociologists have begun to extend their interest in this direction, suggesting that children (in middle childhood) perceive their siblings to be an important source of support, albeit children also report sibling relations to be punctuated by rivalry and conflict (Kosonen 1996; Morrow 1998). Moreover, as we discuss in this chapter, living apart from, as well as living with, siblings may render siblings important to children.

From children's vantage point, family networks form both the context in which family change occurs and constitute an outcome of family change. As we suggested in Chapter 3, family networks following family change afford children the possibility of social ties with other siblings. Children may acquire half siblings and step siblings who either join them in the same household or who live in other households. Some children may have little contact with siblings who live with the other non-resident parent. In the case of foster children, many have siblings who are frequently scattered in a number of different households, because of family change not only because of care orders, and they typically have little or very irregular contact with them. However foster children may gain new 'sibling-like' relationships within their foster care families – with carers' own children or with other foster children.

Just as contact and relationships between children and their parents may vary over time, so too their relationships with siblings are likely to be subject to flux and change.

This study provided an opportunity to contextualise children's accounts of their sibling relations in the networks of children's families (Chapter 3) and for linking children's understandings of sibling relations to household and kinship structures and hierarchies of age and status.

While this chapter draws largely on the case study material, mention should be made also of evidence from the Questionnaire Survey which also lends some support to the importance children placed upon their siblings. In response to a question about the three most important persons in children's lives, over half of children placed siblings in third place (56%), with mothers mentioned in first place and fathers second. In the Questionnaire Survey evidence, siblings also emerged as a significant source of support for children at the start of secondary school. Moreover, as we show in Chapter 8, a good deal of children's contribution to care revolved around siblings. Over four-fifths of those with siblings (92%) said they were nice to their brothers and sisters either every day or on some days. Over a third said they took care of younger brothers and sisters every day, with South Asian origin children much more likely to do so (54% compared with 29% of white children). In the remaining part of the chapter, we turn to the case study interviews and the maps of significant others which children completed and which give some indication of the importance children placed on their siblings. But first we will provide an overview of the nature and range of the support children reported giving or receiving from their siblings.

Types of support siblings give one another

As the research literature suggests, siblings may provide a number of forms of support for one another (Dunn and McGuire 1992). First, they may be important attachment figures providing children with a sense of meaning and ontological security. Second, they act as a key cognitive resource in terms of acting as role models and in the development of skills and intellectual development. Third, siblings may be sources of emotional significance, albeit that warmth is often allied to conflict (Dunn 1988). But what is often ignored is the way in which children engage in 'sentient activity' – to use Mason's term (Mason 1996) in interacting with their siblings, and may provide a confidential ear to one another. Fourth, sibling relations may provide sociability and companionship. Lastly, they may also offer care in a practical sense.

In their accounts of their sibling relations, children rarely articulated the sense of security and meaning which siblings can provide one another, except in the event of unusual and traumatic situations in which children were separated from their siblings. As we shall show, for foster children who had been forcibly separated from their siblings when they were placed in care, siblings typically provided children with an important sense of symbolic attachment even if they rarely saw them. Robert lived with his foster carers, had no current contact with his parents and only irregular contact with his five brothers and sisters. He placed his two brothers and three sisters in the inner circle of his map of significant others. Although his monosyllabic replies to questions about his siblings did not give much away about his feelings for them, his earlier responses to questions concerning the significance of the term 'family' were quite unequivocal. Asked the first word that came into his head when he heard the word 'family', Robert unhesitatingly replied 'brothers' and when asked what he would miss most by not being part of a family, he said he would miss 'not seeing his brothers' and then added 'sisters'. Moreover, when working out who else to place in his map of important people, he included the postman because, he said, he brought letters from his siblings.

Children often clearly indicated the support their siblings provided in terms of cognitive development. Older siblings described helping younger siblings and younger siblings described being helped by older siblings with developing various skills, which typically related to school homework but also concerned the negotiation of social relationships. For example, a girl described teaching her younger sibling about the importance of 'sticking up for herself' which she said was her own discovery. Latasha wanted to transmit this self knowledge to her sister: *'If she's like having problems at school or with friends, I always tell her to stick up for herself . . . because I've learnt to respect – to be happy with myself and that I can actually stick up for myself.'* As Dunn (1988) suggests, children practice reasoning and language skills in the course of their disputes with siblings. The graphic accounts of children in our study of sibling quarrels testify to this and will be discussed later.

Children's accounts also suggested that they sometimes engaged in 'sentient activity' (Mason 1996) in their sibling relations, that is they expressed concern about and empathy towards their brothers and sisters, especially if they were in trouble. Lucy (mixed race, lone mother family) described worrying about her older brother who was currently living elsewhere with his father and was trying to come off drugs. On a more mundane level, Emily was understanding towards her 16-year-old sister because she was doing her GCSEs and described taking over her sister's share of the cleaning. Jasmine described how her mother relied on her to pick up her young brother from school and how, on the way home, she took on her mother's mantle of responsibility when they were crossing the road and another child gave her little brother a bad example by 'turning round in the middle of the road'. *'I goes "Don't teach my brother that because he'll end up getting run over 'cause of you" and I'll tell you I would kill them if that happened'*. Amy described becoming more attentive to changes in her relationship with her brother, following the arrival of her step father and his children. Amy described how she noticed that, following the step siblings' departure from the household, she and her brother became more appreciative of each other when they went on holiday and spent time together: *'And me and [brother] noticed – well, I noticed anyway – that me and [brother] spent so much time together on that holiday.'*

Children also confided in their siblings especially over matters in which their siblings were already experienced, for example children consulted older siblings who had already negotiated the transition to secondary school. A South Asian origin boy, Baldev, was clearly very proud of his 16-year-old sister who was now at college. He mentioned her at every opportunity in the interview. Even his identity at his new secondary school owed much to his sister: *'Because my sister was there basically everyone knew my sister and so everyone knew me.'* Baldev's sister was unusually important to him as a confidant and Baldev showed his appreciation by buying her a mobile phone: *'I can talk to her [about] things – girls that I don't want to talk to my mum and dad about. [Even] if I did go out with a girl. But I can talk to her about everything. And if I didn't want her to go blabbering, she wouldn't. She's kind as well.'*

Siblings as a source of sociability and companionship was another common theme in children's accounts of their sibling relations, albeit their relations were marked also by conflict. Children often described their older and younger siblings as 'playmates' and as people with whom they had 'fun' and with whom they went out, not necessarily as a family. As we shall describe in greater detail later, children's ways of talking about their siblings suggested considerable emotional significance both in terms of positive and negative interaction. Indeed, children described sibling rivalry and quarrelling as part and parcel of 'normal' siblings relation – as two sides of the same coin.

Finally, as to practical care and responsibility for other siblings, children sometimes suggested they cared for younger siblings, albeit not always willingly or voluntarily. However, although they were sometimes resistant to their parents' expectations concerning looking after or minding siblings, their accounts were usually tempered with mention of some positive aspects of the work. Moreover, children were also keen to emphasise the limits on their responsibility for younger siblings. In particular, several children stressed that their mothers did not expect them to look after younger siblings 'by themselves'; that is, they were

suggesting that their mothers were not delegating maternal responsibility for to do so would flout normative guidelines concerning what it
is to be a child.

Positioning of siblings in children's maps of significant others

Children most usually placed their siblings at the centre of their maps
alongside their mothers and fathers in the inner circle.

As Table 6.1 shows, almost all children in each family type placed at
least one sibling in the inner circle, with most placing all their siblings
there. Only a few children distributed siblings across the three circles. In
the cases where children omitted mention of siblings, these mainly comprised step siblings or half siblings who were living in other households,
either with their birth fathers or children of their step fathers from a
former relationship. In most cases children omitted siblings from their
circles where there was little contact. However, some lone parent children omitted mention of new half siblings of non-resident birth fathers
whom they visited. Foster children included their siblings whether or
not they were in contact.

Full siblings

Almost all children placed their full siblings in the inner circles of their
maps of significant others. The positive reasons children gave for their
importance referred to a varied range of social support, as already
described. Some children simply referred to the ascribed nature of
sibling relationships. As David, a white foster boy, noted in response to
the question concerning the importance of brothers and sisters: *'Just
family. Family is important to me.'* A step family child said: *'Because
they are related to you.'* Some children seemed unable to articulate why
their siblings were important.

Those children who placed their siblings in the middle and outer

Table 6.1   Number of children with siblings (full, half and step) who
positioned at least one sibling in the circles (inner signifying greatest
importance) by family type

	Inner	*Middle/outer*	*Not in circles*
Two-parent ($n = 15$)	14	2	0
One parent ($n = 17$)	12	5	6
Step father ($n = 15$)	13	3	8
Foster care ($n = 13$)	11	3	1

circles included two girls living with their lone mothers. Their positioning of their siblings reflected the difficult and complex dynamics which
existed within the family network and which were related to the break-
up of the parents' relationship. But some children simply said they did
not get on with their siblings. A Black foster child, Gail, put her younger
sister with whom she was living in the outer circle *'because she is bossy
to me'* while Emily, a white girl living in a step family, put her older
sister in the middle circle because they argued a lot.

In contrast, Mirza, a South Asian origin boy living with a lone
mother, placed his three older married sisters and his one younger
brother in the middle circle not because he did not get along with them.
Rather, he considered other people to be more significant in his life,
especially during the transition to secondary school. In fact, he placed
six teachers in the inner circle together with seven male friends from his
secondary school. Similarly, Andrew, a white boy living with a lone
mother, placed his four sisters in the middle circle, despite saying that he
got on 'very well' with them. With the exception of his mother, Andrew
limited his inner circle to males including his mother's brother, his
aunt's husband and the football manager of the local team he played
for. Andrew initially omitted his birth father but when asked whether
he wanted to include his birth father, Andrew decided to include his
birth father in the inner circle as well. The positioning of males in the
inner circle could reflect a desire on Andrew's part for male role models,
especially those who shared his interest in football. Moreover, this
desire may have been augmented by the fact that, as Andrew's mother
noted, his non-resident father was neglectful of his first family and often
failed to keep his promises to visit them.

Three foster children did not place their resident siblings in the inner
circle. Gail found her sister 'bossy', while Liam expressed regret that his
sister, who was of a similar age, no longer wanted to play with him. In
contrast, Wayne exhibited extreme hostility towards his resident sister
and wanted to join his elder brother in another foster home; this negative relationship with his sister may have had its roots in the troubled
family history.

Resident half siblings

Children with resident half siblings positioned them in the inner circle.
These half siblings from their step fathers' relationships with their birth
mothers were often much younger. (No step siblings in the study were
resident in children's households on a full-time basis at the time of the
study.) Lenny, a Black boy living with a lone mother, put his five-year-
old half sister in the inner circle of his small map of significant others

which also contained his birth parents (who were no longer living together), his grandmother with whom he lived for part of the week, together with some aunts, uncles and cousins and his deceased grandfather. Asked why he put his half sister in the inner circle, he described with some relish taking his sister to the park – *'where she can run around and play with her friends.'* He also described caring for her despite her status as his half sibling: *'I care for her a lot even though we didn't have the same fathers. I look after her a lot, look out for her. I wouldn't like her getting worried or anything.'* Only one child did not include his resident half sibling, but then neither did he include his other two sisters. Steve dismissed his three-year-old half sister *'because she can hardly speak yet'* and complained about his two older sisters because they *'nick my clothes'*.

Non-resident half and step siblings

As noted above, some children omitted from their maps half siblings acquired by their birth fathers' subsequent relationships, and also non-resident step siblings (through their step fathers or non-resident birth fathers). This was noticeably so if children were not in contact with these siblings but it was also the case for some who were in contact. Andrew, who placed his three resident siblings in the middle circle, omitted all mention of his non-resident birth father's children from his second, subsequent family even though he was in contact with them. Rebecca omitted mention of her non-resident father's son, her half brother, whom she saw when she visited her father during the school holidays. Moreover, Rebecca identified strongly with her father, much more so than with her mother. In addition, the fact that she placed her resident full sister who was nearly her own age in the outer circle was significant. Describing her relationship with her sister as 'not really close', she put this down to the fact that her sister and her mother both shared an interest in 'girly things' which she, as 'a kind of tomboy', despised. The omission from her map of her half brother who lived with her father may indicate some resentment of him, given her strong preference and identification with her father and her problematic relationship with her sister in particular.

Foster children stand out in marked contrast to those who omitted mention of their non-resident siblings. Foster children included in their inner circles all their siblings, many of whom were half siblings, even though they did not live with and, in many cases, had no current contact with them. Absent siblings appeared to have a particular significance for foster children. Some foster children had lived with some of their siblings; together they had once constituted 'a family', but their 'family life' of their siblings and parents had been taken from them and was unlikely to be reinstated. Thus the salience of siblings to foster children may lie in symbolising that they had once been a family, albeit often an unhappy one. As Claire said of her brother who shared the same foster carers: '*He is the one person from my life I live with.*' As to her other half siblings, some of whom were born after she went into care, Claire expressed a wish to meet them but said she was unable to get in touch with them because she did not have their addresses. When completing his map of important people, Jason placed his birth family in the inner circle: his dead father, his mother and his four brothers and sisters with whom he had no current contact.

Sibling ambivalence

While a few children described their relationships with their siblings in ambiguously positive terms, this was not the whole story of sibling relations. Placing siblings in the inner circle did not rule out conflict between them. Most children reported feeling annoyed and irritated by their siblings and typically mentioned quarrelling, fighting and teasing. As Barry, who lived in a recently formed step family, commented about his older brother: '*I just put him there [in the inner circle].*' He then went on to describe very strong negative feelings towards his brother: '*I hate him!*'

This next account of a South Asian origin boy, Niaz, initially suggested a harmonious set of sibling relations. Niaz had two older sisters aged 16 and 18, one younger brother aged eight and one younger sister aged six. Niaz described a particularly good relationship with his older 18-year-old sister to whom he felt he could talk '*about things I can't talk to nobody else about*'. If there was something he really wanted, he said his sister would buy it for him. The only thing he was unhappy about in the relationship was if his sister was in a bad mood and shouted at him. By contrast, he described his relationship with his 16-year-old sister quite differently – as much more playful because they 'messed about' together: '*She's really good like, she plays darts with me, she plays snooker. She always wins.*' He was also grateful that she didn't try to banish him from the sitting room when the adults were out and she had friends home: '*She wouldn't shout at us, that's what we're always scared about, that someone's going to shout, like if she doesn't want us here.*' However, when asked directly, he admitted that she bullied him 'sometimes'.

Niaz's relationship with his two younger siblings was marked by the responsibility he shouldered for helping to look after them, though never by himself, as he pointed out. He described how, the day before the interview, he had been asked to look after his younger siblings upstairs while one of his older sisters entertained her friends downstairs. He admitted being bored by this responsibility, especially when his younger siblings ganged up against him in their choice of TV programmes. As the elder child in charge, he felt he had a right to choose the TV programme on behalf of his siblings but clearly his younger siblings put up a strong fight: *'There's football on – the biggest match of the century, like Man United v. Liverpool in the FA Cup football and they want to watch cartoons and I don't. I have to make them watch football. I'm in charge.'*

Niaz also hinted at sibling rivalries which typically pervade larger families when children compete for parental attention and favour. According to Niaz, his relations with his siblings were complicated by his parents' and siblings' preferences for one another. His description of his younger nine-year-old brother as 'mummy's boy' was symptomatic of this. Although he showed no obvious resentment of his mother in the remark: *'She likes all of us but obviously she likes him so much,'* his admission of occasional bullying of his younger brother may have been significant: *'I shout at him a lot until he does [play with me]. And I always make him do jobs I don't want to do. If I don't want to take the garbage out: "Do it!" And he'll do it for me. He doesn't do it sometimes. That's so annoying. I really feel sometimes I could just kill him and I can't.'* While he described a very good relationship with his second oldest sister, he also noted that it was easy to annoy her, and that his sister had a close affinity with their father, while his younger brother had a similar affinity with their mother. Perhaps this was because she was his father's favourite child? *'Cos like, she likes my dad the best. Cos he [younger brother] likes my mum a lot, she likes my dad a lot. My mum likes him a lot and my dad likes her a lot.'*

Latasha, a Black girl in a two-parent family, was the middle child with two sisters aged eight and 14. She said that they argued all the time. When two of them fell out, the third played an ambiguous role – 'in the middle' – as she describes it. *'Say V [older sister] is not talking [to me], S's in the middle. If me and S aren't talking, V's in the middle.'* Then she gave an example where her older sister used her older age to her own advantage. The incident she reported concerned finding a one pound coin in the street. According to Latasha, even though she herself had found it, her elder sister managed to take charge of it and then spent it on herself. She described her older sister as 'a very convincing person' who managed to implicate herself in her younger sister's find: *'Like I found a pound and she goes "Can we share it? Because if I wasn't walking with you, you wouldn't find it either."'*

Negotiating hierarchies of age

Children framed their relationships with siblings, especially in larger families, in relation to hierarchies of age and birth order. These hierarchies were socially constructed and therefore not immutable. Children typically tried to negotiate their positioning in the social order. While it could be argued that these hierarchies constitute sibling cultures which were distinct from 'family culture', the hierarchies among children in the family were often legitimated by parents who tended to accord greater responsibility and sometimes privileges to the eldest children. Yet at the same time, both parents and children themselves also subscribed to the 'equality' or 'fairness norm' of treating all children in the family the same (Chapter 9). As we shall indicate, parents often abided by this normative guideline by simply refusing to interfere in sibling rivalries.

Those who were elder or eldest children in the household often presented themselves as speaking from positions of responsibility and privilege. On the positive side, they described different ways in which they held sway over their younger siblings and helped in their care – looking after them when they were small and, when they were older, helping them with homework or looking out for them at school. In many cases, children mentioned volunteering to help their siblings. On the negative side, they spoke about the different ways in which their younger siblings sought to challenge their positions in the status hierarchy. Younger sibling tried to violate the privacy of older children – for example, barging into their bedrooms was a favourite strategy. Or they bargained using their young age, for example by behaving in a 'babyish' way in order to attract parents' attention and intervention.

Willy, a white boy in a lone mother household, clearly resented the arrival of his younger sisters because they had usurped his position as the only child. Moreover, he found the responsibility that had been laid upon him as the older brother highly onerous. Nonetheless, he saw the logic of the situation and eventually agreed that his mother's privileging of his younger siblings was 'fair' even though he resented it:

W: *It's, like, when . . . one of my sisters gets sweets, and I don't or something, and then she gets something else, and I don't get nothing, she [mother] says, You're the oldest, you see, you should save your pocket money, and that.*

I: *So do you feel that your sisters get more than you do?*

W: *Yes.*

I: *Because they're younger?*

W: *Yes. Everything that you have when you're young, she's having now, but – I don't know what I was having when I was younger, because I can't remember it.*

I: *You can't remember. Yes. So how does that make you feel, that your sister's getting more than you do?*

W: *I think it's fair, because I had quite a lot when I'm younger. Because I was the first baby, and the first baby always gets treated more, because they think it's the most precious, when you first have a baby. But I think it's quite fair. Because I think I've had more than them all the way over the years.*

In this next example, Claudia, the older child in a lone mother family, clearly demonstrated the double-edged aspect of sibling relations. Claudia put her seven-year-old sister in the inner circle. While she first said that she 'loved' her younger sister, she then noted that '*sometimes she gets on my nerves*'. Then Claudia volunteered an instance where her younger sister had challenged her: '*Like if I'm playing – just like before you came, I was playing my computer and then she asked if she could play it. And then she had a tantrum and she started throwing everything.*' Asked whether she thought her mother was fair when she and her sister quarrelled, she agreed but also went on to suggest that her mother placed upon her, as 'the elder child', undue responsibility. She was clearly unhappy that her mother refused to support her as the wronged party in the quarrel. Claudia resisted responsibility being conferred on her on the basis of her older age and thought that her mother should intervene: '*Sometimes they [parents] have a go at me and Mum will say, "You should know better". They [parents] don't listen to you. They just say, "I don't want to know. I don't want to hear it. You should know better. You are older." But I don't think older's got nothing to do with it. She [sister] starts, I start back on her . . . I'm not standing for it!*' However, in another situation, Claudia accepted her positioning in terms of the age hierarchy and described how she took it upon herself, as the older sibling, to help her younger sister. She did 'favours' for her sister which, she said, her sister, as a relatively 'young child', lacked sufficient skills and status to do herself.

Younger children described the converse side of the relationship with an older sibling. On the positive side, they described how their older siblings would help them and how they, in turn, sought to redress the power imbalance which arose when one was always the giver and the other the receiver. Younger siblings described lending money to older siblings and doing things for them. For example, Hayfa (South Asian origin, two-parent family) described helping her two older sisters and older brother: '*And I have to go up and down, up and down the stairs getting them things. They go, "Hayfa, get this, get that! I'm like 'Okay, I'm getting it!'".*' As already noted, a South Asian origin boy, Baldev, described being able to talk to his older sister about 'everything' and how his sister was especially helpful when he started secondary school. In return he had bought a mobile phone for his sister from the money he earned from working for their father.

On the negative side, younger siblings described how their older siblings used their positions of power over them – shouting at them, ignoring them, bullying them – and how they in turn sought to redress or challenge the age hierarchy: barging into their rooms and taking their possessions. Lujayn (South Asian origin, two-parent household), was one of several 'middle children'. She had to share a bedroom with her elder sister and complained about her sister for shouting and screaming at her, behaviour which she explained thus: *'It's because she thinks – she's older, she's bigger and bossy.'* By contrast, her relations with her younger brother, albeit also involving conflict, she described more positively as 'messing about': *'He doesn't really fight with me. He just pretends to.'*

Siblings argued over scarce resources and older siblings sometimes used their position to ensure their own priority of access. Kevin (white boy, two-parent household) put his seven-year-old brother, with whom he had to share a bedroom, in his middle circle while putting his older 14-year-old brother in the outer circle. He explained this positioning in terms of his older brother's rejection of him as a playmate which he clearly expected of him: *'He never comes to the park, he never comes to play football with me.'* He also complained that his brother was always commandeering their shared computer – *'Like he's always on it, always, always, always'* – and that he took the prerogative in choosing computer games by manipulating their younger brother: *'Like we each got a game at the beginning of the summer. Like he talked my little brother into getting one, and my little brother didn't really want it.'*

Sibling support and household structure

In addition to children's negotiation of their sibling hierarchies, children's relations with siblings were also influenced by structural aspects of family life. One concerns family size. If children lived in a larger family and had several siblings, especially if they were close in age, this could entail responsibility, notably of older for younger children. A large family may also provide opportunities for sociability and friendships. As Morrow (1998) has observed, the accounts of some children of Pakistani origin in her study were indicative of these features of sibling relations. However, how far these were cultural rather than structural features of the families in our study is open to question. Roughly half of the South Asian origin families in our study contained three or more children which made these households rather larger than many other families. As already noted above, the Questionnaire Survey evidence suggested that South Asian origin children were more likely than white children to say they looked after their younger brothers and sisters 'everyday' (54% compared to 29%), while white children were more likely to say they never looked after siblings (25% compared to 13%). However, South Asian origin children were as likely as Black children to say they had been 'nice' to their siblings while white children were least likely to do so (34%, 32%, 22% respectively). Certainly in some of the South Asian origin case study families, children volunteered that they helped care for siblings and considered their siblings as their playmates. Harinder, for example, talked about playing with his cousins who ranged greatly in ages; in his fond reference to playing with his eight-year-old cousin, Harinder considered that there was nothing shameful in mixing with a younger child.

Larger families also increased competition for scarce resources. One particular resource which was of concern to some children who lived in larger families related to sharing a bedroom. A Black boy, Jake, complained that his older brother with whom he shared locked him out of the room when he wanted to watch certain kinds of films on the television. Similarly, Kevin, who shared with his younger brother, complained about having to wait downstairs while his seven-year-old brother went to sleep, but enjoyed being able to play computer games with him in the morning. Latasha complained of a lack of privacy; she said that whenever she did something in their bedroom, her younger sister wanted to know what she was doing. However, there are several examples of children who preferred to share a bedroom with siblings because it meant that they had company and could have fun together.

A second structural feature of sibling relations is the gender composition which, when number of siblings and birth order are taken into account, can produce a variety of combinations and patterns. South Asian origin girls were particularly likely to complain that parents were more strict with girls (see also Brannen et al. 1994). Lujayn complained that it was not fair that her brother was not made to do housework, while Zarina considered it unfair that her brother was given more freedom. Rohini complained she had to go to school accompanied by her parents and that she was not allowed to go to the shops on her own to buy an ice cream. She put this down to being a girl, although her parents' protectiveness may have had something to do with their status as relatively recent migrants and a fear of the new society.

A third feature of sibling relations implicates household structure. Issues around love for, and care of, a younger sibling can bring other issues related to family structure to the fore. In some step families where there were joint children from the mothers' new relationships, the older children in these families were expected on occasion to look after their younger half siblings especially if they were very young, as several of them were. This was evident in one of the step families. In this case, the mother's enlistment of her daughter's support in looking after her young half brother highlighted the daughter's ambivalence towards her step father.

Amy was the middle child in the step family positioned between her slightly older brother, aged 13, and her young half brother aged one. She was the only daughter in the household. She described how her mother expected her to help look after her young half brother, especially when she got in from school. Moreover, Amy's older brother was exempted from caring, not on grounds of his maleness but because of his considerable prestigious extramural activities which took up a great deal of his time. This externally-derived prestige enhanced his status *within* the family, as the older male child, and conferred privilege upon him. However, Amy did not appear to resent this, although it was notable that Amy did not want to attend the same secondary school as her brother but sought to win a place at another school in her own right. Amy said she loved her little half brother but also resented looking after him while agreeing that her mother needed 'a break'. Sounding very much like an overworked mother herself, Amy asserted her own right to have some time off at the end of a hard day at school: '*When I get home from school, I usually have to look after him. Well, I mean, fair enough, my mum's had him all day. But it gets a pain because, like, you've been to school all day. You've done all this hard work. And then you have to come home and look after this screaming baby.*' Amy was torn between considering this a chore and a labour of love, while also taking account of her mother's fatigue – the step father appears to have been exempt from helping with his son.

In rejecting her step father, Amy was aware that her love for her half brother was somehow implicated. Amy had to manage the difficult psychic talk of accommodating that which united the step family as well as that which separated them. On the one hand, Amy asserted that it was 'quite understandable' that her step father should treat her differently from his own child and that he should love him more than herself and her older brother. On the other hand, Amy was conscious that her mother made no such distinction between her children: '*But it's like my mum liking – loving me different than she loves [half brother]. It's all the same. But because me and [full brother] are from a different father than [half brother], it's like we're totally different really.*'

Conclusions

Children's ties with their siblings emerged as strong and enduring. Siblings were only outflanked in importance by their relationships with their birth parents, at least at this time in their lives. While most children did not articulate the way in which their siblings provided them with a sense of meaning and ontological security, when family life breaks down, as had been the case for the foster children in the study, siblings came to represent a symbolic source of attachment for such children. As we have argued, where birth parents had signally failed to care for them, foster children invested great importance in their siblings. Siblings represented continuity in the face of discontinuity and symbolised the family that could have been or had once existed.

In terms of children's positioning of siblings at the core of their maps of important people, children adopted a highly inclusive approach towards the siblings with whom they lived and grew up. Moreover, while some children also included half siblings and step siblings in their maps of significant others when they had not grown up with them, others did not mention them.

The kinds of support which siblings derived from their relationships with one another were varied. Siblings often provided a key resource in terms of acting as role models and in the development of practical skills and intellectual argument. They acted as sources of emotional significance albeit that relations were often marked by conflict. Children also indicated the ways in which they enacted 'sentient activity', identifying their siblings' needs and responding empathetically to them. Siblings provided some children with an important source of sociability, especially where there were several children in the household who were near in age. Children also provided care in a practical sense, particularly of younger siblings, albeit not 'by themselves' and sometimes reluctantly.

However, one of the main features of family life which shaped children's accounts of sibling relations concerned the hierarchies of age and birth order which shaped children's own cultures within their families. Children negotiated access to scarce resources in the household including material privileges and parents' attention. Sometimes they challenged and sometimes they invoked these social hierarchies, depending upon their position within them, and their ability to negotiate them. They sometimes willingly took on caring roles allocated by parents according to children's age and birth order and sometimes they resisted them. Children's negotiation of these hierarchies depended upon a range of different conditions. These included the number of children in the household, the household's structure and the gender permutation of siblings in the household, the latter being particularly significant in South Asian origin families. The research design of the study was, however, not such that it provided a sufficiently controlled set of conditions in which to explore systematically the many different combinations of all these conditions.

7 The importance of grandparents, relatives, friends and others

Family's always there, friends aren't. They can change overnight, but your family doesn't really.

Until recently, there has been little research interest in the significance of wider kin to children (see Hill and Tisdall 1997 for a brief review). By contrast, children's peer relations have received more consideration (Berndt 1986; James 1993; Hill and Tisdall 1997). Only a few studies have focused upon the full range of persons children consider to be important to them. As Morrow (1998) has recently documented in her study of children's views of families, children included a wide spread of significant others which covered a range of kin beyond the nuclear family unit, especially grandparents and aunts, uncles and cousins (Morrow 1998).

As we have already noted (Chapters 5 and 6), as well as parents and siblings – both resident and non-resident – most children included among those they considered important to them (via their maps of significant others) their grandparents and other relatives. They also included friends and pets, while many children also mentioned a range of what we have termed 'formal others' – teachers, family doctors and social workers. Just as Morrow (1998) and others have found (Ahmad 1996), children's inclusion of extended family and a range of significant others was not confined to particular minority ethnic groups but constituted a common feature of children's lives.

In this chapter, we turn first to children's positioning of their grandparents and other relatives in their maps of significant others and the ways in which they justified their positioning. Second, we turn to the positioning and importance of friends, although we should emphasise that friends might have emerged as having more significance to children if the focus of the study had not been family life. Third, we discuss the particular importance children gave to formal others.

The importance of grandparents and other relatives

The inclusion of relatives and grandparents as part of children's every-day worlds is supported by evidence from the Questionnaire Survey. In the Survey, children reported frequent contact with relatives of their parents' generation, namely aunts and uncles, and even greater contact with their own generation, namely cousins. Three-quarters of the Survey children reported seeing aunts and uncles at least monthly (76%), while over half (54%) reported seeing them in the past week (Table 7.1, Appendix). While 71% saw cousins and 48% other relatives on an at least a monthly basis, just under half (48%) and under a third (31%) respectively ticked weekly contact. There were no statistically significant differences by household type with respect to contact with relatives (excluding grandparents).

Rather fewer children in the Survey reported seeing grandparents within the past month (63%), while less than half (46%) reported seeing one or more grandparent within the past week. Given that not all children had living grandparents, it is perhaps not so surprising that grandparent contact was outstripped by contact with other relatives. Household type made a statistically significant difference to frequency of contact with grandparents. Probably because step family children had more grandparents available to them, through their parents' re-partnering, step family children were more likely to report more fre-quent contact with grandparents (71% in the past month) compared with children living in other types of household (64% of children living with both birth parents and 59% of lone parent children). Moreover, reported contact with relatives, including grandparents, was higher than the contact of children in lone mother households with their non-resident fathers (47% weekly and 59% at least monthly).

Contrary to cultural assumptions about the importance of extended families in 'traditional' South Asian cultures, children of South Asian origin reported less frequent contact with grandparents in the Ques-tionnaire Survey. On the other hand, South Asian origin children (and Black children) reported more frequent contact with aunts and uncles, cousins and other relatives compared with children from the white and 'other' minority ethnic groups. It may be that these children were less likely to have living grandparents or to be in regular contact with them because their grandparents lived overseas. (Table 7.1, Appendix). Most of these survey findings were borne out by the case study material, as we shall indicate.

In the case studies, as Table 7.1 below shows, children on average placed twelve relatives (which included grandparents) in their circles, one grandparent, nine friends including one opposite-sex friend, and

Table 7.1   Mean number of important persons children identified in each category by household type

Category	Two parent	One parent	Step parent	Foster	All children
Grandparents					
3 circles*	1.5	1.3	2.2	0.7	1.4
inner circle*	1.2	1.1	1.4	0.6	1.1
Relatives					
3 circles	10.1	10.0	16.6	12.3	12.1
Friends					
3 circles	12.7	6.8	9.5	7.5	9.0
inner circle	8.4	3.1	6.1	6.1	5.8
Opposite-sex friends					
3 circles	0.5	0.9	1.6	1.1	1.0
Formal others					
3 circles	4.2	1.8	2.5	3.2	2.9
inner circle	2.4	1.3	1.6	2.0	1.8

*Differences are significant at 0.05 level

three formal others. The differences between the average for the inner circle as opposed to the average for the three circles is rather greater for friends and formal others than for grandparents and formal others, of whom there were fewer. Differences by household type include the greater number of grandparents and relatives identified by step family children, reflecting their greater potentiality for kinship ties. However, differences were only statistically significant with respect to grandparents.

Most children's maps of their significant others cited a high proportion of other relatives as important to them, with step children identifying rather more other relatives than the other groups, as they did grandparents, followed by foster children. Children in lone mother and two-parent households reported fewer other relatives (Table 7.1). Commonly mentioned were blood-related aunts and uncles, that is, their mothers' and fathers' siblings, who, more often than not, children placed in the inner circle. In some cases, spouses or partners of their uncles and aunts were included in inner circles but, in others, they were allocated to the other circles, signifying less importance. Where their aunts and uncles had children of their own, children typically included these cousins, even when they lived abroad. Zarina included a deceased relative while Mirza included relatives who lived overseas and Willy included cousins he had never met. Harinder, who lived with his birth parents and his paternal grandparents, placed a large number of relatives in the inner circle: five uncles, six aunts and nine cousins. He readily justified their importance to him by describing the different activities he did with them – taking him places, making him laugh, '*you can always talk to them and everything'*. Three children of South Asian origin included relatives who lived in their countries of origin. Several children included as relatives persons who were not related by blood or marriage. Bibi, a South Asian girl, included in the middle circle her mother's friend, whom she called 'Auntie', together with her two teenage children. Niaz, a South Asian boy, included a family friend whom he called 'Uncle' and his 11-year-old son and again, like Bibi, he put them in the middle circle, thereby reserving the inner circle for blood-related kin. In the following section, we focus on grandparents only.

Grandparents

Since the foster children had fewer grandparents, fewer of them placed grandparents on their maps. This was not surprising given the fragmentation of many of their families, their lack of knowledge about their kin (which was revealed when they completed their family trees), and their general lack of contact with them (only two appeared to be in regular contact with grandparents). However, all but two foster children significantly placed their grandparents in the inner circle. In contrast, step family children, because they had more parents, identified the highest number of grandparents in their circles and had more frequent contact (Table 7.2).

The main reasons children said they omitted grandparents from their maps of significant others were that grandparents were dead or that they had no contact with them. Lack of contact was due to grandparents living abroad in some cases but also to family conflict and family fragmentation, as in the case of the foster families and children in lone mother and step father families who had no contact with their non-resident fathers and their 'side of the family'. A few children described their grandparents as 'going a bit funny' or 'getting forgetful' in their old age which they suggested made them feel less close to them. A couple of children explicitly excluded their grandparents' new partners on the grounds that they were incomers to the family, while one girl called a friend of her mother 'Granma' and her mother's friend's lodger 'Grandad'.

Most children placed grandparents in the inner rather than the other circles. But while step family children placed more grandparents on their maps, they were also more likely to exclude grandparents from their maps (Table 7.2). Some step family children excluded their grandparents on their non-resident fathers' side and some excluded their step fathers' parents, even where they had contact with them. Anna had an ambivalent relationship with her step father (albeit she placed him in her inner circle) mainly because, according to her mother's account, she still wanted to live with her birth father.

Table 7.2 Children's positioning of grandparents (GP) by family type

	At least one GP in inner circle maternal/paternal		At least one GP in middle/outer	Contact with at least one GP but not in any circle	GPs dead/no contact at all with any GP
Two-parent	8/15	8/15	2/15	2/15	3/15
One parent	13/17	5/17	3/17	4/17	3/17
Step parent	13/15	4/15	5/15	9/15	1/15
Foster	7/15	1/15	1/15	1/15	7/15

N.B. Most children placed more than one *grandparent* in the circles and had more than one *grandparent*.

Although she had contact with her step father's parents, as she noted – visiting them in the summer and on New Year's Eve – she preferred not to call them 'Nanny' or 'Grandad' *'because they feel like they are not part of the family with us'*. Amy excluded her step father's mother from her map even though she thought her 'really nice' because she did not get on with her step father. However, although Ben excluded his step father's parents from his map *'because I'm not related to them'*, he included his non-resident birth father's new wife's parents and called them Granma and Grandad. As he also explained, he did so because they lived across the road from him and saw them quite often.

While most foster children included their grandmothers in the inner circles of their maps, they had little to say about them. As Wayne said of his maternal grandmother whom he had not seen for two years: *'She was always nice.'* Liam, who saw his grandmother six months ago, said *'I love her to death'* and regretted the infrequency of his visits which was probably because he had so many other people and activities to fit into his life, including the visits of his separated parents and his involvement with his extended foster family. However, he blamed his failure to visit his grandmother on himself, saying he preferred to play football. Other foster children said that the grandparent in question, in all cases a grandmother, was the 'only grandparent' they had or simply that they were 'family'.

While several South Asian origin children and Black children omitted their grandparents from their maps, they did so sometimes because their grandparents lived overseas and they never saw them. Yet some children who only saw their grandparents very occasionally did include them in their maps. For example, although Jahangir had only seen his grandmother, who lived in an African country, twice in recent years, he still placed her in his inner circle while his only comment was that he *'liked her'*. Conversely, while those who had a great deal of contact with grandparents, and often lived near them, tended to place them in the inner circle, not all did. For example, close physical proximity to grandparents did not always guarantee that South Asian origin children placed their resident grandparent in the inner circle. A South Asian origin brother and a sister placed their invalid paternal grandfather who lived with them in their middle circles. The brother was resentful of the heavy demands his grandfather placed upon him: *'We don't really get on a lot. He is always shouting for us, calling us to do this, to do that. And he is always sitting up in his room. We don't see each other a lot unless he is calling me. . . . It's just that when I am doing things he is always calling me.'* By contrast, Harinder was rather positive in his comments about his resident paternal grandparents: *'When she goes away I miss her . . . she's really nice to talk to and everything and be with. . . . Sometimes he [grandfather] talks to me or I just go to see him, see what he's doing.'* He went on to say that he liked living with them: *'Because I don't have to travel a far distance or somewhere. They are right here which is good.'*

Rather more children identified maternal grandparents in the inner circle than included their paternal grandparents. Maternal grandparents, especially grandmothers, were popular with children and were more likely to visit regularly than paternal grandparents according to children's accounts. In the Questionnaire Survey, children were asked with which set of grandparents they got on best with. Over half (53%) said both sets of grandparents, one-third the maternal grandparents, and 13% their paternal grandparents (2% reported not getting on with any). In the case studies, children indicated a marked preference for their maternal grandparents. Lee, a white boy living in a two-parent family, said that his maternal grandparents visited every Sunday, that he regularly stayed overnight at their house when his grandparents let him stay up to watch sport on Sky TV. He described his grandmother as 'really caring' and his grandfather as 'fun' because he shared his sporting interests. However, as some children also suggested in their accounts of their parents' importance (Chapter 5), some children were anxious to demonstrate that they were 'fair' to both sets of grandparents and refused to prioritise one set over the other. Rebecca: *'. . . because I mean, my mum thinks that her family is more important to us than Dad's but I look at them all equal really.'*

In setting out on this study, we were interested to examine whether there were cultural differences in the importance children placed on maternal and paternal lines of kin. In the Questionnaire Survey, we found that, despite our cultural assumptions about the significance of paternal kin in South Asian origin families, South Asian origin children were no more likely to mention a preference for their paternal kin than other ethnic groups; indeed they were statistically significantly more likely to mention (together with the 'other' ethnic group) a preference for both sets of grandparents (66% and 62% respectively, compared to 49% of white children and 47% of Black children). In the case studies, South Asian origin children living with two parents were equally likely to include maternal as paternal grandparents in their maps. In keeping with cultural mores which prioritise paternal over maternal ties, in three cases the paternal grandparents of South Asian origin children lived in the household. However, this did not guarantee a place in children's inner circles as we noted above.

Grandparents provided a sense of symbolic importance to children – giving them a sense of continuity and belongingness – which was particularly evident for the foster children in the study. One boy put it this way: they were *'the next best thing'* if his parents died. Grand-parents were also part and parcel of the everyday worlds of many children and constituted a key source of instrumental and expressive support. They sometimes provided practical care or had looked after children when they were younger. The maternal grandmother of Lenny, a Black boy who lived with his lone mother, still looked after him and his young half sister almost every day as his mother worked night shifts. He noted: *'Because she [maternal grandmother] looks after me a lot. She used to take me to school . . . she can help with my homework, gets food for me and she put up with me after all these years!'* Cliff, a Black boy who lived in a step family, lived with his maternal grandparents during the week because they lived close to his new secondary school. He noted that his grandmother was important to him because she cooked for him and washed and ironed his clothes, while his grand-father helped him with his homework.

In the lone mother group, maternal grandparents had often provided crucial help, both practical and expressive, when their parents' marriages broke down. Lucy, a mixed race girl who lived with her lone mother, and who saw her maternal grandmother frequently, placed her in the inner circle explaining: *'She is like a second mother to me.'* This is because she had lived with her grandmother for two years when her parents' marriage was in trouble. Similarly, Inderpal, a South Asian boy who lived with his lone mother, regularly saw his maternal grand-mother and placed her in his inner circle because: *'If it wasn't for her, we would have been living in a crummy flat when my dad kicked us out.'* Jasmine, a mixed race girl who lived in a step family, placed her mater-nal grandmother in her inner circle and said that she felt close to her grandmother because she used to live with her until her mother met her step father and set up house with him: *'She is really nice and she makes me laugh.'*

As children suggested in talking about their parents (Chapter 5), they were unwilling to be seen to differentiate between their grandparents. Yet they managed to describe them in different ways. Almost always they made positive comments about them except when they omitted them from their maps; negative references included them being 'moany', 'old fashioned' and, as already noted, some were described as 'going a bit funny' in their old age. Children construed grandmothers as key figures of support. They said they were important to them because they were 'very caring', 'really kind', 'nice and cuddly', 'just there for me'. Leila, who lived with her lone mother and only saw her father in the holidays, had a rather small map of significant others. Her relation-ship with her grandmother was, therefore, potentially significant. Leila noted that she got on 'really well' with her maternal grandmother: *'She is nice and cuddly and loving and everything ... I'll always have an open door to her and she'll take me out and everything.'* Rohini recalled with affection her maternal grandmother with whom she used to live in South Asia: *'She tells me advice and she tells me stories. Like she knitted a jumper with wool and she made a little dog with wools and I like her.'* Salome, who lived with her lone mother, brother and twin sister and who, because of family troubles, had no contact with her birth father or his family, included her maternal grandmother in her rather small map. She said she felt closest to her grandmother *'because we've got older and we're not, like, running all over the house. We're really sensible.'*

While grandmothers were portrayed as loving and affectionate, grandfathers were described as 'funny', 'smart', 'generous', 'jokey' and, in one case was contrasted unfavourably with the grandmother, as 'strict' and, in another, as 'angry'. Leila described her grandfather as 'funny' while adding: *'Because he used to be a teacher and he is really smart.'* Salome very much respected her grandfather; she said he was important to her because he gave her money and took them to *'really expensive restaurants ... And if he doesn't want us to do anything, I don't do it because otherwise I know he's going to get really angry.'*

Grandparents' roles in children's lives were described as similar in many key respects in giving children money, presents, taking them out. Several children suggested that grandparents 'spoiled' their grandchildren – indulging them with generous presents, often money, and letting them get away with things. Ceri said: *'When people get old, they really like children and stuff and we are really special to them. And they spoil us and everything.'* Rebecca commented: *'They take us out and ... let us get away with things.'*

The giving was not all one way however. As Elliott described, his paternal grandmother gave him *'an enormous amount of money'* (£20) when she retired which he felt unable to accept: *'I said I can't have this. She needs it more than me ... So I just gave it back and she gave me five pounds of it.'* Some children offered help to their grandparents. Serena said she helped her maternal grandmother with cooking and cleaning; Claudia did shopping for her paternal grandmother; Anton helped with hoovering and shopping; Rohini described getting her grandmother's medicine when she used to live with her overseas: *'... and like if her legs were painful I just pressed them up.'*

Thus, to sum up, grandparents were important to children for many reasons and in several ways. However, regular contact nor indeed living with grandparents necessarily guaranteed their importance to children, and neither did having several sets of grandparents. In some cases step children included their new grandparents in their maps of significant others, while mostly they did not. Grandparents were considered generally more important if they were related by blood. Maternal grandparents appeared to have the edge on paternal grandparents while paternal grandparents did not appear to figure more significantly among South Asian origin children, contrary to assumptions about cultural mores. Grandparents provided children with a sense of symbolic continuity and belongingness even when these features of children's lives seemed most stretched, as in the case of foster children. Grandparents were important to children in both practical and expressive ways. They had often provided practical care when children were younger or when they had experienced family difficulties, notably housing them when their parents' marriages had broken up. As a consequence, they became emotionally important to children. On the whole, children described their grandmothers as kindly supportive figures who were very special to them, while grandfathers were portrayed in more quirky ways as funny, jokey, clever. Grandparents' support was also perceived as undifferentiated (by gender) and both grandfathers and grandmothers were reported as sources of gifts, money and indulgence. In return for their special position as grandchildren, children also reported concern and care for grandparents, notably doing jobs for them and being concerned about them.

The importance of friends

As other studies have shown, friends make a central contribution to children's well-being, giving children confidence, enjoyment and a sense of belonging (Hill and Tisdall 1997; Borland et al. 1997). Friends are important at times of difficulty, and studies have suggested that having friends to turn to who have been through similar experiences is important to children (Mitchell 1985; Laybourn et al. 1996). In this study, friends were covered as part of a study of family life and were only touched upon in the context of children's discussions of the importance of a very wide range of people.

It is perhaps significant that, on average, children identified more friends than other categories of ties. However, as the Questionnaire Survey evidence suggests, children in the study vary in the extent to which they spend time with family and friends, with over half of children saying they spend time partly with friends and partly with family followed by over a quarter (26%) still reporting spending time mainly with family and under a fifth mainly with friends (Table 7.2, in Appendix). Children's reported time patterns vary by ethnic origin with South Asian origin children more likely to report spending time with family.

In the case studies, we found considerable variation in the number of friends children mentioned, with three children including no friends (two were foster children) and eight including large groups of 12 or more (six of whom were boys). In the Questionnaire Survey, four-fifths of children agreed with the statement that they were happy with the number of friends they had. As Table 7.1 shows, there are differences, albeit not statistically significant ones, in the average number of friends reported by children living in different types of household. Two-parent children, with the highest average number of friends, reported on average twice as many friends as the lone mother group (12.7 compared to 6.8), followed by step father children (9.5) (who identified the largest average number of opposite-sex friends in their networks, albeit the range is small).

The average number of friends for the foster care group (7.5) was low and close to that of the lone mother group (6.8) (Table 7.1). As a study which followed up children who had been in care showed, friendships may be more difficult to develop for such children: a psychological explanation for the low average for foster children relates to the severing of their close family ties which, it is argued, requires foster children to put all their energies and personal resources into building ties with their new carers and carers' families (Hodges 1996). This leaves little energy or space for creating other ties, notably with peers. In our study, foster children's friendships may have been adversely affected by being placed in care or by changes in placement. In a couple of cases, it was clear that foster carers were very wary of the children in their care making 'unsuitable' friends who might lead them into further danger.

The lone mother group placed the fewest number of friends in their inner circles and the lowest number in the three circles combined, albeit the differences were not statistically significant. Four lone mother children reported few or no friends in completing their maps while several included friends who were of different ages from themselves or who were outside the categories which most children used to identify friends (see below). The low reporting of friends in this group may be a chance finding since, as far as we know, there is no research which sheds direct light on it. However, it needs stressing that all the children in the study had recently experienced, or were about to experience, disruptions in their lives with implications for their friendships – namely the transition to secondary school.

It is likely that the actual number of friends children had was less relevant to them than the quality of their friendships, as the greater differentiation of friends across the three circles suggests, that is compared with other categories of ties. Having one or more 'good' or 'best friends' may be more important to children than having many friends. We did not ask children these questions directly. However, it was notable that, in completing their maps, children did not always spontaneously identify a 'best friend', although in the Questionnaire Survey 87% reported having one. Some groups were more disposed to mention best friends in drawing up their maps than others. Two-parent children were most likely to mention a best friend compared with the other groups (15/15 compared to 8/17 in the lone mother group, 7/15 in the step father group, and 5/15 in the foster care group). We found no such differences in the Questionnaire Survey. As Lenny, who was living with his lone custodial mother commented: *'I don't have best friends. Friends are friends to me.'* Leila, similarly living with her lone custodial mother, noted: *'I like my friends as much as each other. I couldn't pick one out.'*

In placing friends on their maps, children tended to identify friends who were of the same age and same sex as themselves. Many identified friends made through their old primary and new secondary schools and who were usually in the same class. But this was not always so. One girl who lived with her lone mother and brother mentioned friends of the opposite sex, who were in fact friends of her much older cousin. Several lone mother children mentioned friends who were much younger than them. For example, Zarina, a South Asian girl who lived with her lone mother, included the neighbour's three small children. Two other girls living with lone mothers mentioned friends who were much older than themselves – grown-up women who were friends of their lone mothers.

As research suggests, friendships are strongly gendered. From middle childhood, girls' friendships have been reported as being more intensive while boys are more extensive (Hartup 1992). For boys, the incentive to have friends is the fear of being without friends and of being excluded from the group. Compared with girls, there is a tendency for boys' friendships to be patterned within larger groupings although they may also engage in dyadic relations. Especially for boys, 'being friends' is often publicly enacted through shared participation in games and rowdy behaviour. Within the public context, boys have learned not to be demonstrative in their relations with one another (James 1993: 226–7). In our study, six boys and two girls included large groups of friends in excess of 12 members. For example, Lee, a white boy living with two parents, included 17 boys whom he had known either at primary school or 'all his life', reserving the middle circle for ten friends he had got to know very recently at his new secondary school. Baldev, a South Asian boy living in a two-parent family, included everyone in his inner circle: his large kin network, 31 children in his class at secondary school, and a further 29 children from his primary school. At the same time he identified three boys as 'special friends' who had accompanied him from primary to secondary school. Jahangir, a South Asian origin boy in a two-parent family, placed his immediate family and his extended family in the inner circle, reserving the middle circle for 15–20 friends from his secondary school, and a similar number of people in the outer circle whom he said were members of his mosque. Andrew, a white boy from a lone mother family, included in the outer circle the local football team for which he played, while reserving a place in the inner circle for the football club's manager, and a place in the middle circle for four friends – two older boys who lived downstairs and two boys he had known since primary school.

Exactly where children placed friends on their maps may be indicative for some children of 'closeness'. While almost all children located their birth parents and their siblings in the inner circle, indicating their great importance to them, they tended to distribute their friends across the three circles. This differentiation of friends was most evident in the two-birth-parent group, only two of whom placed all their friends in the inner circle, in contrast to 8/15 foster care children, 7/15 step family children and 5/17 lone mother children. The fact that so many of the two-parent group differentiated between friends' importance may relate to the preponderance of South Asian origin children in this group. As the Questionnaire Survey data clearly also showed (noted above, see Table 7.2 in Appendix), South Asian origin children were statistically significantly more likely to mention spending time with family members and were least likely to spend time 'mainly with friends' (and also most likely to report spending time alone). As Sunita commented in her interview: *'Friends are important but not as important as family,'* and Niaz commented: *'[Friends] can never be as important as my family. Never. Out of 100 I give my family 100%. That's how much I like them to be close to me. My friends about 60%.'* Baldev made a similar point: *'Well (first) it's my family, then it's my relatives, then it's my friends.'*

The justifications children gave for the importance of friends are indicative of different meanings to friendship and their relative importance. Friends could provide children with a sense of continuity in their lives. Several children mentioned friends they had known from earlier periods of their lives. Two children living with lone mothers mentioned friendships which went back to their early years at nursery. Another girl mentioned a friend she had known from her nursery days and, even though she had died a few years ago, she still counted her as her 'best friend'.

Having friends

Some of the foster children mentioned the importance of 'having friends' perhaps because they were least likely to be able to make and maintain contact with friends due to the disruptions in their lives.

Several foster children mentioned 'friends' they had literally only just met or friends with whom they had no contact or no chance of further contact. There was also an additional factor for some children who said they had to negotiate with their foster carers when they wanted to have friends home. Liam, a white foster boy, said that his friends were only allowed into his foster home 'half way'. He remarked: *'because if you ain't got friends, what have you got in school?'* Claire, a white foster girl, said that friends were necessary *'otherwise you're really lonely'*. A girl who lived in a step family noted the importance of solidarity in a conflictual and competitive world: *'because if you never had no friends, you'd be alone in the world. Everyone would be arguing and fighting.'* Lujayn, a South Asian girl who lived with two parents, emphasised the importance of friends as an insurance against feeling 'left out'.

The start of a new school is clearly an important time in which children have to re-position themselves in peer groups. As children suggested in their remarks in response to a vignette portraying an isolated child in the school playground (Chapter 2), the hierarchical structure and conformist culture of school life may act as constraints against children acting in inclusive ways towards other children. As Lujayn noted *'If you're at school and you're hanging around by yourself, everybody would tease you.'* However, while having friends was considered important, Lujayn also said that her family was more important to her. Ceri, a white girl, commented: *'If you don't [have friends], then nobody really likes you. It'd be really horrible because you'd just have to sit and eat lunch all day by yourself.'*

The sociability benefits of 'having friends' were a particular theme also. Several children mentioned the importance of friends as people to 'have fun with', 'hang around with' and 'spend time with'. As one child said, *'Otherwise you'd be bored'*, while another recognised potential dangers: *'friends can get you into trouble.'* Kevin suggested that friends were important because they are interwoven into everyday life: *'You see them every day at school. Like you would with your family. You talk to them as much really. You play with them. You have fun with them.'* For Lee, his friends were his family: *'Some of my friends are like a family to me. Because we're always together and they're fun to be around and we can always relate to things.'*

Being friends

The process of 'being friends', as contrasted with 'having friends', was also a significant theme in children's accounts. Many children talked about friendship in terms of relationships and the sources of support these relationships provided. For some purposes, friends were seen as providing similar support to family: *'[friends are] people who are always there for you.'* A South Asian boy living with his widowed mother noted that it was important to have friends *'because they stick up for you and it's like family and all'.* However, several South Asian origin children suggested that they looked to their families for support rather than to their friends. Harinder, a South Asian origin boy living in a two-parent household, had several friends whom he had known for at least five years. Nonetheless, he said that family was more important to him: *'Family's always there, friends aren't. They can change overnight, but your family doesn't really.'*

For others, friends provided an alternative source of support to family in some particular respects, namely as a safe and trustworthy repository for confidences which children found difficult to talk about to their parents: *'to tell them things you can't tell your family,'* (Sally, living with a widowed mother). *'Tell them your problems and secrets, about boys,'* (Debbie in foster care). *'People to tell secrets to,'* (Jordan in a step family). Adam felt safer talking to his friends than to his foster carers: *'It's like if you don't feel safe talking to [foster carers] then you've got friends to talk to and that.'* Kevin noted: *'It's someone to talk to other than your mum. Because there's some stuff you can talk to your friends about, but not your mum.'* Niaz felt a similar need to discuss topics which he felt unable to discuss with his family: *'They're people you can talk to about personal things, things you can't talk to your family about.'* Best friends were mentioned as the persons children, especially girls, were mostly likely to provide them with support when they started secondary school.

Four step family children alluded to the importance of talking to friends who 'understand', although they did not say what about. Daniel, a Black boy living in a step family, talked about his three close friends – all boys – as *'someone else to talk to, like they understand and all that. Like they won't laugh at you because I know I can trust them.'* Emily, a white girl in a step family, identified 20 friends – all girls which she distributed across the three circles, and noted: *'Because they're there for you to talk to them about stuff you can't tell your mum.'* Amy, a white girl in a step family, talked about the help she found in turning to 'a special [girl] friend' who had experienced a similarly difficult transition, namely becoming a step family: *'She's gone through it. Like her mum's got remarried and had another baby. And it's like she's gone through the same things and we've helped each other through like. The past two years have been really difficult for both of us.'*

Limits to friendship

Children's accounts of friendship referred to a number of clear limitations. As already mentioned, some children were resistant to the notion of a best friend while most children clearly had a preference for friends of their own sex and own age. Some articulated this same gender preference as a clear principle which shaped their choice of friends. For example, two girls said that they were only comfortable talking about 'personal matters' to other girls, while boys too made references to 'boys' talk'.

In this study, it seemed to be circumstances rather than preferences that constrained children's friendships. For some, the main constraint was a parent or carer who encouraged particular friends but not others, or who discouraged children from bringing friends home or from visiting or sleeping over at their friends' homes. Debbie complained that her foster carers would not let her stay at the houses of two boys she was friends with. Several South Asian origin children mentioned their parents being more restrictive with daughters than sons. One South Asian girl said that religious differences meant it was difficult to be friends with a particular girl.

A very significant constraint upon children's friendships concerned whether they and their friends would continue to go to the same schools after the transition to secondary school. This transition was particularly difficult at the time in the two local authorities in London where the study took place. There was fierce competition for places at local secondary schools and few children could be certain of gaining a place at their local schools unless they already had siblings there. For these reasons, children's friendships were often severed when they went to different secondary schools which, for many children, was a source of some considerable regret to them, especially to those whose friendships had lasted right through primary school. Sunita, a South Asian girl living in a two-parent household, placed in her inner circle three 11-year-old girls who had accompanied her from her primary to her secondary school. But she placed others in the middle and outer circles friends who had gone to different secondary schools, only one of whom she had managed to keep in touch with.

Foster children and a few other children had clearly moved house quite a lot and, as a result, had lost contact with friends. Claire, a white foster girl, included a lot of relatives in her map (but not her birth parents), very few of whom she now saw. She also included her foster carers and their children, placing them alongside her relatives in the inner circle. The handful of friends she also included, as well as her best friend, were from her last school. She rarely saw them now because they no longer attended the same school and because, as she said, *'they live far away'*. Adam, a white foster boy, included fewer friends on his map. In fact these friends – he put three in the inner circle – were children who had been fostered with him in an earlier placement but with whom he had no current contact. He said: *'I want to try and see them. I'm going to ask my social worker if I can go to see them.'* One foster girl included as 'her friends' her foster carers' relatives and their friends.

Children's friendships were often uncertain or insecure not only because of geography but also because friendship was to some extent seen as a matter of 'choice'. Several children contrasted family relationships, which they saw as ongoing and secure, with the instability of friendship. Harinder, a South Asian origin boy who had a large extended family both within and beyond his household, placed only two friends on his map while including five household members and 21 relatives. As he noted: *'Family are more important because family is always there and friends aren't. They can change overnight but your family doesn't really.'* Chloe, who lived in a step family, reflected wistfully on the many different friends she had got to know in the various social arenas of her life – namely the three neighbourhoods she visited to see her grandmother, her birth father, and her step family: *'All the time I'm getting used to somebody. Yes, and then they stop being your friend.'*

The fact that some children had few friends may reflect their unpopularity with other children. Salome, a white girl living with her lone mother, had moved schools several times because of being bullied. She identified only two sets of friends, who also happened to be blood-related, who lived a long way away and whom she saw only a few times a year. Inderpal, a South Asian origin boy, included only one friend in his map. This friend had been very important to him, he said, in helping to protect him from bullies: *'If it wasn't for him I wouldn't have been able to survive.'* However, he put this boy whom he had known since nursery in his middle circle, reserving the inner circle for his mother, brother, pets, grandmother and aunts and uncles.

To sum up, friends were important to children. With some exceptions, children chose friends who were the same sex and age as themselves. While some children attributed importance to large groups of friends, others highlighted particular friends or best friends. A number of children, particularly those of South Asian origin, suggested that family was more important than friendships, a finding also born out by the Survey evidence. Friends had different meanings for children. As James (1993) has so delicately described for younger children, there is a process by which children may be said to develop different 'capacities' for friendship. Among younger children, friendship acts as a classificatory mechanism by which a child marks out his or her place within a social space; children 'have' friends as a means of creating social inclusion and awareness of 'otherness'. By contrast, older children are more directed towards 'being friends'. In this latter case, friendship is not only a means of social classification but is also a relational process whereby the emphasis is on connections with individuals rather than with groups. For some children in our study, 'having friends' was the most important thing and they included large numbers of friends in their maps, especially the boys. For other children, 'being friends' was more important; children sought individualised relationships with other children to turn to and confide in. Many children noted friends who went back a long time and thus provided them with a sense of continuity in their lives. But children's friendships were negotiated in the structural context of home, school and the wider community. External events in children's lives, notably the transition to secondary school, altered and, in some cases, disrupted children's friendships. Foster children who, together with single parent children, included fewer children in their maps had few long-term friends because of the changes in their lives; they sometimes included friends they had only just made or friends they had lost contact with. But these changes shaped the friendships of other children also, albeit to a less-marked degree. Moreover, unlike family relations, as some children noted, friendships are largely a matter of choice and they depended upon the will and whim of the other as well as the self. A few children had virtually no friends which may have reflected their vulnerability in school and other peer group settings.

The importance of formal others

Not surprisingly, children mentioned fewer formal others than friends and relatives, with just over half the sample putting at least one such person on their maps (Table 7.1). The average number of mentions for the four groups ranged from one to four persons in all three circles and between one and two persons in the inner circle (Table 7.1). Two-parent children mentioned the largest number on average and, again, lone parent children mentioned the fewest persons.

These formal ties, to which just over half of the sample attached importance, consisted in three different types of professionals: teachers, doctors and social workers. Teachers were easily the most commonly mentioned (26 children), followed by doctors (11 children). Four foster children mentioned their social workers, with one foster child including a Guardian *ad litem*, another a school dinner lady from her former primary school, and another the organisation *Who Cares Trust*, which supports children in care. A further foster child mentioned the postman *'because he brings our post'*, notably letters from his brothers and sisters whom he rarely saw. A girl living in a lone mother household mentioned a family counsellor, while one boy from a two-parent family mentioned the football manager of the local team he played for, and a South Asian origin boy living with two parents mentioned the members of the mosque to which he and his family belonged. As with other types of social ties, children were more disposed to place these formal others in the inner rather than the middle or outer circles, although the tendency was less marked than for other categories of persons. While children's responses to questions about the importance of these professionals in their lives were brief – the questions came near the end of the interview with the series of questions about children's significant others – children's accounts provide some insightful clues.

Teachers

Many of the teachers children mentioned were closely connected with their personal welfare: they were their former class teachers in primary school or their current tutors in secondary school. In addition, some children mentioned specialist teachers, for example, tutors who taught them at Saturday schools and, in one case, a music teacher and in another a horse riding teacher who provided individual tuition. A foster boy included a support teacher from his last school: *'[She] helps me in class and that. . . . She was just like a friend.'*

In some cases, children said teachers were important because they had been supportive in relation to a particular problem or event. For example, a white girl living in a lone mother household placed a teacher and counsellor in the inner circle; both had been important in helping her to come to terms with the abuse she had suffered.

Several children distinguished between teachers who were 'kind', whom they liked, and teachers who were 'horrible' whom they disliked. Yet 'horrible', teachers also figured in children's networks which indicated a certain ambivalence on children's part towards teachers whom they usually described as strict. While disliking strictness, they also respected it and saw it as necessary to learning. Claudia, a mixed race girl living with her lone mother, placed four teachers in the outer circle including the former head teacher of her primary school. One teacher Claudia described as her 'favourite', while another she described as 'kind' because she joked with the children. She also placed yet another teacher in the outer circle and described her as 'horrible in some ways but funny and nice in others', while the fourth teacher whom she put furthest away in the outer circle she considered almost irredeemably 'horrible'. However, in justifying her positioning in the map, Claudia depicted her as having some redeeming features: '*She was kind to me once, no twice – once when we were reading a book and I got interested in it and asked her something . . . she was very kind to me and read the book to me.*'

Children mentioned teachers whom they respected for helping them to learn. Indeed two of the main challenges children had encountered were their SATs (Standard Attainment Targets) and gaining a place at secondary school, which for those living in the two local authorities covered by the study was far from an automatic transition. Amy, a white girl in a step family, said: '*The best teacher I had was . . . got me through my SATs and through getting into secondary school . . . I could talk to her like I could talk to my gran. . . . She taught me the most.*'

The following cases of two South Asian origin boys are instructive in understanding the importance of formal others in some children's lives. Both boys and their families were members of a religion (Islam) which endorsed learning and education as a key goal in life. Yet despite their families' supportive backgrounds which stressed the importance of education, or rather because of their backgrounds, both boys mentioned the importance of teachers whom they regarded as instrumental in motivating them to learn.

Niaz was a Moslem boy of South Asian origin who lived with two parents. Education was strongly endorsed at home with learning closely linked to the study of Islam. He said his parents were anxious that he both prayed and studied hard: '*My dad always wants me to pray. And I can pray and I do pray, but not enough. . . . My mum says to pray, but not as much as my dad. She says more to work harder. She says in your spare time you should read books more. And I am reading books more. She says to write things down on the computer or in your handwriting. Improve your handwriting and I do things like that.*'

Yet the key person in Niaz's life who, by his own account, had motivated him the most to pursue his studies was a supply teacher from his primary school whom he placed in the inner circle: '*In primary school, we didn't get no homework until we had a supply, because our teacher had cancer and so she had to go away into hospital. But we got a supply, he was very, very helpful. He was my favourite teacher in the school. . . . If he hadn't been at school, I don't think I would have been that clever. I don't think I would even have been in [current secondary school]. He's told me everything that I really want to know. Like he, just something. I could put him as my best friend. Someone I know a lot, so –*' Niaz emphasised the importance of this teacher in being able to motivate him: '*He talks about things in such a different way. Like most teachers, say, "He was born on such and such a day, he done this, he done this." He says, "He was pretty cool, can you imagine doing that?" He makes up really weird stuff and you like to think, "What would that be like?"*'

And you get your work done.' Niaz went on to describe the importance of his teacher in terms of making pupils work hard and in terms of fairness – treating all pupils the same – while Niaz also suggested that the teacher was special to him: *'And it's not like ... he doesn't pick on anyone and he doesn't have favourites. Some teachers have favourites, they like love someone and they don't like that person. He's not like that. He treats everybody fairly and things like that. And if you're not working hard enough, he'll tell you. He won't just bring it and say, "That's nice", but he doesn't mean it. He'll tell you if you're not working hard. He won't say, "You're not working hard", he'll say, "You're working hard," but he'll ease into it, he'll tell you clearly. He won't make you feel bad. But he'll tell you how to improve, things like that. He was really good to me.'*

Mirza's mother was widowed. He belonged to a family and culture where considerable importance was also placed on the study of Islam. He lived in a large extended family with two of his older siblings and their partners in overcrowded housing. At the start of the interview, he emphasised that education and sport were very important to him: *'I like to do everything, but if I haven't got the time, then ... , as I said, the most important thing is, really ... the right thing is I should get my education. ... Because if I have my education thing when I grow up, I can have more time to do ... the stuff I want.'* At the beginning of his interview he reported that he had once thought he would go to a religious boarding school to study Islam. However a series of events changed the course of his life. At the time when his peers were seeking places at secondary school, he and his family returned to Bangladesh where his sister's marriage was to take place. His father stayed in Britain to continue working and died suddenly. When Mirza returned, most of the secondary school places were allocated and he had to go to a school low down the pecking order where he was bullied. He reported losing concentration in his studies.

Significantly, Mirza put six subject teachers from his secondary school in the inner circle and one in the outer circle and explained: *'It's basically – why I'm good in lessons is because of the teacher ... It depends on what teacher. And, even though I'm good, but in – if I'm good in that lesson, I might not like that teacher. But mostly the lessons I'm good in, the teachers are – that's the teachers I like.'*

Family doctors

Despite the considerable pressures on the National Health Service at the time of the study, and the prevalence of group practices in primary health care (family doctors), several children (9/63) mentioned their family doctors when filling in their maps with all nine placing them in the inner circle. Children's rather brief accounts of why they included their general practitioners suggest several reasons. First, some children had clearly been attending the same GP for many years and felt at ease with them. Second, some children saw their GP very frequently for a significant, persistent health problem which in itself may have led to the development of a special relationship. As Clark, who lived with his mother and brother, noted: *'Because he's been my doctor since the hospital found out I had [particular disease] . . . Because he's friendly and I've know him a long time and I'm used to him.'* A third reason may relate to the efforts made by the GP to strike up a rapport with children. As Zarina noted: *'I can talk to my doctor. Yes, he's really nice to me. He gives children lollies.'* A fourth reason may relate to how recently the children had seen a doctor, with those who had recently visited the doctor more likely to identify him or her. A South Asian origin girl, Hayfa, placed her GP and the emergency services along with three teachers in the inner circle. A month ago she had fractured her ankle and her GP had told her to go to the emergency services. In the event, Hayfa was disappointed because the hospital did not provide her with crutches, until her GP interceded on her behalf.

Conclusions

This chapter has suggested that children considered a very wide range of people to be important to them. Children's significant others extended well beyond their immediate families of origin. However, variation was found in children's inclusiveness of significant others. In accordance with the smaller family networks of lone parent children, these children also identified fewer persons as being important to them; they included fewer persons overall, fewer friends and fewer formal others compared with children living in the other types of families. Foster children mentioned few grandparents and relatively few friends, with a couple of children mentioning their social workers. Two-parent children mentioned more friends than other groups, while step family children identified the highest average number of persons overall, grandparents in particular.

Children's significant others were important to them in different ways. Grandparents emerged as significant figures to children, especially maternal grandparents, while contrary to cultural assumptions, South Asian origin children were as likely to mention maternal as paternal grandparents. Regular contact with, or indeed living with a grandparent, failed to guarantee grandparents' importance to children, nor was having several sets of grandparents significant, as in the case of step family children. Grandparents were generally seen as important if they were related to children by blood. Grandparents provided children with a sense of continuity and belongingness even when these features of children's lives were absent, as in the case of foster children. Grandparents were important to children in symbolic, practical and expressive ways: in being 'there for them', in providing practical care, notably when children were young or their parents' marriages were breaking up, and they were important to children emotionally. Grandmothers were depicted as kindly, supportive figures while grandfathers were portrayed in more quirky ways – as funny, jokey, clever. But children were anxious not to be seen to discriminate between them. Grandmothers' and grandfathers' support was also perceived as undifferentiated; both grandparents were seen as providers of gifts and as 'spoiling' their grandchildren. In return for their special position as grandchildren, children were concerned about and helpful to grandparents, notably doing jobs for them.

Perhaps more surprising was the high regard in which children held their relatives – especially their blood-related aunts and uncles. In most cases these persons were individually identified and often placed in the inner circle together with cousins, while other circles were reserved for non-related partners of their aunts and uncles. Indeed, in the Questionnaire Survey, contact with these relatives was more frequent than with grandparents and non-resident fathers, although they were in most cases more numerous.

Somewhat intriguingly, while friends were frequently mentioned by children, rather fewer were mentioned on average compared with relatives, with the exception of the two-parent group. Moreover, the significance of friends was much more variable. Rather surprisingly, few children talked much about the importance of 'best friends' (with the exception of a few girls). With some exceptions, children mentioned friends who were the same sex and age as themselves. Friends had different meanings for children (James 1993). For some children, 'having friends' was the most important thing and they included large numbers of friends in their maps – as a source of group inclusion, self identity and sociability, especially for boys. For other children, 'being friends' was more important, providing them with a means of relating to others on an individual basis – an opportunity to confide and as a source of emotional and moral support. However, friends were seen by some children to be less important than family, particularly by South Asian origin children. Many children noted friends who went back a long time in their acquaintance and thus provided them with a sense of meaning and continuity in their lives. But children's friendships were negotiated in the structural context of home, school and the wider community. External events in children's lives, notably the transition to secondary school, altered and, in some cases, disrupted children's friendships. Foster children who, together with lone mother children, included fewer children in their maps, had few long-term friends because of the changes in their lives; they sometimes included friends they had only just made or friends they had lost contact with. But these changes shaped the friendships of other children also, albeit to a less marked degree. Moreover, unlike family relations, as some children noted, friendships are largely a matter of choice and they depended upon the will and whim of the other as well as the self. A few children had virtually no friends which may have reflected their vulnerability in school and peer group settings.

Finally, children included among their significant others some 'child professionals' who played an important role in some children's lives: teachers who were helpful to children who sought to learn, family doctors who were supportive to children when they were ill, and social workers upon whom some children, notably foster children, were dependent for their care and well-being.

8 Children's contribution to family life

I love her. I'll be there for when she's old and that's it.

The increasing recognition of children as reflexive, competent social actors is leading to renewed scrutiny of the contribution children make to the different social arenas which they occupy. In this chapter, we will examine the diverse ways in which children make a contribution to family life. In the relatively small literature which exists on this topic (Brannen 1995; O'Brien 1995; Morrow 1996), there is a concentration on children's material help in families which reflects the earlier emphasis on mothers' caring as work. In this chapter, we will extend our interest in children's contribution to cover care in a broader sense, with a special focus on what Mason (1996) has termed 'sentient activity': the ways in which children are sensitive and respond to others' emotional needs. Moreover, the chapter attempts to examine children's beliefs and justifications for providing material help (or not). It also addresses the issue which is intrinsic to the negotiation of caring practices and identities, notably with respect to motherhood, namely how far caring orientations are associated with a sense of responsibility or commitment towards others, and whether altruism is part of children's practice of family life. As research has suggested (Goodnow and Delaney 1989; Goodnow 1991), learning to take responsibility for others is key to understanding gender differences in terms of children's later contributions as adults to the domestic division of labour. Are children encouraged to be interdependent and to help others out of a sense of altruism or ethic of care, and how far are they encouraged to be independent and look after themselves? This is not an easy issue to address and involves a broader consideration of the ways in which childhood as a gendered phenomenon is socially constructed, by children and adults alike.

Since, normatively speaking, parents' job is to care for children rather than the other way round, it is crucial that we examine children's expectations and rationalities for helping (or not) in relation to their parents' (that is, mothers') expectations. In order to understand the parameters under which children engage in caring, we have focused upon a critical instance of care, whereby the expectation that children contribute to family life might be said to overstep the mark. By asking the question whether parents should discuss their problems with children – a question put to children and mothers alike – we hoped to be able to generate reflexive accounts about what it means to care and to be a child. Thereby we hoped to illuminate not only issues of reciprocity within households and families but also how the construction of children as carers illuminates the meaning of childhood itself.

In these endeavours, we draw upon a variety of sources of data from the Questionnaire Survey and from the interview case studies. Some of the questions posed via the two research methods were broadly similar and were asked in similar ways, while other questions were posed differently. Some questions were only asked via one method only.

Children's orientations towards helping at home

As a measure of children's orientations towards helping at home, we draw on three types of data: children's general normative views about giving help; their rationales for helping; and the significance of financial inducement.

Children's views: whether they ought to help parents

As we described in Chapter 2, in response to a vignette which portrayed children being asked to help in a family-run business, children seemed to be suggesting that the 'proper' work for children of their age (the start of secondary school) was school work rather than household work. While most children agreed that a child in that situation should help her parents after school, many qualified their responses and suggested that children should only help 'a bit'. In the Questionnaire Survey, two-thirds of children said children should help 'a little' or give 'some help' with household work, while a third said they should do 'a lot' and only 3% saying 'none at all'. Mothers' views were largely similar to those of children. Moreover, in response to the vignette, children were also sceptical about parents' long working hours and considered the 'proper' job of parents was to spend time with their children and help them with their homework.

Children's reasons for helping

Children were asked, both in the Questionnaire Survey and in the interviews, their reasons for helping (or not) with household work. In the Survey, they responded to closed questions (which were pre-coded) and in the interviews to open-ended questions. The Survey included intrinsic reasons for helping (children said they liked to help their parents) and extrinsic reasons (they were told to help, or they were paid to help) (Table 8.1). In both the Survey and in the interviews, children suggested the importance of intrinsic reasons notably to do with the ethic of care – they helped parents because they needed help and as part of the mutuality of family life. In the interviews, some children mentioned the importance of helping as a way of learning how to look after themselves. Instrumental reasons for helping – being told to help and being paid to help – were ticked less often in the Survey and were not mentioned in the interviews.

With respect to the Questionnaire Survey data, children's gender, whether they were at primary or secondary school, their ethnicity and their parents' employment all statistically significantly influenced the reasons children gave for helping. Girls and primary school pupils were statistically more likely than boys and secondary school pupils to say they liked helping, while girls were more likely to say they helped because everyone in the family helped. South Asian origin children were more likely to say they were disposed to be helpful to their parents' compared with other ethnic groups, while white children were more likely to say that they helped because of payment. Similarly, children whose mothers worked full time were more likely to report helping because they were told to do so, compared with children whose mothers were not in paid work. No statistically significant differences were found with respect to household type, birth order and number of siblings.

The notion that it was right to respond to parents' need for help at home is reflected in the comments of a number of children, including some children whose lone mothers were particularly in need of

Table 8.1   Children's reasons for helping with household work: Questionnaire Survey

	% (n)
To be helpful to parents	47 (443)
Enjoys helping	55 (447)
Everyone in the family helps each other	46 (390)
Told to help	32 (302)
Gets paid	18 (178)
Other/preparation for independence	7 (44)

children's help since they had no partner in the household with whom to share the work. Clark, a Black boy living with a lone mother, may have been reflecting on his own family circumstances when he commented: '*Um, because if you're living with a single parent, then you can't expect her to do everything. So I reckon children should help out occasionally.*' Leila, a mixed race girl from a lone mother family, stressed the importance given to everyone in the household pulling their weight, especially when the mother was the sole provider, albeit she thought children's contribution should be limited: '*Because they [children] are living here too. So they've got to contribute because they eat off the plates and everything. And the mother will put clothes on your back and everything. So I think they should contribute, to an extent. I don't think they should do too much.*' A South Asian origin boy, Inderpal, who lived with a lone mother: *Yes, I think that's quite right to help around the house because you can't . . . what's it called? Let your um, parents do all the work because, um, they're getting old and they spend like – what's – all their life looking after you.*'

In response to being asked why they helped at home, half the children in the Questionnaire Survey indicated that they liked helping. However, asked the direct question, also in the Survey – Do you like doing household jobs? – more than half ticked the 'sometimes like/sometimes dislike' box and 16% disliked doing them. Only just over a quarter said they unequivocally liked doing household tasks (27%). For example, Claudia, a mixed race girl living with a lone mother, suggested in her interview limited enthusiasm for household work: '*If their parents need help, they should help. But if their parents say "Just leave it. I'll do it. I'll do it", then they should just leave it.*' Rebecca, a white girl from a lone mother household, found housework a strain and only did it because of payment: '*It's [a] big [house] although she [mother] lives on her own. It's a strain on us because we've given up all our spare time . . . if we don't do it, we don't get a pound kind of thing. I think it's too much, too much pressure on me and [my sister].*'

As parents typically suggest, housework is seen as a means of preparing children for taking responsibility for themselves (Goodnow and Delaney 1989; Goodnow 1991), a theme also noted by children (Table 8.1). For example, Marsha, a Black girl from a step family noted that it was important for *girls* to learn how to cook, clean and do the ironing '*because sooner or later they're going to have to do it for themselves*'. Cliff, a Black boy in a step family, was thinking about the future when he would be supporting himself or living with a partner: '*You're going to have to do housework anyway. So, it's a good way to start.*'

Children's views about payment for housework

As noted above, only 18% of children in the Questionnaire Survey ticked payment for housework as a reason for contributing. While the interview question was posed differently (children were asked whether they thought children ought to be paid for housework), two-thirds (only 33 of the 63 children were asked the question) thought children should not receive payment and only six children were unequivocally in favour. (Mothers' views were broadly similar.) Of the six South Asian origin children asked the question, only one boy disagreed with payment and thought that hard work should be rewarded financially (see also Brannen 1995; Song 1996). Most of the reasons for opposing payment related to the mutuality of family life and children's acknowledgement of what their parents did for them: *'because it's your own family, you're doing it for your own good'*, *'because it's your own house'*, *'because their mum and dad work for [children]'*, *'because they pay for our food and our clothes. . . . The mortgage and bills'*. Children's reasons in favour of payment were usually to do with gaining privileges in the sibling hierarchy (older siblings sought payment for greater responsibility while younger siblings sought equality with older siblings). Three children made the link between housework and paid work: *'Like when you're older you have to work for your money.'*

Thus, while most children suggested they ought to help at home, on the whole they considered that their contribution should be modest. The most popular reasons for contributing to household work were to do with 'the ethic of care' – helping parents because they needed help or because of mutuality and reciprocity of family life. The intrinsic aspect of a caring orientation was expressed in terms of 'liking to help' although a direct question suggested that children were more ambivalent than they first appeared. Instrumental orientations to providing help received little support from children in that payment for housework appeared to transgress the ethic of care and the mutuality of family life.

Children's assessments of their contributions to care

In the Questionnaire Survey, children were asked to assess the size of their contribution to household work and to report on the frequency with which they carried out specific household tasks. The Survey also covered a series of more general aspects of giving care not only to family members but also to classmates and elderly people.

Housework

Children's views of how much they helped broadly matched their assessment of how much help they thought they ought to give. As noted, two-thirds said they should provide a modest amount of help, so two-thirds in the Survey considered that they did 'some or a little' housework (32% considered they did 'a lot' and 3% none at all). Those most likely to say they did a lot were those from larger families (three or more siblings). Mothers' views about whether they expected their children to help in practice broadly reflect children's own views, with three-quarters of mothers interviewed agreeing that children should make a modest contribution. Mothers' low expectations reflected a number of factors: that their children in practice did very little even in the few tasks they were meant to do, notably tidying their own bedrooms; or that they considered that, as children, they should not be expected to work except as a minimum self-maintenance or as preparation for adulthood.

It is difficult to assess whether children's assessments are borne out in their reports of how frequently they carried out specific household tasks (Tables 8.2). However, it does seem to be the case that children carried out self-care tasks more frequently than family-care tasks. Between roughly a third and a quarter reported performing self-care tasks such as clearing away their own dirty dishes on a daily basis, while the figure falls to under a fifth for family-care tasks such as making something to eat for someone else and vacuuming/dusting. Around four-fifths reported doing self-care tasks, either every day or some days in the past week, while two-thirds to three-quarters carried out family-care tasks.

Children's contribution to household tasks was influenced by a

Table 8.2 Children's contribution to household tasks 'in the past week'

'Self-care' tasks	Every day %	Some days %	Not at all %	N
Make something to eat for yourself	37	55	8	802
Clear away own dirty dishes	31	46	23	799
Tidy/clean own room	28	56	16	811
Wash own sports kit	8	24	68	799
'Family-care' tasks				
Lay/clear table	26	49	25	797
Wash up/fill or empty dishwasher	21	43	36	791
Make something to eat for someone else	18	60	22	803
Vacuum or dust	16	57	27	800

number of factors, although no one factor was influential across the board. Compared with white children, black children and South Asian origin children were statistically more likely to do certain family care tasks (hoovering/dusting for both groups and laying/clearing the table for South Asian origin children). Girls were statistically more likely to do certain tasks than boys (that is, clearing away their own dishes and making something to eat for others) but, unlike other studies of older young people, they were not more disposed to do more family-care tasks overall than boys (Brannen 1995). However, we also asked children whether they carried out the tasks *without being asked*. We found that girls were statistically significantly more likely than boys to do five of the eight household tasks without being asked (three family-care tasks and two self-care tasks). It was noticeable that foster children were not expected, according to their carers' accounts, to have too much responsibility because of their difficult past childhoods. However, two foster children (Wayne and Gail) were vociferous in complaining about being expected to do too much housework although their accounts did not suggest that they did a great deal more than other children. As other studies have found (Wittner 1980), foster children were wary of being exploited – of their carers using them as a source of unpaid labour.

Although most children seemed opposed in principle to payment for housework, we found only partial corroboration for children's views in practice; half of children (56%) in the Questionnaire Survey reported being paid 'sometimes' for housework while 12% reported 'always' receiving payment, and a third were never paid (32%). In the interviews, a quarter of the mothers reported paying their children 'sometimes' for housework; similarly, a quarter of the children said so, with four saying that their payment came as part of their pocket money. Two South Asian origin boys noted that their parents gave them some for doing 'little things' when they were younger. Salome, a white girl living with a lone mother, was paid in theory, if not in practice. However, mindful of poverty and of her mother's current statuses as a lone mother and a student in particular, Salome was reluctant to take the full amount she was owed.

S: *But if it's a really poor family, and your mum and dad tell you to help clean the house, and the child's expecting money, I don't think they should get it, because if it's really poor and the mortgages are high, they don't really have the money, so -.*

I: *So you get paid . . . ?*

S: *I only get paid for doing the washing-up.*

I: *How much do you get?*

S: *40p.*

I: *Are you happy with that amount?*

S: *Yes I am. . . . That's a lot of money for Mum, because she hasn't got that much money. She doesn't earn that very much, and then there's [her mother's] college fees and everything. So I don't really mind that it's 40p.*

Caring activity

Whether children participated in more general caring activity is a little-researched and perhaps more interesting issue. In recent years there has been interest in children who act as carers for their sick parents, for example, African refugee children who look after parents affected by AIDS (Chinouya-Mudari and O'Brien 1999). We asked children a set of less specific questions about helping and being nice to family and to other people. On some caring activities, children reported higher frequencies than for household tasks, with half reporting giving help every day to their mothers and over a third to their fathers. Similarly, for the same frequency, over a third said they were nice to or helped their classmates, and over a third looked after their pets. Over half said they took care of younger brothers and sisters some days a week and nearly two-thirds reported helping an elderly person (Table 8.3). Caring activities which were less commonly reported were looking after pets and looking after siblings mainly because some children either had no younger siblings or had no pets. In fact, 39% of eldest children and 35% of middle children in families reported looking after younger children every day and four-fifths at least once a week.

Reported performance of housework and caring work were highly associated ($r = 0.45$; $p > 0.001$). Not surprisingly, children living in lone mother households were less likely to report helping their fathers, while South Asian origin children, most of whom lived in two-parent households, were statistically significantly more likely than other ethnic groups to report helping their fathers. When birth order was taken into account, South Asian origin children who were the oldest or middle children in the family were significantly more likely to look after siblings every day than other groups, while South Asian origin and Black children were more likely to report being nice to brothers and sisters every day compared with white children and 'other' children (Chapter 6) (See also Morrow 1998).

In terms of reported frequency therefore, children made a considerable contribution in terms of frequency of doing household work and being caring. However, also by their own accounts, they regarded their contribution as modest.

Table 8.3 Children's contribution to general caring by frequency

	Every day %	Some days %	Not at all %	N
Help mother/step mother/female foster carer	50	47	3	820
Be nice to/help classmates	37	57	6	818
Look after pets	37	21	42	800
Help father/step father/male foster carer	36	48	16	800
Be nice to brothers/sisters	26	62	12	815
Take care of younger brothers/sisters	25	30	45	775
Help an elderly person	16	56	28	815

Taking responsibility

In understanding the ethic of care among adults, responsibility is a key concept (see, for example, a discussion by Smart and Neale 1998). In conceptualising children as agents of care, we may also examine whether children see themselves as taking responsibility for helping others. As we have already noted, the notion of children having responsibility thrust upon them was contested by many children (Chapters 2, 5 and 9). At this point in the life course, many children considered a great deal of responsibility for children's care and upbringing (material, moral and emotional) still to lie with their parents. As their responses discussed elsewhere in the book suggest, children had absorbed messages concerning parents spending time with children, that parents should 'be there for' children and that they should not work too hard (Chapters 2, 5).

In order to examine children's sense of responsibility, we asked a number of different questions, but only with respect to household work. First, we asked children in the interviews which household jobs they took responsibility for. We found that while seven children said they were not responsible for any jobs, the majority only mentioned one task, the most popular task being tidying their own bedrooms followed by vacuuming and washing up. Other tasks ranged from looking after pets and babysitting to ironing, polishing, and cleaning the cooker.

Another approach adopted in the Questionnaire Survey was to distinguish between those household tasks children performed and those they did 'without being asked'. We repeated the same set of tasks but on different pages of the questionnaire so that children could not easily copy their answers from one question to the other. Around four-fifths of children reported doing the following self-care activities at least once a week without being asked: making something to eat for themselves, clearing away own dirty dishes, tidying/cleaning own room. Between a half and two-thirds reported doing family-care tasks at least once a week without being asked: laying/clearing the table, washing up/emptying the dishwasher, making something to eat for someone else and cleaning/vacuuming. When these responses are compared with responses to the simple frequency questions (Table 8.1), a fall off in frequency emerges for family-care tasks and only a slight reduction in frequency for self-care tasks (Table 8.1, Appendix). For example, 75% reported laying or clearing the table every day or some days of the week but only 63% reported doing it without being asked to do so. There were slightly smaller differences for cleaning, washing up and making something to eat for someone else, while differences were less for self-care, for example tidying or cleaning own room.

The third approach involved asking children during the interviews whether they sought to exempt themselves from household tasks or delegate responsibility to others, notably to siblings, or whether siblings passed on jobs to them. Responses from both older and younger siblings suggest that delegating responsibility was a common practice. Some 16 older siblings in the Interview Study said they passed on jobs and 12 younger siblings said their older siblings transferred jobs to them. Children in the middle of the sibling age hierarchy reported both practices. In some cases, children said they helped siblings because they needed help but expected that help to be repaid: *'Like if I need help, I do ask them'* (South Asian origin girl, two-parent family). *'When [older sisters] have got a lot of course work and stuff, then I have to do it [housework].' (How do you feel about it?) 'OK, 'cos I can tell them "I done your part of the work and now you've got to do mine"'* (South Asian origin girl, two-parent family). *'The only way I have to do hers or she'll have to do mine is if she's sick and I'll just quickly hoover her room for her and that's it really'* (Black girl, step family). Unusually, a South Asian origin boy living with a lone mother asked his younger brother to do his share of the cleaning because he said his little brother liked cleaning: *'He's more clean then me. He is, he's a house fanatic, he likes cleaning.'*

In many cases the aim was to avoid the task or to ensure that the work was shared equitably, for example with younger siblings seen as 'spoilt' or 'lazy'. Considerable bargaining went on among siblings over money involving bribes and requests for payment. In this next case, Claudia, a mixed race girl living with a lone mother, did not offer payment to her younger sister but her sister clearly expected it; when money was not forthcoming she 'told on' her sister to their mother. *'I'll say [to sister], "Could you do the washing up?" And then she'll say, "OK I'll do it." And then after that, she'll go, "Where's my money then?" And I'll say, "I never told you I'd give you money." And then she'll tell my mum.'* Scott, a white boy in a step family, had a complex set of bargains in place: *'Sometimes we'll have a deal. Say if he [brother] wants something of mine, or wants to borrow it, I'll say, "You have to do certain stuff" and that. And then he'll do it and I'll get more pocket money for it.'*

It is difficult to reach any clear conclusion about children's responsibility for household work. On the one hand, there was rather a small difference between the frequency with which they said they did tasks and the frequency with which they said they did tasks without being asked. Moreover, there was a discernible fall off in the frequency of doing family-care tasks. Most children volunteered only one task for which they were responsible in practice, although the latter finding is likely to reflect the methodology (an open-ended question in the interview as compared with a list of tasks provided in the Questionnaire

Survey). Furthermore, there was evidence of children transferring tasks to siblings and using money as a means of bargaining to get others to do the work. Many children clearly considered household work a site of contest in which they sought to limit their work responsibility. This conclusion supports other evidence discussed in the chapter, notably children's qualified support for the norm that children ought to help at home and their assessments of their contribution as modest. On the other hand, as we have shown, children's contributions to household work, especially to general caring, were considerable, at least in terms of frequency.

Children's accounts of supporting their parents

As we discussed at the beginning of the chapter, we were also interested in whether children provided parents (and others) with emotional support. We attempted to capture children's ways of 'being caring' towards their parents by a general question: Are there any things you do for (parent/carer) or give him/her? In addition, we have also searched the transcripts for other examples where children showed an appreciation of their parents and expressed concern and care for them. Some of these accounts have already been referred to, for example children's understanding of their lone mother's financial position and their need for help with housework.

Children's accounts of the help, care and concern they give parents fall into three categories. One set of comments focuses on concrete, practical forms of support. A second set of comments provides empirical evidence that children are sentient actors (Mason 1996) since children displayed considerable understanding of their parents' situations and feelings and seek to respond accordingly. A third set of comments focuses on their appreciation of what parents achieve for them and their desire to reciprocate.

Children gave many examples of providing practical support: doing shopping, washing the family car, helping with housework, looking after siblings and elderly grandparents. A number of children referred to buying presents for parents, siblings and other family members. Several children thought of practical ways of helping their parents in the future when they grew up. Elliott, a Black boy in a lone mother household, considered how he would help his mother when he got a job: *'If I had a job, I would look after my mum . . . if she needs help with her bills or anything like that, I would be glad to help.'*

Several children suggested that they wanted to help their mothers with housework because, for example, their mothers were in full-time employment: *'It's not fair. They go out and work all day, then they have to come home and do everything for you'* (Anna, a white girl, living in a step family). Ben (a white boy living in a step family), whose mother was convalescing after a major operation, wanted to make sure that he did all the jobs which involved lifting and carrying: *'So Mum don't have to do it.'* As noted earlier in the chapter, several children described not wanting to take pocket money because their lone mothers could not afford to give them any. In Chapter 7, Elliott, a Black boy living in a lone mother household, described returning his grandmother's gift of money because he thought she could not afford it. Several step family children mentioned looking after their young half siblings to relieve their mothers of some of the care.

While these children talked about the practical nature of the support with which they provided their mothers, their accounts also testify to the practice of identifying the need for help and of understanding their parents' situations and feelings. Elliott was able to see his family's poor financial position from his lone mother's perspective. Anna understood how tired her mother was when she arrived home from a long day at work and took her mother's part: *'It's not fair.'* Ben understood the effect of a hysterectomy upon his mother's ability to lift heavy things. Amy was not a very willing carer of her young half brother, but displayed considerable ability to put herself mentally in her mother's shoes. Lone mother children were mindful of their mothers' financial situation and sole responsibility for the housework.

Several children showed understanding of their parents' disposition to worry about their children and sought to help dissolve their worries. Baldev, a South Asian origin boy living in a two-parent family, was mindful that he should telephone his mother or father if he wanted to stay late at his friend's house: *'Because you don't want to worry your parents.'* He was also mindful of the worry his older sister might cause their parents and had purchased a mobile phone for her. Two girls described how they had come to realise how much anxiety they had created for their mothers by not telling them their whereabouts on particular occasions which had since led them to become more thoughtful about letting them know.

Children's accounts provide plenty of empirical evidence of giving mothers emotional support albeit that, compared with mothers' accounts, they were often rather understated. This may well be because children were the givers of such support while the mothers were the grateful recipients (see next section). Providing a listening ear to problems was, according to three girls, an important way of being helpful to their mothers. Latasha, a Black girl living with two parents, noted: *'If she [mother] finds she has any problems she'll talk to me a little bit.'* Leila, a mixed race girl living with a lone mother, understood how much her mother needed someone to turn to (she said her mother felt that 'men don't understand') and how much she provided her mother with a sense of meaning and security: *'I think I'm her security. I think she can always talk to me and everything. Because my brother isn't around, he's at my dad's.'* Zarina, a South Asian origin girl living with her lone mother, was concerned that, in general, children should understand parents' problems and indicated the way in which she was offering an understanding ear to her own mother: *'Because sometimes my mum speaks about her problems to me. Her deep inside secrets to me. And I understand them. So all parents should . . . they should inform the children as well, 'cos otherwise they might not know. They might get a shock. The problem is that parents should understand children as well. And children should understand parents. Some parents say it so high that children don't understand it. But some parents say it so softly, in the children's point of view.'*

A third theme evident in children's remarks about their care of their parents refers to their appreciation of what their parents did for them. Several South Asian origin children talked in terms of respect for and loyalty towards parents but other children spoke in similar ways. In appreciating what parents did for them, children expressed a willingness to please them, for example by not going against their wishes (Chapter 9) and a wish to repay their parents. As we have emphasised in other chapters, children seemed to be remarkably loyal to their parents. A girl in the Questionnaire Survey wrote about helping her parents with housework: *'It gives me a chance to do something for my parents instead of them doing things for me.'* Another wrote: *'I help my parents because I love them and I would do anything for them.'* In response to being asked what she did for her mother in the interview, Serena, a Black girl living with her widowed mother, simply said: *'I love her and I care for her and I look after her.'* As Claudia, a mixed race girl living with her lone mother, noted, love was the only means available to her of reciprocating her mother's care: *'I love her, help her and that's it because I can't feed her because I ain't got no money.'* Lee, a white boy living with two parents, described what he had to offer. Just as mothers talk about 'being there for their children' and children talk about mothers 'being there for them', so Lee said he would 'be there for his mother', and not only now but also in the future: *'I love her. I'll be there when she's old and that's it.'*

Children as sentient actors: mothers' views

We also sought to examine whether mothers conceptualised their children as sentient beings: as having the competence to understand, empathise with, and offer emotional support to others. In particular we asked them the question: Have there been any times when [your child] has been helpful or understanding to you? Because of the framing of the question, mothers interpreted children's ability to be actively sentient in terms of its effects on themselves. As their accounts indicate, in some cases they were clearly surprised at their children's competence to be caring persons. Mothers often very vividly described their children's sensitivity to their feelings and moods and the ways in which they felt supported by them, in emotional terms but also through their appreciation of the symbolic importance of caring gestures.

Making a cup of tea was one such culturally symbolic gesture which, in stressful situations, constituted a significant means by which children offered mothers emotional support. Niaz's mother (South Asian origin, two-parent family) described such a stressful situation and her son's response: 'Like, I'm a diabetic. Sometimes if my sugar level is high, then he knows I'm not feeling well. I say, "Niaz, I don't like noise or something." Then he will take both [younger] sisters out from the room and say, "You must not make any noise, Mummy is not feeling well." He will go and make a cup of tea for me. He'll bring the tea, sit down next to me and say, "How are you feeling, are you feeling better now?"' (How do you feel when Niaz is like that?) He makes you cry, it's really nice.'

Several mothers described the support they had received from their children during the difficult time of family change. Jasmine's mother described how her daughter supported and advised her when her marriage broke up, noting that she continues to do so: 'Yes, when I split up with my second husband Jasmine knew I was upset and she was quite good. Obviously, I didn't want it to be a burden to her, she was only small, she was only 7. But, you know, she went, "Mum don't get upset, everything will be alright, you've got us." So then I thought maybe I put a bit too much on her. . . . I mean, I could tell Jasmine anything now and she would sit down and listen and she would sort of try and advise me even though she's [only] 11, she would. You know, if I moaned about [step father] she says, "Well, have it out with him when he gets in then, you know." She is pretty good like that.'

Similarly, Daniela's mother described her daughter's emotional support when she was receiving treatment for cancer: 'I mean, yes, the times when I have been ill. She has been there . . . And you know, she was very, very supportive. I mean, when I had radiotherapy and I really wasn't well, I used to flop into bed. And she would come in and she would say things, "Do you want this Mum? And do you want that Mum?"' Ben's mother, who had had a hysterectomy, also valued her son's support: '*When I came out of hospital [after hysterectomy] he was a Godsend. I mean, he couldn't do enough for me.*'

In the next quotation, a mother in a step family was clearly as surprised by her son's understanding of her emotional distress during the televising of Princess Diana's funeral as by his solicitous action: '*Yes, the funeral of Princess Di, I was sitting there, I was watching it . . . and when Elton John sung I started crying. And then when her brother done that speech . . . I was really upset. And he was sitting there, he was looking at me. I'm going "You don't understand, Barry, this is a really sad occasion." Children don't understand this. And then he went up the road to my friend and said, "Can you come down to my mum, she is crying?" He sent her down, you know. Things like that he does. He is really good. If he feels he has upset you, he'll make you a cup of tea.* (How does that make you feel?) *To think that he thought about you, run up the road, and you know, done something. It's nice. He is very thoughtful like that.*'

Others also described their children as learning to be caring persons. A foster carer described with great pride the way in which Claire, a foster girl, was learning to express concern for others, which she considered to be a significant milestone in a foster child's life. She described Claire's response, which included a solicitous offer of a cup of tea, when her carer felt unwell: '*If I'm not well, something like that, she is very good. She'll make me cups of tea, well she can't at the moment* [because of broken arm] *but she'll say, "Do you want a cup of tea?" and things like that. "What can I do for you?" She'll draw a picture: "Hope you're better soon." And all that, yes. That's the compassion coming out.* (How does that make you feel?) *Brilliant, wonderful. I mean, she could do anything naughty if she does that sort of thing! Because I think anything they do wrong is sort of cancelled out by the way they come back and act like that.*'

Willy's lone mother described her son's caring nature as a central facet of his personality – 'he is just him' – which greatly pleased her. She commented: '*He is just him. He bought me a thimble yesterday and a little mug with "I love mum" on it. Now, I wouldn't think that my son would go out and do that, and yet he's done that. They all had a fiver yesterday because we went to Southend and he bought me them. Out of his fiver. Well, he didn't have to do that and yet that's him, you know? He'll come and sit with me and, you know [gestures a cuddle] . . .* (How did that make you feel, when he bought you the present?) *Good, yes, it does make you feel good.*'

In these and other quotations, mothers suggested that their children had considerable understanding of their feelings and situations and sometimes their problems. Zarina's lone mother (Zarina was quoted in the last section as listening to her mother's problems) noted: '*She is like a companion to me, like a close friend, where you talk, discuss. She understands you, your feelings and all that.*' As we will suggest later, this somewhat goes against mothers' responses to another question concerning the appropriateness of discussing adults' problems with children. Here, the discourse of children's right to a protected childhood clearly overlays many mothers' views of how they ought to bring up their children. Yet, within their descriptions of everyday life, many mothers also drew upon specific examples of care and support which their children provided. Moreover, they interpreted their children's gestures of support within the discourse of the ethic of care in which caring (as in motherhood) is a sentient activity involving emotional intelligence as well as practical competence. The imaginative understanding of others' feelings and responses is a key skill in providing social support which, often combined with practical activities, is also emotional and symbolic. Moreover, many of their comments also testify to the spontaneity and unsolicited nature of children's contribution to care.

Discussing adult problems with children: children's and mothers' views

Whether mothers and children thought it appropriate for their mothers to discuss their problems with children reflects underlying social constructions of what it means to be a child and the 'proper' way to bring up children. We put a critical question to both children and their mothers: Should parents talk to children about their own problems? Children were equally likely to be in favour, to disagree, or to say 'it depends'. By contrast, more mothers said that they disagreed with disclosing their problems than said either that they agree or that 'it depends' (Table 8.4). Comparing mothers' and children's responses, there was rather less consensus among children than among mothers. Moreover, it was also the case that few of the reports of the mother/child pairs coincided (Table 8.4).

When children's and mothers' responses to these questions are examined by household structure, some differences emerge. Unsurprisingly, given their troubled family lives, only one foster child favoured parents discussing their problems with children and three two-parent children compared with seven lone mother children and six step family children. The supportive attitudes of some children may arise because they had been through household change and discussed it with their mothers. Similarly, more lone mothers (6/15) agreed with discussing their problems with their children as compared with other mothers

Table 8.4 Children's and mothers' responses to the question: 'Should parents talk to children about their problems?'

	Children	Mothers	Number of matching accounts
Agree	17	14	5
Disagree	18	27	8
It depends	16	18	4
Don't know	2	1	–
No Answer	10	0	1
n	63	60	18

(4/13 two-parent mothers, 3/14 step family mothers, 3/14 foster carers).

Many of the reasons children gave in favour of or against discussion of their parents' problems were similar in emphasis to those of mothers, if not in frequency. Both mothers and children emphasised that discussing adult problems with children depended upon the kind of problem, while both groups seemed to have in mind similar types of problems, in particular problems in their parents' relationships leading to possible break-up of the family. Mothers and children also referred to children's competence in being able to understand or take on board their parents' problems. Children and mothers discussed the issue in terms of children's 'sensitivity'. All three arguments were used, especially by children, to favour as well as to disagree with disclosure of adult problems to children.

It depends on the problem

For some children, the issue was the severity of the problem. Some children thought parents should talk to them if the problem was 'bad' or affected the children, while others asserted they should only disclose 'simple' problems or those that were 'easy to understand'. As well as relationship problems, many children had in mind money problems. Some children were opposed to the discussion of money problems, while others were very much in favour. Marsha thought it very important that parents explain their financial situation so that children could be sensitive to this and hence not make unrealistic demands upon their parents for 'all the latest things': '*Well, yes, they should let the children know what problems they are having, like, financially. Because children nowadays, they like to have all the latest things out. Now, if the parents talk to the children and say, "Look, we don't have the money for getting all these things, you have to understand this, I have to work for how*

*many hours" they [children] should understand what their parents are
trying to get at. Parents can't always go out and get all the stuff what
children want.'*

Others, especially some boys, thought that private and personal
matters should, in principle, be kept confidential to the persons concerned. At issue here was not children's status and 'nature' so much as
the privacy aspect. Andrew, a white boy living with a lone mother,
simply said it was *'none of children's business'*, whilst Amos, a Black
boy living with a lone mother, similarly said: *'I wouldn't want to
know.'* Baldev (South Asian origin, two-parent family) said: *'Parents
don't tell you all of it because some stuff has to stay to themselves.'* A
foster boy clearly found his foster carer's disclosures about her own
childhood helpful but went on to say that talking about her sexual relationship was taboo: *'[Foster carer] talks to me about her life sometimes
because she was adopted. But not like, she might have private things
that she don't want to speak about. In some ways they should, but not
in all ways.* (But what does it depend on do you think?) *They can have a
private life, about things that they have done in their sex life, whatever.*
(And they should not necessarily talk to children about that?) *No.'*

A mixed race girl in a step family said that parents should talk about
deaths in the family but not *'personal stuff'* suggesting that relationship
matters were for parents only: *'Like it's adult problems, like, if you've
just had an argument with your husband, like – it's nothing to do with
you really.'* However, she then went on to qualify this, perhaps thinking
of her own past family situation: *'Like if your dad's beating up your
mum, then you probably would like react. If you've got a phone, then
you probably would try and phone the police or something like that.
But you shouldn't really interfere in your mum's problems.'*

Yet other children thought that children needed to know about relationship and money problems as soon as possible in order to be aware
of any implications for themselves. Lujayn, a South Asian origin girl in a
two-parent family, was concerned that adults should forewarn children
of impending money problems: *'Yes, I think they should but if they do
have any money problems they don't want to tell us. They'll tell each
other, but then when it gets really harsh, then of course they would have
to, but it has never happened.* (Do you think they should really tell you
about it?) *Yes.* (Why is that?) *Because you need to know what is happening around your house. I mean, if you are living with them, yes. So
you need to know what is happening. Otherwise you don't know why
they are down and upset.'*

Latasha, a Black girl in a two-parent family, mentioned the 'right' of
the child to know about parents' relationship problems before 'drastic
things happen': *'I think that parents should. I think that the child*

should have a right to know that, if there is a problem with the marriage or so-and-so happened at work or whatever, I think it's important that children should know, so that they are ready for any drastic things to happen. (Do you think your parents do that?) *I don't think they do . . . I know that, when I'm an adult, I'm going to share everything with my child. I would ask them to help me with my problems and everything.'*

Several mothers' accounts suggested that childhood was a time when children ought to be safeguarded from the problems of the adult world and the worries and burdens it was seen to bring. As Scott's mother, a white mother in a step family, said: *'I don't think they should learn too quick. They should still have their childhood.'* Barry's mother, a white mother in a step family, noted: *'. . . you can't put an old head on young shoulders and, basically, those kids are going to have enough problems when they get older.'*

Not surprisingly, several foster carers emphasized the importance of allowing children 'to have their childhood', as one foster carer put it, especially given the privations which foster children had experienced in their birth families and by being taken into care. Wayne's white foster carer defined children in general, and foster children in particular, in terms of their 'otherness'. Perhaps because Wayne was temporarily placed with her, she thought that Wayne ought to be concerned less about his carers than about his own parents, despite the fact that he rarely saw them: *'Of course when [someone Wayne knew] died, we had to say [tell him] . . . But I don't feel it's right that they should know all the ins and outs of our problems: a) it's of no interest to them; b) they've got enough problems of their own; c) adults don't discuss problems with children. That's for adults to deal with basically. And it would have any impact on them as well. They've got their own family, their own – however inadequate we think it is. It's their family . . . So you don't put any more worries on their shoulders. You protect them from that, don't you?'*

Children as competent beings

Some children also defined themselves in terms of the developmental paradigm of childhood. In exempting themselves from 'knowing', several referred to their young age, their implied immaturity and lack of competence in understanding adult problems. Willy, a white boy in a lone mother household, whose mother said *'children shouldn't need to know'*, considered children 'not old enough' to know about parents' problems: *'I think she thinks we are not old enough to know adults' problems yet.* (Do you think she is right?) *Yes, I think she is right because kids won't know adults' problems. Like, they might have problems with . . . they* can't have a baby and you haven't got much sperm, and that is confidential. You shouldn't be telling your kids stuff like that.' Rohini, a South Asian origin girl living with two parents, said: 'No, *we're not that big to know their problems or something. Like it's OK if you're 15 or 16 but not now.*'

By contrast, other children considered that children, like grown ups, 'needed to know' about private troubles, with several children referring to the break-up of parents' relationships as an instance where children should be included in discussions. Jordan, a white boy in a step family, noted: '*I think so. (Why do you think that?) Because children, like, with problems, like, if their mum and dad have just broken up, they should tell them and not lie and say they have gone away or something like that.*' Leila, a mixed race girl living with her lone mother said: *Yes, I think they should because if it's like, in the home, a problem in the home, then the children will be affected and I think they should know.*'

Some mothers and several children suggested that children 'knew anyway' about many of their parents' problems. Harinder, a South Asian origin boy living in a two-parent family, said: '*They can see it in your face that something is not right.*' His mother thought that families should not have secrets and that children had considerable competence in understanding: '*That's what you call a family. If you want to keep secret to yourself, that's not a family then. (But sometimes parents might think, perhaps children can't understand). No, I think the children are more clever than us. They got young brains, they know more. And if you tell them your problem rather than hiding them, then they're beginning to understand more.*'

Children's 'sensitive nature'

In addition to constructing children as incompetent or in need of protection, some mothers' and children's accounts referred to children as being overly sensitive. While there was an admission that children picked up that there were problems in any event, children were seen as special or different from adults because they might take adults' problems too seriously. Latasha' mother (Black, two-parent family) described children in this way: '*No. [Mother was opposed to disclosure]. But they are sensitive anyway, they are going to pick up if [father] and I aren't getting on and we are arguing all the time, even though you try not to argue when the children are around . . . they are still sensitive.*' Jake's mother also thought children were 'sensitive', again to parental relationship problems, but felt such problems should not be discussed because children might feel under pressure to take sides: '*Not really, not great details because kids are not, they observe, they are sensitive. They know when things are not right. Certain things you can tell them. Like now, my most senior brother is ill – their uncle – and they need to know. They ask me from time to time. "How is he?" What is happening and so on. I tell them. Things like that. But if it's maybe a problem between the couple, husband and wife, arguing, a misunderstanding, no I don't think that children should be dragged into that because they will tend to take sides with one parent or the other and it's not good for them.'*

Like mothers, some children agreed that children should not be stressed or burdened by the problems of their parents or made to assume responsibility for the problems. Salome, a white girl living with a lone mother, whose family had been through some difficult times, said: *'No, I don't. Because if the children have got their own problems and they are really, really worried, they just don't want to have more things dumped on their chests.'* As noted above, foster children were more disposed to disagree with adult disclosure than other children, probably reflecting their own highly stressful family experiences. Claire, a white girl in foster care, noted: *'I don't think so, because that puts pressure on the children. It's different with children talking to adults.'*

By contrast, other children suggested that talking about problems was preferable because they considered it was generally good to vent feelings and offload problems rather than keeping them locked inside, while some said that disclosure was more likely to lead to a solution. Lucy, a mixed race girl living with a lone mother, commented: *'Yes . . . because otherwise they are just going to get really stressed and they will be, like, a load of problems on them and then they will get angry with you and it would, then it would put stress on you.'* Cliff, a Black boy living in a step family: *'Yes, it will help them to get out of themselves, instead of bottling it up and not letting anyone know that they have a problem. Because if you don't let anyone know, then they can't sort it out.'* Kevin, a white boy in a two-parent household, said: *'They should because that might solve the problem and make them feel better and stuff.'*

Concerned not to transfer their problems to their children and put undue burdens on them, mothers did not emphasise the value of venting feelings or offloading their problems. Indeed, Jasmine's mother who was quoted at length earlier, where she described the support she had received from her daughter when her marriage broke down, gave an ambivalent response to the question about parents discussing problems with children: *'They shouldn't burden their children with certain things because they've got to let them be children. But I think discussing certain things if the mother is upset or something and the child says, "What is wrong?" maybe the parent should say because I think it helps children in future, their future relationships or their own home life. I think it gives them more confidence.'*

Conclusions

While most children suggested that they ought to help at home, on the whole they gave only qualified support to the idea, suggesting that their help should be modest. The most popular reasons children gave for helping were to do with the ethic of care – helping parents because they needed help or helping as a 'normal' expectation of being part of a family. The intrinsic aspects of care were expressed in children 'liking to help', although a direct question suggested that children were more ambivalent than they first appeared. Instrumental orientations to providing help (payment for housework) received little support from children in that payment for housework was seen to transgress family mutuality, with more support from white children than other ethnic groups.

Childrens reports of their contributions to care in practice suggest that, while they made a considerable contribution in terms of reported frequency to household work, especially contributing to their own self-maintenance, they reported a higher frequency of general caring – both caring for and about other people, including mothers, fathers, siblings, classmates, elderly people and pets. It was difficult to assess how far children were doing household tasks out of a sense of responsibility. Few children volunteered many examples of tasks for which they assumed responsibility, but most said they did household tasks without being asked, although the frequency fell for family-care tasks done without being asked (compared with tasks done without this proviso). Passing on jobs to siblings was also commonplace and part and parcel of sibling rivalries and hierarchies.

However, the interviews were punctuated with examples where children displayed competence in understanding their parents' feelings and situations. Almost in passing, children noted the ways in which they provided support to their mothers, lone mothers especially. Children described being caring in three different ways: providing concrete, practical forms of support to parents; understanding parents' own situations and feelings and responding accordingly, often in practical ways; appreciating what parents did for children and wishing to reciprocate.

Mothers, as the receivers of support, elaborated upon the support children provided. Mothers' descriptions of their children suggest that children are capable of understanding the feelings and situation of the other, and they drew considerable emotional comfort from their children's gestures of support, epitomised in cups of tea proffered at the right moment and in times of stress and crisis. Mothers invested these supportive, highly appreciated moments with symbolic meaning. Sometimes mothers noted surprise that their children were so emotionally intelligent. Mothers' descriptions also testified to children's love and affection being spontaneous and unsolicited. Just as affective, emotional and symbolic sources of support are central components of care with which mothers seek to provide children, so children also show that this is what they can offer mothers.

Nonetheless, when the issue was raised as to whether children should be expected to be privy to parents' problems, mothers' responses (and to some extent children's also) were in the main rather different. Consonant with the view that childhood ought to be a time of protected 'innocence' and freedom from stress, many mothers and some children were opposed to parents 'burdening' their children with their problems. Some mothers who thought it wrong to burden children contradicted what they had earlier said about their own practice. For some mothers and children, it depended upon the problem, but most seemed to have in mind difficulties in parents' relationships and financial problems. But here there was no consensus, with children split between those who viewed such matters as personal and confidential and not to be disclosed, on the one hand, and those who considered that children needed to be prepared because they might be implicated in adults' problems, for example the breakdown of their parents' relationships. Children who mentioned parents' money problems in some cases subscribed to the benefits of childhood ignorance while others were keen to know about the problems. That children were especially 'sensitive' was a view taken by some mothers and children although, again, what were seen to be the consequences of this varied. For some children, sensitivity meant being aware of, but not being able to cope with, adult problems and so they wished to be protected from them. Others were unequivocally in favour of venting feelings and offloading problems.

On balance, we would suggest that mothers and children view childhood at this time (11–13 years) as a protected period in which children should only be engaged in a modest amount of household work and responsibility. Children's rationalities for contributing, while being in part embedded in the mutuality of everyday life, also relate to notions of self-responsibility and self-care. However, what is perhaps more interesting is the ways in which mothers valued other aspects of children's contribution, namely the comfort and sense of meaning and value they derived from their children as caring, sentient beings. Children themselves testified to their emotional intelligence in a variety of, albeit often under-stated, ways. As the boy quoted under the title of the chapter suggested, just as children want their mothers to 'be there for them', so children seek to 'be there for their parents': *'I love her. I'll be there for her when she's old and that's it.'*

9 Children and mothers' regulation

> I don't really argue with them about rules. They are the parents, so I just have to get on with it.

In recent years, sociologists of childhood have placed emphasis on children's reflexivity and their potential contribution to society, and to constructing and making sense of their own lives and the world around them (James and Prout 1990). In reconceptualising children as social actors, this is not to argue that children are now seen to wield more power *vis-à-vis* adults, but rather to understand them as having the potential and the competences to exercise power.

It is difficult to situate the study of children's regulation in a study of care because the concept of 'care' tends to be separated off from the concept of control and is sometimes juxtaposed with it. Moreover, the study of mothers' care has reflected particular theoretical concerns. For example, in the 1970s and 1980s, feminist sociologists focused upon the neglect of women as carers and the invisibility of caring as work (Chapter 1). From a feminist perspective, therefore, parental regulation of children may be understood as part of mothers' work in caring for children and as evidence that mothers care about their children. By contrast, from the perspective of a sociologist of childhood, parents' regulation of children may look like explicit 'policing', as James et al. note: 'Just as soldiers are drilled persistently even beyond basic training, so children are required to eat, sleep, wash and excrete at specific and regular times' (1998: 55).

Children's lives are lived within the structural context of power in which adults regulate children's bodies and minds. In their general status as children, and in their particular statuses as sons and daughters, children's ability to act autonomously and their access to resources are constrained. Within the household and family, children's 'participation' takes place on unequal terms. From an interactionist perspective, as Berger and Luckman wrote in the 1970s: '. . . it is the adults who set the rules of the game. . . . The child can play the game with enthusiasm or with sullen resistance. But alas, there is no other game around' (1971: 154).

Bernstein's work, which began in the 1970s, continues to be salient to the analysis of children's regulation and the different modes in which control in its communicative forms is exercised. By making crucial conceptual distinctions at the levels of structure and discourse (classification and framing), Bernstein identified mothers as central agents of cultural reproduction and analysed their role in preparing children for the public education system (Bernstein 1975: 131). Locating his structural analysis within the changing shape of the social class structure in Britain, Bernstein identified different forms of caring and regulation which, put simplistically, are contingent upon the distinction between 'visible' and 'invisible' forms of control. These modes of control are enacted as communicative strategies so that, for some parents, the particular form of communication is congruent with the particular form of control. Bernstein identified differences within the middle classes as well as between social classes. For example, for the new middle-class parents (teachers and social workers working in the public sector), their occupational power is based upon knowledge and communicative strategies rather than economic power, communication as control is invisible and leads to the construction of children's identities as 'personal' and to flexible role performance. Bernstein contrasts the communicative strategies of the new middle classes with the communicative control strategies of the old middle classes which emphasise children's individual rather than personal identity (Bernstein 1975).

In the context of renewed interest in children's agency, it is important to continue to problematise the construction of the 'autonomous child' and the trend towards self-regulation. From children's perspectives, mothers' regulation may be perceived differently from the ways mothers intend and practice the regulation of their children. Visible forms of control may not be perceived as such, however, by children themselves, who may not 'feel' controlled – that is, when their expectations converge with those of parents, By contrast, invisible forms of control may be interpreted by children as controlling even though the overt adult intention was not to appear controlling.

Within the limits of the study, it was not possible to investigate in any depth how children and their mothers discussed parental control in relation to the particularities of children's lives, nor indeed to observe directly the different discourses in which control was embedded. In this chapter, we examine the 'public' rather than the 'private' accounts of children and their mothers concerning definitions of parents' 'rules' and 'strictness', including children's reports of how they responded to mothers' control. Since mothers largely set the limits to children's everyday family lives, we give considerable attention to the accounts of the mothers. Moreover, since the study did not include fathers, we have not addressed the role of fathers in regulating children, although there is evidence from the Questionnaire Survey to suggest that children perceived their mothers to be as important as fathers and, in the case of lone mother households, more important in exercising discipline (Chapter 5).

In the first section of the chapter, we consider mothers' views about rules and the ways in which they justify rules or lack of them. In the second section, we examine the issues from mothers' perspectives: the kinds of issues which they say attract rules and the different approaches mothers reported in exercising control over their children. In the third section, we turn to children's views of rules and their mothers' regulation, and their accounts of the ways they responded to mothers' reported modes of control. In the final section, we present some case studies to exemplify the different combinations of mothers' approaches to regulation and children's responses. Because of the powerful evidence that social class influences the ways in which mothers exercise control over children (Bernstein 1975, 1996), we have indicated the types of occupations in which mothers were employed. As we noted in Chapter 1, most of study families are working class according to both mothers' and fathers' occupations. However, given the study design, it was neither our intention nor a feasible possibility to assess the influence of social class systematically.

Children need guidelines: mothers' views and justifications

In the current public policy context prescribing parental responsibility, it seemed to us that mothers would be likely to set considerable store at this time by their ability to set standards and boundaries for their children. Mothers unanimously claimed that children 'need rules'. However, at the same time, mothers were wary of being 'too strict' with their children. Rather, they said, children needed 'guidance', a view which supports the general contention concerning the 'negotiated' nature of family obligations in late modern society (Finch 1989). Asked a direct question, many more mothers said they were quite strict (26/58) or not at all strict (19/58) than said outright that they were strict (13/58). In their accounts of regulating children, mothers portrayed themselves as 'flexible' while, at the same time, exercising control. (Similarly, as we shall show, more children put mothers in the 'flexible rules' category than in the strict or no rules categories.) As Latasha's mother noted: '*You need to have some form of control, not in a bad way, where you restrict them from doing everything, but there have to be guidelines*' (Black mother, two-parent family, cashier). Daniela's mother: '*I just guide them sort of . . . a little bit of shove the right way. I mean, I don't like saying, "You must do this"* ' (white mother, step family, non-employed). Even teaching children 'right' from 'wrong' was seen to involve following guidelines rather than clear-cut moral principles: '*I think they need some guidelines, because otherwise they wouldn't know, you know, right from wrong and you've got to have a structure*' (Steve's mother, white, step family, postwoman).

For many mothers, rules were more about setting boundaries or 'not overstepping the mark' – mechanisms by which mothers indicated to children what was expected of them (Ribbens 1994). As noted above, Steve's mother spoke in terms of the 'need for structures'. Amos' Black, non-employed lone mother regulated her son by verbally clarifying the boundaries of acceptable behaviour, while not appearing authoritarian: '*When there is something wrong I tell them, I talk to them about it, but I don't rule them.*' This next mother explained that rules were there to set the limits to children's negotiation – 'a little bit of boundary' rather than a hard and fast principle: '*You've got to have a little bit of a boundary you know. What I mean is, if you're going to keep on over-stepping the mark in your house, you're going to do it outside. And what you can do with your parents, you can't do outside, so you've got to know what limit you can go to*' (Black lone mother, care assistant). Yet, as we discuss later, while the discourse that most mothers drew upon suggested that they did not want to be *perceived* as dictatorial or strict, clearly some mothers saw themselves as very much in charge, albeit for their children's 'own good'.

Mothers' justifications for regulating their children reflect those identified by Ribbens (1994) in her study of families with seven-year-olds: the need to constrain children *qua* children; the need to make children 'fit for' and 'fit into' the public world; the need to indicate to children (and to others) that they are loved and properly cared for. In relation to the first social construction – children 'in need of constraint' – mothers in our study described children as potentially anarchic if left to their own devices, a view held by mothers in other studies (Backett 1982; Ribbens 1994): '*. . .if they [children] don't have rules, they get out of control. They won't listen, they won't do what you want*' Zarina's mother (South Asian, lone mother, bank clerk). '*If children don't have rules they step all over you*' (Lucy's white lone mother, social worker). '*You have to let them know what the rules are, really, because they are living in your house and you have to let them know that somebody has to be in charge, else it would be a riot!*' (Robert's white foster carer).

In relation to the second social construction – children need rules at home in order to help them to negotiate life outside the home – mothers perceived the public domain to be permeated by rules and assumptions which children have to learn and put into practice. *'I mean, when you go to work, there is rules, everywhere you go there is rules, so there should be rules in the house'* (Sally's white lone mother, non-employed). *'It doesn't matter where they go, there's always rules. There's rules at school, there's rules at a club, there's rules at football, there's rules at work. There's rules on the train, there's rules on the buses . . . rules everywhere. If they're not used to it at home, then, when they go out elsewhere, they're going to find it very hard to abide by the rules'* (Scott's white mother, step family, non-employed).

With respect to the third social construction, having rules was a symbol of showing children that their mothers (and fathers) loved them and cared for them 'properly'. Taking responsibility for children seriously – inculcating moral principles, protecting children from danger, making children feel secure – was part and parcel of what they considered criteria for being a 'proper parent'. *'I am strict by my children's definition because I love them and will not allow them to behave or have the same thing as children whose parents don't love them. The reason why I say the parents don't love them . . . you can't love your child if you allow your child to be in environments that you know are not created for them. You can't love your child if you don't discipline them. When I say "discipline" I don't mean battering them or any physical discipline, I mean look out for them basically. You can't tell your child you love them if you are not prepared to look out for them'* (Marsha's mother, Black, step family, non-employed).

In addition, mothers also justified rules in terms of their own social status as the main or sole carer. Several lone mothers and mothers in two-parent households said that, as the sole or main carers on a day-to-day basis, they needed to exercise control over children. Since Clark's father was rarely in contact and provided no practical or financial support, Clark's mother felt she 'had to be strict' with Clark: *'. . . because with a male figure they'll listen more. Um, as a female I find that they listen to you less. Even when their dad comes to visit, which is rare, he'll just talk to them once and they'll jump, but I have to talk two, three times and, you know, I'm still not heard, you know'* (Black lone mother, school meals assistant). Similarly, Barry's mother made it clear that, as the only resident birth parent, she considered herself to be in charge: *'I like things to be done my way. I think it's easier that way. You can only have one person to rule a home and in this house it's me'* (white, step family, cleaner).

Mothers who lived with children's step fathers also said, in some cases, that they chose to be in charge of their children rather than place responsibility upon their partners. Emily's mother was adamant that her new husband should not take on the role of substitute father since he had his own children to contend with: '. . . *we agreed that since we both had separate sets of kids, and they both had other parents, that we weren't going to act as substitute parents for the other one's children. So, I mean, [step father] is another adult. He will, you know, he will help and support and look after and whatever else if I'm not around, but it's only if I'm not around. Otherwise we've sort of got this idea of, you know, significant adult, which is . . . a positive thing, you know, there is another significant adult who cares about you, but not as an alternative parent . . . So there is a very clear distinction between my role with them and his role'* (white, step family, university lecturer). A troublesome relationship between a step father and a step child could create dilemmas for mothers, inhibiting them from appearing as 'too strict' to their children, as in the following case. Amy's mother said that she felt that, because her daughter did not get on with her step father, she had to be 'softer' with her than she used to be as a solo mother, or else Amy would perceive her to be siding with her step father: '*I think I was probably more strict when I was on my own. I think sometimes the tension between [step father] and Amy and the feeling of being piggy in the middle actually makes me probably a bit softer on her, to be honest*' (white mother, playgroup helper).

For rather different reasons, foster carers felt they ought to be strict with foster children namely because they felt their parents had failed to provide children with 'proper' boundaries. Wayne's foster carer described how she had to teach Wayne and his sibling basic routines: '*Yes, I'm quite strict . . . it's the only way I can keep sane. . . . So I thought, 'Don't go over the top, this is their norm.' So for the first few nights they went to bed quite late and I accepted them getting up early. And then I sat down and said 'Look, this is what you are used to, but this can't go on.' So you take a firm line, you say, "Right, bed at this time and I don't want you getting up before say, six in the morning. You've all got clocks in your rooms."* '

In the case of Debbie, who was rapidly embracing teenage culture, her foster carer said she continued to be strict with her. Moreover, Debbie's carer particularly disapproved of Debbie's liking for short skirts, parties and boyfriends. Even though she considered she ought to let Debbie have a say in decisions, she felt this was unwise because Debbie would overstep 'the mark': '*Well I think she can have a say, we can sort of discuss things, but I don't know that she'll have a say, because I know what her say would be. It's usually the opposite of what we would like, you know, to stay out or to dress in something that we say "No".*'

Mothers' conviction that children require guidelines and boundaries were filtered by a range of different ways of viewing children and parenthood: children were viewed as anarchic and in need of constraint; children were constructed as future adults who needed to learn to abide by rules in the public sphere; setting rules and boundaries was a key criterion by which 'proper parenting' was judged. Mothers' views of the need to guide their children were also shaped by their particular situations: lone mothers, as solo carers, felt that they had to set boundaries for their children, while mothers living in step families similarly noted it was their responsibility to guide their children rather than expecting their partners to do so. Finally, foster carers justified rules on the grounds that foster children needed to be clear about the expected norms in their foster families, especially if they had lacked clear boundaries in their families of origin.

Rules and regulation: mothers' views

Types of rules

Mothers' rules for their children reflected their aims as parents. First, they had rules to encourage children to become self regulating, for example about observing time schedules and behaving 'properly'. These rules were often specified in terms of age-appropriate criteria. Second, since mothers at this time in their children's lives still retained responsibility for their health, lifestyles and educational progress (homework especially), they sought both to inculcate children with a sense of personal responsibility while at the same time protecting children from risk. Knowing children's whereabouts emerged as a critical worry for mothers of teenagers (Brannen et al. 1994) and also was a non-negotiable issue among these mothers of younger children. Because of mothers' concern about the risks of public environments, notably traffic dangers and child abuse, they required their children to tell them their whereabouts. Jake's mother said: '*Well, they can't go out without letting anybody know and I need to know when they are coming back. I tell them when to come back. I want to know who he is going with. In fact, he can't leave the house without letting me know. I need to know because of his safety*' (Black, two-parent household, a dental nurse).

Several mothers included in their list of rules normative expectations concerning children's proper behaviour: good manners, respect for other people and honesty. Especially those whom we later term as 'negotiative mothers' spoke in terms of 'basic ground rules' implying that other matters were open to negotiation. The fact that these mothers are middle class is not surprising given Bernstein's theory concerning invisible modes of control among new middle-class families (Bernstein 1975). Emily's mother talked about basic ground rules involving respect for others and letting each other know where they are: *'I think you do need some basic ground rules to do with, you know, safety, to do with how they behave towards other people. You know, basic things, but I try not to add on them too much, really. I think [step father] thinks that they [children] have a ludicrous amount of freedom and that I don't control their behaviour enough, like how long they spend on the phone. But, you know, in the end I'm more interested in . . . will they respect the rules that I've got about . . . not just taking off and disappearing off to a friend's house without letting anyone know than I am about, you know, whether they spend two hours on the phone'* (white, step family, university lecturer). Leila's mother, another negotiative mother, also mentioned the following ground rules: children's safety – rules about 'coming and going', honesty, pulling one's weight, being part of the family – which represent a mix of protection and socialisation issues: *'Main rules I have, I like safety. Really important. So things like coming and going, never do it without absolutely letting me know where they are, when they're going to be back. Safety is a very important one for me. Honesty is another one and that kind of covers stuff like, you know, why they are doing things and then working that out for themselves as well. . . . What rules do I have? I think it's about coming and going and being part of the family and pulling your weight. Putting something in as well as taking it out and not seeing it as a one-way process. Probably those are the things that never really change. Almost everything else can be negotiated, I think'* (Black lone mother, hospital administrator). As Leila's mother intimated, apart from ground rules, other issues were negotiable.

Regulative approaches

As noted above, social constructions or typifications of what a child 'is' shape the ways in which mothers bring up their children. Ribbens (1994) classified the mothers of seven-year-olds in her study in terms of a threefold typology: as 'directive', 'negotiative' and 'adaptive'. Directive mothers sought to control children directly on the grounds that they needed discipline and constraint or else the 'little devils' would run wild. In contrast, mothers who adopted a negotiative approach construed children as 'small people' – as individuals with similar rights to those of adults. They sought to 'negotiate' with children, taking account of children's wishes and views rather than exerting control unidirectionally. An adaptive approach was contingent upon a view of the 'specialness' of childhood, a period of relative innocence in which children needed freedom from restriction. In adopting an 'adaptive approach', mothers saw their task as providing children with the 'right' kind of environment to develop their 'natural' selves.

Our study focused on a later period of childhood than Ribbens' study and therefore mothers' approaches to children are likely to be different. The adaptive approach did not appear to figure. Rather, mothers' accounts of the ways they exerted control over children were largely characterised along a continuum from directive to negotiative. We have used the term 'directive' to cover mothers who, although in many cases they regarded themselves as flexible and as listening to children's point of view, suggested that they made the decisions. 'Negotiative' mothers, by contrast, are those who treated their children with some degree of equality, discussed rules and decisions with them, and took account of their wishes and concerns. These mothers suggested that the final outcome was a compromise. The difference lies not only in their view of childhood but also in their construction of the structural relationship between adult and child – as hierarchical or equal – which was an issue which they did not explicitly elaborate upon a great deal, and whether they took children's wishes into account, an issue which many did explicitly refer to. It should be kept in mind, however, that regulation was but one of many issues covered by the study and that our classification was based upon how mothers chose to present these matters, rather than upon a systematic interrogation of their practices.

These limitations notwithstanding, we classified 35 of the 60 mothers as 'directive' and 25 mothers as 'negotiative'. Two-thirds of the two-parent and foster care mothers (9/14 and 9/13) were classified as directive, compared with half of the lone mother group (9/18) and around half of the step family group (8/15). Given foster carers' formal role *vis-à-vis* social services, and their relatively short-term and potentially impermanent relationship with foster children, it is perhaps unsurprising that foster carers sought to spell out rules and boundaries and to define their sphere of responsibility clearly. Proportionally, more Black mothers were classified as directive (14/17) compared with South Asian origin mothers (7/11) (all in the two-parent group) and a little under half of the white mothers (15/32).

Some mothers classified as *'directive'* clearly portrayed themselves as the main arbiters of decisions concerning children's lives, while others asserted children's right to state their point of view but not necessarily to influence the outcome. Willy's mother was in the former group where the mother's word was not open to question: *'I have always said, "I am mum, I do as I please." They are the child, they do as they are told. When they are an adult, they can do as they please as well. You know, I can't have them running around like banshees because this is my house.*

Table 9.1   Mothers' regulative approaches by family type

Family type	Directive	Negotiative	N
Two-parent	9	5	14
Lone mother	9	9	18
Step father	8	7	15
Foster carer	9	4	13
Totals	35	25	60

N.B. There are three pairs of siblings in the study and therefore only 60 mothers.

You know what I mean? If they don't like the rules, that is just tough' (white lone mother, barmaid). Rebecca's mother was among the larger group of mothers who were in favour of children having a say but still made the decision themselves: *'I mean, obviously, like, if it's about them they've got to have some sort of say, really, you know, because it's about them, really. But overall, I think it's up to parents really, because their parents are still their guardians. It's still important really to make the decision for them'* (white, lone mother, home help). Leroy's mother acknowledged the 'political correctness' of listening to children but was opposed to children having a say in decisions: *'If I had my way they shouldn't have no say, but I suppose it's nice to hear their opinions, do you know what I mean? Whether or not I like it, I suppose it's nice to hear what they have to say'* (Black lone mother, non-employed).

Being directive on some matters did not preclude the possibility of negotiating with children over other 'less important' matters. *'No, I don't think I'm strict in all aspects. Certain areas, yes. Something I think is really, really important, that is going to affect him in life or now or whatever, I'm strict. Something I think doesn't really matter, I explain to him and. . . Sometimes with things I'm strict, he cries and says it's not fair and blah, blah,blah, he goes on. I just let him cry. At the end of the day he still comes back to me and then I explain to him . . . Some decisions, yes, they can have a say. It is important. It will help them to understand and to follow whatever decision it is.. But some things, as a parent, you are just responsible and you have to do it'* (Jake's mother, Black, two-parent family, dental nurse).

By contrast, 'negotiative mothers' not only valued the child's opinion but would try to negotiate a compromise with children. Baldev's mother said: *'. . . I think if the parents sit with the children and the children sit with the parents and have a bit [of a] chat, then we have to do a bit [of] compromise, you know. It's not a big deal. If the children wants to do something else [from parents] they can do [it]'* (South Asian, two-parent household, non-employed). Tracy's mother had a similar view:

'*I think they [children] should have a say. If, you know, if you are going to put your point over, they have got to put their point over as well. Yes, I mean ... if I make a rule or I'll say something and they don't like it, I don't say to them, "Shut up, I don't want to listen." I'll listen to what they've got to say and if it comes across to me that ... perhaps they are a bit right, you know, then I will say, "OK, we'll compromise about that," you know*' (white mother, step family, data processor).

Some negotiative mothers made mention of adjusting rules to suit the child's individual character, age, or birth order. Emily's mother described not having negotiated with her older daughter since she had been less assertive at Emily's age: '*I think Emily in particular has a strong feeling about, you know, if she thinks she is being disempowered, then she is rampant. And so she insists on, you know, we have to negotiate quite a few things. I think sometimes she thinks she doesn't have enough of a say. The things that we negotiate at the moment are mostly to do with "Can she go out? Where can she go?", what restrictions I place on that*' (white, step family, university lecturer). Lucy's mother similarly had older children and acknowledged that younger children might 'need' different kinds of control: '*What I realise now is, what I felt was right for one isn't necessarily the same for the other child. They are all different and they have different needs. Um, and I also think it would be fair to say, although I hate to admit it ... you don't always get it right the first time anyway and sadly, perhaps to my detriment, you learn with the first one and then you realise with the next one that it, you know, it needs to be a bit different*' (white, lone mother, social worker). Leroy's mother (Black lone mother, non-employed) noted in her interview how proud she was of the strict way she brought up her elder son but, according to the interviewer's note, the mother was not at all strict with her young daughter who was present during part of the interview. The child's gender is also likely to be a significant factor, as in the latter case, but was not easy to elucidate given that few families contained siblings of both sexes.

Rules and regulation: children's views

Types of rules

To some extent, the kinds of rules children mentioned in their interviews reflect the concerns of their mothers. Children referred to a variety of rules while a number said their parents had no rules but, on closer questioning, described quite specific expectations. One type of rule was about time deadlines which related to children's status as 'children' as well as to time schedules related to family life: bed time, meal

time, homework time, television time, praying time, and, most importantly, homecoming times. Some rules referred to codes of personal
hygiene. As several foster children noted, their foster carers had rules
about brushing their teeth and changing their underwear, matters
which may have been neglected in their own families. Other codes concerned personal behaviour – showing respect for people (not being
rude, not swearing, not hitting siblings, keeping the volume down on
the TV) and treating the physical environment of the home 'properly'
(cleaning up the kitchen after making a snack, putting things away, not
playing football in the sitting room). As Scott noted, his parents
expected him to behave 'properly' in the house: *'Like when you're
eating, don't put your feet up and like I'm not supposed to be wearing
my shoes ... you're not allowed to wear shoes in the front room'.*
Another type of rule referred to helping in the house, especially the
requirement that children tidy their bedrooms, while several children
reported being expected to clean the house and to do the washing up on
a regular basis.

A very frequently reported type of rule reflected their mothers' and
carers' concern with risk and safety. A key rule for children in the study
was to let parents know their whereabouts and not to be out after dark.
One South Asian girl complained that she was not allowed to go out by
herself, had to be accompanied to school, and was subject to frequent
surveillance from parents when alone in the house (parents phoning in
to check up on her). Another South Asian origin girl referred to several
of the above issues: *'I have to go to bed, and I have to eat all my food, be
healthy. And if I'm late home from school, I have to call them and let
them know I'm late and stuff ... basic rules really.'*

Several children were unable to think of any rules and, when asked
whether there was anything they would like to do that their parents
would not allow them to do, they explained that, by and large, they conformed to their parents' expectations. Lujahn, a South Asian origin girl
(two-parent, working-class family) exemplified this group of children;
she made it quite clear that she conformed to her parents' wishes:
'Because if they tell me to do something, I do it. So there's no discussion.'

Perhaps not surprisingly, very few children volunteered examples of
infringing parents' rules or of sanctions imposed by parents. In the
interviews, children, like adults, sought to present themselves as
morally deserving. Lenny was unusually expansive. He described how
his mother was strict about not hitting his sister or 'back chatting' his
mother and gave homework as an issue where his mother might impose
sanctions: *'Like I mean, if she takes away my computer, it's not fair. I'm
doing my homework and she thinks I'm not doing that much homework. But she thinks it's the computer and the telephone ... sometimes*

she agrees and sometimes she takes [the computer] away' (Black boy, lone mother who was a nursing auxiliary).

Flexible mothers and compliant children

The claim made by many mothers that they were generally flexible in their application of rules was endorsed by children. As other studies of older children have also found (Brannen et al. 1994), and as we found in the Questionnaire Survey, only a minority of children portrayed their parents as strict (12%) while two-thirds (69%) said their parents' rules were flexible and a fifth (19%) that they had no rules. Boys were more likely than girls to say that their parents had strict rules (Table 9.2). Similarly, in the interviews, the majority of children said their parents had flexible rules (49/63) or no rules (5/63), while only a minority said their parents had strict rules (9/63). However, more foster children, reflecting their foster carers' self descriptions, described their carers as strict (5/15, compared with none in the step father group, 2/15 in the two-parent group, 2/18 in the lone mother group).

While children did not consider their parents to be strict, asked a rather different question in both the interviews and the Questionnaire Survey, several children wrote down examples of 'things that they would like to do but that their parents would not allow them to do'. A particular complaint concerned lack of freedom outside the home. Yet, elsewhere in their interviews, children chose not to criticise their parents.

Kevin portrayed his parents as 'not really strict' but, as Kevin suggested, their relaxed approach may have reflected the fact that he largely conformed to his parents' expectations. In this sense, the rules were internalised and taken for granted. But, as Kevin's account also suggested, he had to be home by a 'certain time', while noting also that his parents did not set specific times: *'They [parents] are not really strict. They don't like to tell me a certain time that I have got to be in when I go out. They just say, "Don't be out all night" because I go to play football down at the park or something. They just say, "Don't be there for ages." They send me to bed, yes, but they don't mind when I go to sleep, you know. I'm just not allowed to be down here after a certain time.*

Table 9.2   Children's perceptions of parental rules (Questionnaire Survey)

	Girls %	Boys %	All %	N
Strict rules	9	15	12	104
Flexible rules	70	69	69	593
No rules	21	17	19	161

N.B. Significant difference at 0.02 level

They give me pocket money and they still buy me stuff. So they are not really strict, no' (white, two-parent household, mother a playgroup helper).

In accordance with the requirement to be self regulating, many children suggested there was no need for parents to be strict, implying that most of the time they conducted themselves appropriately. Baldev said: *'We don't really have rules because me and my sister we do our work anyway and we're doing well in school, so. And we help around the house, so basically, we don't have any rules'* (South Asian boy, two-parent family, mother a canteen assistant). Ceri expressed a similar position: *'We never come home late anyway'* (white girl, two-parent household, mother an educational psychologist).

By contrast, some children suggested that their mothers were directive and inflexible. Rebecca suggested she did not get on with her mother: *[Mother] always goes up to her way in the end'* (white girl, lone mother a home help). In a different vein, two boys confessed to misdemeanours which they suggested required their mothers to be strict with them. Daniel suggested that, after school, he preferred going to the house of his non-resident father who appeared to be much less strict with him compared with his mother, who told him off, giving an example: *'Like when my brothers or me have been naughty at school, or like, when our room is not tidy or when we leave things there and that. Those kinds of things'* (Black boy, step family, mother a bank clerk). Similarly, Lenny noted: *She [mother] is strict in her own ways. It depends, like, if I backchat to her and if I've been naughty to my sister, like hitting her or teasing her or something. Or say I get a bad mark and I ain't doing that well in that lesson'* (Black boy, lone mother a nursing auxiliary).

Three-fifths of children presented themselves as largely conforming to their parents' 'directiveness' (36/63), while two fifths suggested that rules were more open to negotiation (27/63) (Table 9.3). Daniela noted: *'I don't really argue with them [parents] about rules. They are the parents, so I just have to get on with it'* (white girl, step family, mother non-employed). No children presented themselves as totally rejecting of or disobedient to their parents' rules. A few children complained less about the rules *per se* as about the fact that their parents would not listen to them. Rebecca complained: *[Mother] knows but she won't listen to me, no. I've tried to – I mean, she thinks that lately, because I'm growing into a woman, she keeps on getting this idea that I've got an attitude problem. So she shouts at me even more.'*

Rather more foster children suggested that they conformed to their carers' rules, reflecting the accounts given by their foster carers, while in the other three family types, equal numbers of children either conformed or negotiated (Table 9.3). But however children portrayed their

Table 9.3   Children's responses to parental rules by family type

Family type	Negotiates	Conforms	N
Two-parent	7	8	15
Lone mother	9	9	18
Step father	8	7	15
Foster carer	3	12	15
All children	27	36	63

mothers and foster carers, only a few were overtly critical of them. On the whole, most children considered them to be generally 'fair' although a few mentioned examples of unfairness, particularly concerning altercations with siblings.

Mothers' modes of regulation and children's responses

The conceptual distinction between mothers' directive and negotiative approaches to the regulation of their children and children's responses to the two regulative modes can be captured in a matrix (Figure 9.1). The vertical axis represents mothers' regulative approach (directive and negotiative) while the horizontal axis indicates children's responses (compliant and negotiative).

(A) Directive mothers–obedient children

A majority of children (17 boys and 14 girls) fell into the top left-hand quadrant in which mothers were classified as directive and children as conforming to their mothers' wishes. Mothers directive approaches differed: some mothers showed a need to be in total charge while other mothers 'explained' their rules to children and did not present themselves as strict. Yet other mothers described 'advising' their children. Most children in the quadrant, with a few exceptions, suggested that they largely complied with their parents' rules.

Willy's mother (white, lone mother, barmaid) was very much in charge and wanted Willy to understand this. Willy said he was unable to negotiate with his mother over what he could or could not do. '*It might be something you really like [to do], but your mum says, "Oh well, we'll do something I like for a change." But we always do something that she likes because we don't get a say in anything.*' Willy's mother confirmed Willy's view of her, making it clear that, as the only adult in the household, she felt entitled to expect unquestioning obedience from her children.

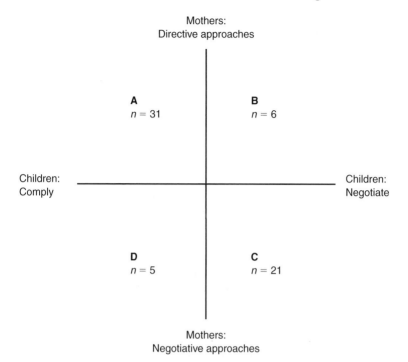

Figure 9.1   A matrix of maternal control strategies and children's responses

I have always said, 'I am mum, I do as I please.' They are the child, they do as they are told. When they are an adult, they can do as they please as well. You know, I can't have them running around like banshees because this is my house. You know what I mean? If they don't like the rules, that is just tough. We seem to have this under-standing, me and my children, that, you know, they know when mummy is annoyed. I don't have to shout and scream. I just look at them and they know they have gone over the mark. But, yes, we have to have rules. (What are the main rules you have for the chil-dren?) Just to behave yourself. They are just kids and kids have to be kids, I know that, but the main rule in this house is to behave yourself. And that's it. And if you don't behave yourself, then you get done. (And would you say that you are strict or not really?) I would say I was, yes. I have to be, because I don't like disrespectful children. I really don't like them. They have to respect an adult and to get that respect you have to be tough. If they mouth you off and you ignore it, they think they can mouth anybody else off. I can't have that. They have got to understand that you are the adult and

*you make them rules for their own good. Not for you. Not because
you want to be nasty or anything, it's because no one will like them
if they can't respect an adult* (white, lone mother, barmaid).

Daniela's mother (white mother, step family, non-employed) is an
example of a directive mother who 'explained' her rules to her daughter
but admitted that she had 'very strict views on things': '*I wouldn't say
that I'm strict in the way that I would be obsessively strict with them. I
would say [to children], "Well, no, you know, we don't do that." But
again, in the same way, I couldn't be like some of these parents – which
I know people are like it – "Do this thing" and they [children] never
know why they have got to do it. They never know why you shouldn't
do something. They never explain anything, you know, and I'm not like
that. I explain everything.*' Daniela herself made it clear she accepted
her mother's and step father's rules without questioning them: '*I don't
really argue with them [parents] about rules. They are the parent, so I
just have to get on with it.*' Elliott's mother (Black lone mother who was
a secretary) also explained her rules to her son: '*I try to talk to him and
let him know why I'm doing it and why he can't do it and why I don't
agree with him doing it. And we can sit down and work it out from
there. I sit down and talk to him and reason with him, to make him
understand why ... I wouldn't like him to do it.*' Elliott himself
accepted his mother's rules as 'normal' for someone of his 'age': '*My
mum treats me like a normal 12-year-old.*'

Hayfa's mother (South Asian, two-parent household, mother a playgroup supervisor) is an example of a directive mother who 'advised' her
children and did not consider herself 'strict'. Nonetheless she expected
to have the greater say in what they did. '*I don't leave them free that
they can go anywhere, but I'm not strict. I just teach them that this thing
is good for you and this is not. And they know it.*' When asked what
happened when the children did not take her advice, she said proudly:
'*They always take my advice; they know I'm right.*' Hayfa described her
mother as 'sort of strict' and made it clear that she accepted her
mother's rules as reasonable: '*I'm alright [about rules], suits me.*'

As already noted, most foster carers felt they ought to provide foster
children with a 'proper' framework for family life which involved
spelling out the kinds of behaviour they expected from them. While
most, but not all, foster children (12/15) said they conformed to their
'strict' foster carers' rules (9/13 foster carers were classified as directive), some were clearly resentful of, albeit obedient to, restrictions
upon their freedom. Wayne's carer said she had to restrict Wayne's
activities outside the house because he acted in an 'irresponsible' way
and she wanted to protect him from making undesirable acquaintances

who might harm him. Wayne clearly resented being restricted and complained bitterly about a lack of freedom outside the house: '*At the moment I am not allowed to go anywhere, I've got to stay on this road.*' Debbie's foster carers insisted on 'standards' which Debbie interpreted as restrictions. While, on balance, Debbie suggested that she conformed to her foster carers' rules, she was very unhappy about doing so and turned to the interviewer for sympathy: '. . . *they treat me like a little kid and that. I'm not allowed out or something. They won't even let me have a boyfriend. Don't you think that is a bit sad?*'

Some children described how they 'learned' to comply with their parents' directiveness. Marsha (Black girl, step family, mother non-employed) said: '*Usually, when she [mother] asks us to do something, we do it. But if we don't do it, she talks to us and tells us why we have to do it and then the problem is solved. And then, the next time when she asks us, we just do it, because we know why we have to do it and what we get out of it.*' Marsha's mother corroborated her daughter's account and contrasted Marsha favourably with her older, rebellious sister: '*She knows, what is the point of disobeying me and she is never going to get to do anything? She tells me exactly where she is going and what she is doing. She learned that. So she tells me [where she is going] and she knows she can get to go [out]. She says she is going to be here seven o'clock, she's here seven o'clock. She says she is going to be with [friends], she's going to be with [friends] and nobody else. She's not going to take a D-route to anywhere, you know.*'

Some children who complied with their parents' expectations said their parents had no explicit rules. Sisters Lujahn and Sunita (South Asian, two-parent household, mother non-employed) both said their parents had no rules. Their father, who spoke on behalf of his wife who had a poor command of English, corroborated this statement, explaining that he was opposed to being strict with his children in the way he considered common amongst parents of similar cultural backgrounds. Yet, this father was still 'directive' in the sense that he expected the children to obey him: '*I think because I haven't made any rules, sometimes, you know, when you say something to them, they won't listen to you. If I say it twice, then they say, "I think he means that". They know that I'm a bit cross, they'd better do it.*' The children confirmed that they did as they were told. As Lujahn said: '*If they tell me to do something I do it, so there is no discussion.*'

(B) Directive mothers–negotiating children

In the top right-hand quadrant, a small number of children indicated that they sought to negotiate with their directive mothers (three boys and three girls). Mustafa's mother (South Asian, two-parent household, a shop assistant) said her children often refused to listen to her, while her husband was more authoritative: *'One shout [from father] and everybody sits up. They are all scared . . . but I have to shout about three or four times.'* Mustafa confirmed that his mother would shout at him to make him do things but most of the time, *'they let me do everything.'* Jamie's foster carer regarded rules as very important and considered herself to be strict. However, Jamie said he could change his carer's rules by sulking or crying.

The other four children in this quadrant, of which three were Black, appeared to engage in lengthy and often successful negotiations with their mothers, even though their mothers adopted directive approaches. Chloe's mother (Black, step family, a dressmaker), considered herself very much in control: *'[Chloe] knows she's got to do the housework, she's got to wash up, she's got to share everything. They know not to push it . . . Yes, they can have their say but at the end of the day, what I say goes!'* For her part, Chloe described how she set about negotiating with her mother about going to a party of which her mother disapproved:

I: *. . . if your mum said to you, 'I don't want you to do that' can you talk to her about it, or do you have to stick by her rule, and that's it?*

C: *No, I sit down and talk to her. I ask her why and she, like, tells me. And if it's a fair reason then I don't bother with it again.*

I: *Does she sometimes sort of change her rules and let you do things because you talked about it?*

C: *Yes, if I talk to her and she is a bit more settled about it. Because there is, like, a party what goes on every half-term. And at first she goes, 'I don't know if you can go Chloe.' And I ask her why and then she goes, 'I just don't know, I think you're a bit too young.' And I go, 'But mum, I've got all of those people I mentioned, my older sister and [step father's] children, we'll all go together.' So she let me go.*

Like Chloe's mother, Latasha's mother (Black, two-parent household, cashier), while claiming to be flexible and to listen to her children's opinions, considered herself to be in control. Like Chloe, Latasha would sometimes conform and sometimes negotiate, depending on whether or not she herself considered the rule reasonable. Bibi's mother (Black, two-parent household, a social worker) hinted that 'all would be well' as long as the children abided by her rules: *'I mean, I do describe the sort of things my children are expected to do. I know my students in college laugh because they think I'm strict. But I'm quite popular with the students because, again, it's the same thing. Most of the kids are*

Black and if I say I've got the same expectations as their parents, I think they do understand what I mean. They know I won't be flexible on that. But if you do observe those rules, then I'm a very generous person.' Bibi, while wishing to negotiate rules with her parents, acknowledged that her scope for changing their minds was constrained by her parents' veto. She had decided that conforming to rules in the present could act as a useful tactic for establishing a fund of goodwill in her parents which might make them more lenient at some future time: '. . . *when they say no [you can't go out] you just give up, it's not worth it. Then you've got a better chance of being let out next time.'*

(C) Negotiative mothers–negotiating children

In the bottom-right quadrant, a group of children constituting one third of the interview sample (12 girls and nine boys) said they were able to negotiate rules on a regular basis. Mothers generally set in train the negotiation process by acknowledging that children's point of view was a very important consideration, as was the case with Harinder's mother (South Asian, two-parent family, school special needs assistant):

I: *Does he [child] sometimes disagree with the decisions you make?*
M: *I encourage that. I think it's quite important, yes. I think it's important for me to listen to what they have to say. I quite value that, I think. Even if they are disagreeing it doesn't mean that I think it's right, but I still like to listen to them and give them my point of view.*
I: *Would you in the end sometimes change your mind about things? . . . Would you change your rules?*
M: *I think I would. I mean, that is the whole point of listening to them, really, and trying to understand a child, their point of view, as well.*

Harinder, while generally accepting of his parents' point of view, said he could negotiate a change and felt his parents were not very strict: '. . . *like sometimes they'll say "Do your homework" so I'll have to go and do it. Or [they say] "Go and do this." I might say, "Can I do this first?" and they'll say: "Yes". And then you do it.'*
    Baldev's mother (South Asian, two-parent family, mother a canteen assistant) also felt that children had the same right as parents to give their point of view: '*I think if the parents sit with the children and the children sit with the parents and have a bit [of a] chat, then we have to do a bit compromise, you know. It's not a big deal. If the children wants to do something else they can do something, isn't it?*' Baldev confirmed that he was able to negotiate household rules but that he only did so occasionally since he was generally in agreement with his parents:

I: *If you wanted to do something and they [parents] said 'No, you can't do that', could you talk to them about it?*

B: *Yes.*

I: *Will they listen to what you have to say?*

B: *Yes, they listen but if we realise they are in the right we understand. Then, if we have our own opinion we talk about it and then we settle on something.*

I: *And do they sometimes change their rules?*

B: *Sometimes, not often. Normally they are right.*

Jasmine's mother (white, step family, non-employed) felt that children should be allowed to give their opinion and that parents should compromise: *'If say they [children] think something is not right, I think the parents should discuss why the children are not very keen on it, umm, work together, I'd say, really.'* Because Jasmine thought that age and experience made her mother the best person to decide on the rules, we considered placing Jasmine in quadrant D (negotiative mothers/conforming children): *'Older people should tell you [what is] right really, because, like . . . I'm only 11, like, just say my mum is, like, twenty six years older than me . . . so really my mum knows better than me . . .'* However, we decided to place Jasmine in this quadrant since she also indicated that she tried to negotiate with her mother: *'I beg her [mother] until she says "Yes".'*

(D) Negotiative mothers–conforming children

In the bottom left-hand quadrant, a very small number of children (three boys and two girls) said they usually conformed to their parents' rules without questioning them, while their mothers' accounts indicate a preference for a negotiative approach. All five children said there was no need to negotiate because the household rules were reasonable. Three of these children lived with foster carers and they were all well integrated into their foster families. Liam had lived with the same foster carers for two years and had built up a close relationship with them. Liam's foster carer felt it was important to discuss rules with children: *'They should be able to say something, because it's their right as well. You can't have parents domineering the whole thing. You can't do that, it doesn't work. It doesn't work.'* Liam had no problem with his foster carers' relaxed approach since, as he suggested, this was what he had been used to at home with his birth parents: *'They [carers] are not strict, they are easy going . . . They've got simple rules . . . don't jump around in the front room, don't fling yourself on the sofa because you'll break it. I mean, all the rules that we had at home, we've got here, as if we are a good family, because we are, really.'*

Conclusions

In accordance with normative trends in modern family life, mothers and foster carers considered that, in order to learn to regulate themselves, children required 'guidelines' rather than rules. Mothers across different household types, cultures and social classes all subscribed to the desirability of regulating their children. The reasons they gave for exercising control over children varied. In some cases, the reasons were structural: the absence of the birth father from the household, the expectation that step fathers should not automatically act as substitute parents, and the need to ensure that children know what is expected (particularly evident among foster carers). Other justifications for providing children with rules or guidelines reflected mothers' social constructions of childhood, adulthood and parenthood: the need to constrain children's innate anarchic nature; the need to prepare children for a public world organised around rules, implicit and explicit; and the need to be, and to be seen to be, 'proper parents'.

Most children did not view their mothers as strict in accordance with mothers' views of themselves, with most children describing their mothers as flexible – 'a bit strict'. Others at first suggested that their mothers had no rules, but then went on to demonstrate how they had internalised their parents' expectations. Most children aged 11 to 12 years clearly regarded their parents' guidelines as reasonable and acceptable. The kinds of issues which mothers and children considered should be subject to regulation broadly overlapped and reflected the twin aims of parenting: to ensure that children should learn to be self regulating and, at the same time, protecting them from risk and danger. Children referred to rules about the time scheduling of their everyday lives as children; to parents' expectations concerning their personal hygiene, their behaviour towards persons and things, and the help they were required to give in the household.

Most mothers insisted that the 'right approach' to controlling their children involved listening to children's points of view. Most mothers did not regard themselves as having 'set rules', nor did they expect blind obedience from their children. In accordance with the dominant discourse of motherhood as 'caring', mothers rarely drew upon the language of 'strictness', with its connotations of domination and disempowerment. However, as we have argued, this apparently liberal attitude can easily conceal different forms of control which mothers exercise over children. We found it useful to classify mothers' approaches to their children's regulation as more or less 'directive' or more or less 'negotiative', according to whether mothers presented themselves as having the major say in decisions concerning their children, or whether they made decisions on the basis of a negotiated compromise. We found that foster carers and mothers in two-parent families were more likely to be directive while lone mothers and step family mothers were equally likely to adopt either approach. Listening to children's views meant that some mothers adjusted their decisions to take account of children's views and wishes while other mothers, although they also claimed to consult children, clearly made the decisions themselves. In these latter cases, the discursive strategies – 'discussing', 'listening', 'letting children have a say' were not predicated upon democratic practice which appeared to characterise the practices of the negotiative mothers. Yet, we want to stress that whatever the regulative approach adopted, the emphasis placed by mothers on the language of consultation, while recognising the right of children to be consulted, also constituted a strategy of control aimed at ensuring children's continuing compliance to their expectations.

The story which children told about their responses to parents' regulative approaches was largely one of congruence. In the main, children portrayed their mothers in similar ways to those described by the mothers themselves. They appeared to accept that most of their mothers' expectations as 'reasonable'. Some children suggested that their parents' rules and expectations were implicit. In effect these children had internalised parents' expectations and guidelines. Moreover, in the main, children portrayed their parents as 'fair' and considered that they were listened to.

When we examined children's and mothers' accounts together, we found some interesting variations. However, in only 11/63 cases were children's responses out of kilter with parents' regulative approaches. Directive mothers matched compliant children while negotiative mothers matched negotiative children. Only six of the 63 children suggested that they attempted to negotiate with their directive mothers and five children presented themselves as compliant while their parents and carers suggested a willingness to take account of children's wishes. This picture of congruence is powerful evidence, whatever the causal directions, of both mothers and children speaking from the same script.

There is one further point to be made which concerns the manifest and latent aspects of power and control (Bernstein 1996). Where the directive mothers made clear what they expected from their children and where they explained the reasons for rules and guidelines, this process rendered the rules transparent to children. By contrast, where mothers presented themselves as ready to negotiate the rules, it may well be there were no rules as such or it may simply be the case that mothers were not making them manifest. Under this condition, because the rules were opaque, children would have to 'read' the rules for themselves.

Moreover, if children interpreted an apparent lack of rules as giving them the power to set the parameters to their own autonomy, then they might seriously overestimate their own power if it turned out that rules existed but were unspoken. According to Bernstein's analysis (Bernstein 1975, 1996), negotiative mothers can be understood to be exercising control covertly over their children. However, within the constraints of this study, we can only suggest this as a probability rather than examine it thoroughly.

10 Conclusions

In the book we have sought to offer an account of children's perspectives on caring and family life in all its contemporary diversity. The book's central theme is the way care is thought about and provided in the different contexts of family life and children's views of care as givers and receivers. Based on a community sample of children living in London during the transition to secondary school, the study on which the book is based provided extensive data on children's views and experiences. The work also afforded intensive evidence drawn from in-depth interviews of groups of children who, over the course of their lives, had been through experiences of family change: becoming a lone mother household, becoming a step father family and going into foster care. The book covers a number of themes to which we return in this concluding chapter.

Children's normative beliefs about care: as givers and receivers

Care as an orientation and practical activity is an expression of the mutuality of the human condition; that is, we depend upon others for our welfare and well-being. It is also an expression of moral commitment that we ought to act towards others in caring ways. In the study, we examined children's understandings of the possibilities for, and the constraints upon, translating a commitment to care into action through a set of hypothetical, typical situations. In a school context (a vignette set in a school playground), children considered that they ought to care for one another. However, as new entrants to secondary school, children were weakly positioned and occupied low statuses within the hierarchical structure of the school, with its formal hierarchies of age, physical size and ability, and its informal cliques and peer groups. In the critical situation of trying to make new friends in a new school and to become part of a peer group, children showed some awareness of the context. They suggested the pressures upon children to conform to institutional and peer group cultures, in which difference and 'otherness' are looked down upon, and which could militate against acting in caring and inclusive ways, including in children's own schools.

With respect to the public world of the marketplace (a vignette showing children queuing in a shop), children considered how norms relating to the apparently even playing field of consumption, based on the assumption that all parties have money to spend, ought to over-ride differences which exist between customers, whether they be children, elderly people or middle-aged persons. In discussing how they thought children ought to be treated – that is, just like other customers – children testified to adults' often disrespectful ways of treating children by ignoring them as if they were less important.

With respect to the conduct of family change (a vignette showing a father leaving the marital home), children's views concerning how they considered parents ought to behave when their relationships broke down were strongly child-focused. More children thought that the father should stay than thought he should leave. All children emphasised the negative effects of the father's departure on the child, with all children suggesting the child would be very distressed initially and half of the children saying they would still feel this way a year later. However, children were also pragmatists and considered that they should live with the parent who, on the basis of past evidence, proved to be more caring, especially in terms of everyday availability. Moreover, in line with their view that family life ought to be chiefly about children, they considered that children ought to be taken into consideration by parents when they made decisions affecting children's family lives and living arrangements. Almost all children considered that children ought to have a say in such decisions as divorce.

Children's views about providing help to parents (a vignette set in a family business) drew upon commonplace meanings and social constructions of parenthood and childhood. Here children prioritised their commitments in relation to their status as school pupils over their commitments to helping their parents, and they considered they should make only a modest contribution. Reflecting general normative models of what it means to be a 'good mother', children considered that parents' first priority was to 'care'; that is, to give children time and attention. Providing for them as breadwinners and working long hours in the family business were not matters which children foregrounded since these conflicted with the requirement upon parents to be 'proper' parents – to be at home with and for their children, including helping children with their homework. Here again, children painted a normative picture of family life in which they located themselves as the central figures.

Children's positioning of themselves in relation to adults in the vignettes offer powerful insights into children's views of the way adults too often treat children in our society: how we may disregard children's presence in public places and how, when we make decisions which affect them, for example at divorce, we can forget that children also have feelings, views and wishes. Children's positioning of themselves in relation to other children suggests how children may have difficulty in practicing the ethic of care. These difficulties arise in the context of the hierarchies and cultures which exist in schools and which are largely shaped by the adult world.

Of course the views children expressed in these vignettes, especially the view that children's interests and perspectives should take priority, were idealised points of view. Just as adults assert principles which they negotiate often rather differently in practice, so children asserted normative principles which they interpret differently in their everyday lives. The strong normative emphasis upon the 'child-centredness' of family life, which may be understood also as an assertion of children's political interests as a collectivity or social category, was only part of the picture. In the conduct of their everyday lives, children showed, and were shown to be, strongly orientated towards other people. In talking about the ways in which they made a contribution to care in family life, particularly the provision of emotional support to parents, children showed themselves to be emotionally intelligent in placing themselves 'in the position of the other': they clearly identified and displayed competence in understanding their parents' feelings and need for support. However, it was children's mothers who elaborated upon this, not surprisingly since they were at the receiving end of children's emotional competence. Moreover, as some children suggested, their motivation for giving emotional care and a desire to understand the world from their parents' perspectives in some cases arose out of their wish to anticipate and so be able to manage the consequences of parents' actions. Those who spoke about wanting to prepare themselves in the event of problems mentioned parents' financial situations and relationship breakdown.

The meaning and importance of family

Children's representations of family life suggest that love and care, especially that provided consistently and on an everyday basis, are far more important to children than family structure. Most children held inclusive notions of family which encompassed different types of family forms, including lone parenthood and step families. In contrast, children did not consider childless couples to constitute 'proper families' but regarded them rather as 'families in waiting'. Children were generally critical of unitary notions of a 'proper family' particularly its connotations of conformity and cornflake packet images of happy families. Those who lived in lone mother and step families had more inclusive views of family forms compared with children living in two-parent, that is more traditional, types of, families and those who no longer lived with either parent (foster children). Children's criteria for family life included: the presence of children; living with at least one parent; a sense of security and a place to belong; and, most important of all, being able to give children unconditional love and care – *'people who never ever don't care about you'*, as one child put it. In short, more important to children was the way family life is lived than what family life ought to look like.

Nonetheless, children considered parents to be very important to them and their expectations of them were high. Interestingly, children's ways of talking about parents drew upon public discourses of gender equality, fairness and equal opportunities, for children constructed parenthood and parenting as largely 'gender free'. Children considered that mothers and fathers ought to provide children with the same types of care and to be equally involved in family life. By contrast, children reported less normative consensus on parents' labour market participation, expressing conservative attitudes on the one hand, notably stressing mothers' place in the home, and a less gendered approach on the other, suggesting that both mothers and fathers should be employed part time when children are small. Moreover, in line with these normative views of parenting, children were reluctant to differentiate between their own mothers and fathers for fear of being unfair to one or other parent. Yet, in reporting their everyday realities, lone mother children especially suggested that, more often than not, their mothers were more involved in their everyday care and, as a consequence, they considered them to be more important in practice. In this very real sense, household structure does makes a difference to children's lives.

On the other hand, no matter what type of household form children lived in, children still considered both their birth parents to be very important to them. They described their parents and carers' importance in a variety of ways, emphasising the importance of love and affection, although other key aspects of parenting such as security and setting boundaries (control) were assumed or understated. It was foster children, who lacked the continuity of at least one parent, who most starkly made the case for parents' importance: by including parents they rarely or never saw in their inner circles of significant others in spite of the most unpromising circumstances and relationships. As for adults who act *in loco parentis*, for example, step fathers, children suggested that these adults had to earn their importance in children's eyes and lives; for children's part, care and its reciprocity were matters to be worked at.

Next to parents, siblings figured large in children's lives. While most children did not articulate the ways in which their siblings provided them with a sense of meaning and ontological security, foster children whose family lives had broken down testified to the way their often absent or unknown siblings constituted an important source of symbolic attachment for them. In the face of discontinuity, siblings represented continuity; they symbolised the family that 'might have been' or had once existed.

Children's descriptions of their everyday lives suggested that they both gave support to and received support from siblings; they positioned siblings at the centre of their circles of significant others but recounted relationships marked by a combination of cooperation and contest. Siblings were said to provide a key resource in terms of acting as role models and in the development of practical skills and intellectual argument. Siblings sometimes acted as sources of emotional significance and sociability, especially where there were several children in the household who were near in age. Children engaged in 'sentient activity', that is, they identified their siblings' needs and responded empathetically to them. Children also provided their siblings with care in a practical sense, particularly younger siblings.

Children showed some reluctance to take on such caring roles, however, and were careful to note that they did not look after siblings 'by themselves'. Thus they argued for limits to children's responsibility according to normative notions of childhood as a 'protected time'. As already noted, a central theme of many children's accounts of sibling relations was contest and rivalry. For example, in negotiating access to scarce resources, including material privileges and parents' attention, children challenged their siblings and contested their siblings' claims to such resources. In this process, they not infrequently invoked hierarchies of age and birth order, depending upon their position within them, the number and spacing of siblings, and the different gender combinations.

Children talking about family change

The study sought to shed light on the processes, as well as the contexts, which shape children's experience of family change, albeit for many children their parents had separated or the family had become a step family some long time before the research project took place. While some children reported on the events of family change, sometimes in especially graphic terms, especially when it was totally unanticipated and parents had not prepared them for the event, others were reluctant to talk about these events or claimed not to recall them. For some children, the events were indeed far in the past.

Children's silence and reticence in responding to our questions about family change is, however, a matter for interpretation. As children hinted and as their mothers stated more explicitly, children did seem reluctant to think of their parents negatively or to criticise them openly. We can interpret children's reticence and silence in relation to the research process – as responses to us as adults and as researchers, and in terms of a desire to be seen to be loyal and fair to both their parents, resident and non-resident. (This non-judgemental view was also evident in their normative views of parenting and parenthood.) On the other hand, children's silence and reticence may be interpreted in terms of the 'gestalt' of the stories they may have been telling themselves about their lives. In the case of foster children (and to some extent, some of the lone mother and step family children), children revealed themselves over the course of their interviews to be ambivalent about their non-resident parents: while still loving their parents, they were not happy that parents had absented themselves from their lives or with the little effort some parents made to see them. A few foster children did not wish to see their parents. Yet, in many cases, they identified their non-resident parents as key persons in their lives; they loved them but at the same time felt disappointed, angry and betrayed by them.

Family life beyond the household

Children at this point in their life course seemed in many cases to be still strongly connected, in practical and emotional senses, to their families. This is not surprising since moving to secondary school often disrupted ties of friendship and local community. Some children who had a strong family orientation clearly had not yet felt the need to strike out and seek new activities and relationships beyond their families.

Children's descriptions of their ties with their kin during later childhood suggest that they defined family boundaries inclusively and loosely. The number of persons children identified as important to them suggests that their significant others extended well beyond the limits of the household. From children's vantage point, families not only provide children with parents, they afford opportunities for ties with siblings who sometimes live with them and sometimes live elsewhere. However, children's ties with kin were generally not within their control. Within and between different family forms, children's ties with non-resident parents and siblings were, in fact, very variable. Moreover, while for some children family networks were clearly subject to change, for others family networks were much more static. For example, some children had never known their step or half siblings, while others' contact varied over time. As far as foster children were concerned, having siblings they rarely or never saw did not detract from their importance. Rather, siblings represented a source of meaning and symbolic attachment to the families they had lost, and reflected idealised notions of a 'proper' family which they had never experienced.

Children's range of significant others to whom they attached great importance (those they placed in the inner circle) also covered a host of other people including grandparents, blood-related aunts and uncles, friends, and those we termed 'formal others' (teachers, doctors, social workers). Children indicated that their significant others were important to them in many particular ways. Grandparents emerged as significant figures, especially maternal grandparents, while contrary to cultural assumptions, South Asian origin children were as likely to mention maternal as paternal grandparents. Neither regular contact with, nor indeed living with a grandparent, guaranteed that children placed them in their inner circles of significant others. Step family children, who had the largest family networks on average, stressed the importance of blood ties and rarely included 'grandparent-type' relationships acquired through their step fathers in their circles of significant others.

Grandparents were considered by children to be important in symbolic, practical and expressive ways: in 'being there for them', in providing gifts and practical care, notably when children were young or, in some cases, when their parents' marriages broke down. Grandmothers were, on the whole, depicted as loving, kindly, supportive figures while grandfathers were portrayed in more quirky ways – as funny, jokey, clever. In return for the 'specialness' of being a grandchild, children sought to be concerned about and helpful to their grandparents. Perhaps more surprising was the high regard in which children held relatives – especially their blood-related aunts and uncles. In the Questionnaire Survey, contact with these relatives was more frequent than with grandparents and non-resident fathers, although this is probably because their aunts and uncles were more numerous and not all children had living grandparents.

By contrast, the significance children attributed to friends was much more variable. Rather few children talked about 'best friends', with most children mentioning friends who were the same sex and same age as themselves. Friends had different meanings for children (James 1993): 'having friends' brought group inclusion, and a sense of social identity, especially for boys, while 'being friends' provided children with relational resources – opportunities for confiding, a sense of personal identity and emotional and moral support. However, for some children friends were less important than family, particularly for some

South Asian origin children. Many children mentioned 'old friends', whom they had known since nursery, who provided them with a sense of meaning and continuity in their lives. Since children's friendships were negotiated in a number of different contexts – home, school and the wider community, they were subject to the ebb and flow of external events which could alter and, in some cases, disrupt children's friendships, notably the transition to secondary school. Some children, particularly some of the lone mother children, appeared to have few friends or few long-term friends, perhaps because of family change. The friendships of foster children showed pronounced characteristics which were undoubtedly related to their life histories as foster children: some included friends they had only just made, some mentioned friends with whom they had lost contact, while some children were very indiscriminate and included all the children in their classes at school. Moreover, as several children across the different family forms suggested, friendships were largely a matter of choice but depended upon the will and whim of the other as well as the self. At a time when children's social networks were undergoing change – that is, during the transition to secondary school – children seemed to consider friendships to be less dependable compared with family relationships which were seen as more reliable, despite disruption caused by parents' divorce.

In addition, children included among their significant others professionals who delivered public services to them. According to some children, these adults played an important role in their lives: teachers were seen to be helpful to children when they sought to overcome obstacles in learning; family doctors were seen to be supportive figures in times of illness; for foster children, social workers were seen as persons to turn to, for example, a postman was valued for bringing news of a foster child's non-resident siblings.

Children as active contributors to care

We have suggested that children are active members of family life and also contributors to care. However, children's views of childhood as a time when children ought to be freed from work, though not from school work, shaped their views about helping at home. While most children suggested that they ought to give some help at home, on the whole they gave only qualified support to the idea, suggesting that their contribution should be modest. However, the reasons children gave for helping related to the ethic of care – helping parents because they needed help or helping as the 'normal' expectation of being part of a family. Children also mentioned intrinsic aspects of care in terms of 'liking to help' although a direct question revealed that children were more ambivalent than they first appeared. Instrumental orientations to providing help (payment for housework) received little support from children, with more support from white children than other ethnic groups, in that payment for housework was seen to transgress family mutuality.

While children made a considerable contribution in terms of reported frequency to household work, especially contributing to their own self maintenance, they reported a higher frequency of general caring – both caring for and about other people including mothers, fathers, siblings, classmates, elderly people and pets. It was difficult to assess how far children helped out of a sense of responsibility although it is likely that being kind and nice to others constituted more spontaneous acts of care than doing housework. Few children volunteered many examples of tasks for which they took charge, yet most said they did household jobs without being asked, although frequency of doing tasks without being asked was lower for tasks done for others than it was for self-maintenance. Passing on jobs to siblings was also commonplace and part and parcel of sibling rivalries and hierarchies.

While children's contribution in material terms may well be modest, the interviews were punctuated with examples where children displayed competence in understanding their parents' feelings and situations. Almost in passing, children noted the ways in which they showed understanding and the support they gave parents. In some cases, they indicated that they appreciated what their parents did for them and wished to reciprocate. However, as already noted, it was mothers, as the receivers rather than the givers of this support, who elaborated upon the impact on them of children's gestures of support. Mothers portrayed children as sentient actors who, often remarkably in their eyes, understood their feelings and situations and they drew considerable comfort from their children's symbolic gestures, epitomised in cups of tea proffered at the right moment and in times of stress and crisis. Just as affective, emotional and symbolic sources of support are central components of care, with which mothers sought to provide their children, so children also demonstrated that this was what they sought to provide for their mothers. Children testified to their own emotional intelligence in a variety of, albeit often under-stated, ways. As one boy noted, just as children want their mothers to 'be there for them', so children seek to 'be there for parents'.

Despite this evidence, many mothers and some children viewed later childhood as a protected period in which children ought not to perform 'proper' work, and in which children's 'special' status and sensitivity needed to be safeguarded. In addition, mothers' and children's rationalities for contributing to housework work and care, while being in part embedded in the everyday mutuality of everyday life, also referred to notions of self responsibility, self care and independence; in short they made reference to the developmental paradigm of children as 'adults in waiting'.

Children and parental control

As we argued at the beginning of the book, the concept of care has traditionally been separated from the concept of 'control' and vice versa. But care and control may be seen as two sides of the same coin: parental regulation of children may be understood as ways in which parents care for and about children while, from the perspective of children being regulated, care may be largely interpreted in terms of the exercise of control. Moreover, as we have also argued, just as adults and children interpret and translate the ethic of care into negotiated practices, so children were seen by mothers and children to need general boundaries to 'guide' behaviour rather than hard and fast, explicitly articulated rules to 'govern' behaviour. In accordance with the ethic of care, many mothers were, in principle, against strictness, with its authoritarian connotations, and sought to portray their approaches as child-oriented; they considered it important to listen to children's views and wishes. In practice, mothers trod a tightrope between wanting their children to learn to regulate their own behaviour while, at the same time, being proactive in protecting them from risk and danger.

However, according to both children's and parents' accounts, there were differences in emphasis between the modes of control which mothers adopted: on the one hand we identified 'directive' approaches – where mothers presented themselves as having the major say in decisions concerning their children and, on the other, we typified mothers as 'negotiative' where decisions were made by parents and children as negotiated compromises. We found that foster carers and mothers in two-parent families were more likely to be directive, while lone mothers and step family mothers were equally likely to adopt either approach. Thus, while all mothers claimed to listen to children, the discourses of 'discussing', 'listening' and 'letting children have a say' were not necessarily predicated upon democratic practice.

Children's responses to parents' regulation were largely congruent with their mothers' approaches. Compliant children matched directive mothers, while negotiative children matched negotiative mothers. Moreover, children in the main portrayed their mothers in similar ways to those described by their mothers. Where their mothers were overtly directive, most children suggested that their mothers were 'fair' and 'reasonable' while other children suggested that they had internalised parents' rules and expectations. There were, however, some cases of non-congruence. Only a few children suggested that they attempted to negotiate with their directive mothers and, similarly, a few presented themselves as compliant when their mothers appeared willing to take account of children's wishes. This picture of congruence is powerful evidence, whatever the causal directions, of both mothers and children speaking from the same script. However, where mothers presented themselves as ready to negotiate rules, it may well be that they were not exercising control. Alternatively, it may be that mothers were not making their control manifest. In this situation, because the rules were opaque, children would be required to 'read' the rules for themselves. Moreover, if children interpreted an apparent absence of rules as giving them the power to set the parameters to their own autonomy, then they might seriously overestimate their own power if it turned out that rules existed but were unspoken. It is possible, therefore, that negotiative mothers were exercising control over children in covert ways.

In conclusion, there are a number of clear messages about how children view and experience family life. First, children emerge as active co-participants in care and co-constructors of family life. Like adults, they make sense of the rules which guide caring behaviour and negotiate them in relation to particular contexts and situations. They make sense of their experiences of family life and family change. However, children do not necessarily talk about, much less explain, their family relationships in the research encounter. Second, in terms of how they think family life ought to be conducted, children are strongly child oriented, asserting the centrality of children to family life, and the need to prioritise the interests, needs and concerns of children. Third, in interpreting what it means to be a member of a family in practice and what it means to care, children show themselves to be pragmatic actors: on the one hand accepting different family forms as long as parents provide them with love and affection, and on the other hand they show themselves to be capable of exercising the ethic of care – of 'putting themselves in others' shoes', notably understanding the needs and feelings of their parents. Fourth, children apply highly inclusive and loose definitions to notions of family, placing importance on a wide range of kin beyond the household and also including pets, friends and professionals. Relations with family and especially with siblings are thus very important to children at this point in the life course, while friendships are subject to flux and change as children move to secondary school.

Finally, we wish to make two further points, one about our research design and one about methodology. The research design refers to the inclusion in the study of a group of children who, in some senses, could be seen to have 'lost' their families, that is the foster children. Having this group in the study served to illuminate the salient meanings and often taken for granted significance of families to children, especially the importance of parents and siblings. The methodological point is that while we sought to make children authors of their own life stories, inevitably our methods limited this ambition, notably the procedures whereby adult researchers required children to carry out tasks and answer our many questions, however sensitively we tried to do this. Moreover, a methodology which seeks to invoke reflexivity needs to match the inclination of research participants to engage in reflexivity at the time the research dictates. Children did not generally position themselves as commentators *on* their lives, nor did they often engage in detailed narratives of their past experiences. Children were living *in* their lives and getting on with the business of changing schools and negotiating their everyday routines. We tried to create as little disturbance as possible in their rhythms and concerns. Thus the story which we have told of family life, as children see it, is a 'between the lines story' based on children's often elliptical reports. Yet, while children may have been less discursive than their mothers in speaking about family life, they provided a particularly impressive body of knowledge to which we have tried to do justice.

Appendix

Chapter 1

Table 1.1.1   Differences in secondary school samples (Questionnaire Survey)

	School 1 % n = 215	School 2 % n = 232	School 3 % n = 140	Sig.
Lone parent children	23	17	40	0.001
Asian origin	4	27	5	0.001
Black children	22	26	22	0.001
White children	65	40	52	0.001
Girls	38	41	41	Not sig.
Children with fathers in work	81	86	78	Not sig.
Children with mothers in work	66	73	56	0.01
Children in no earner households/one part-time earner	30	21	40	0.001
All fathers mentioned in higher status jobs (RG I and II) as % of those in work	10	50	15	0.001
Mothers in higher status jobs (RG I and II) as % of those in work	27	48	22	0.001

Table 1.1.2   Differences between primary and secondary schools (Questionnaire Survey)

	Primary % n = 349	Secondary % n = 592	All % n = 891	Sig.
Pupils living with lone parents	22	25	24	Not sig.
Asian origin pupils	23	14	17	0.00
Black pupils	26	24	25	0.00
White pupils	43	52	49	0.00
Girls	57	40	46	0.00
Fathers in work	81	82	82	Not sig.
Mothers in work	59	68	63	Not sig.
No earner households/one or two part-time earners	26	24	25	Not sig.
Higher status fathers	34	30	31	Not sig.
Higher status mothers	30	35	34	Not sig.

Table 1.2   Children's ethnicity by self-report (Questionnaire Survey) (N = 895)

Ethnicity	%
White	49
Black	25
Asian	17
Other	10

Table 1.3   Children's household type by children's ethnic origin (Questionnaire Survey) (N = 891)

	Asian %	Black %	White %	Other %	Total %
Two-parent	90	47	68	61	66
One parent	8	40	20	31	24
Step parent	1	11	11	5	9
Other	1	2	1	3	1

Significant difference $p < 0.001$.

Table 1.4   Resident mothers' employment (Questionnaire Survey) (N = 837)

	Asian %	Black %	White %	Other %	Total %
Full-time	35	38	32	18	33
Part-time	20	26	27	35	27
Paid job	5	5	9	8	7
Non-employed	40	31	32	39	34

Significant difference $p < 0.00$.

Table 1.5   Resident fathers' employment (Questionnaire Survey) (N = 652)

	Asian %	Black %	White %	Other %	Total %
Full-time	70	71	68	63	69
Part-time	10	16	14	19	14
Paid job	3	1	4	4	3
Non-employed	17	12	14	14	14

Differences not significant.

Table 1.6   Occupational classification of resident parents (Questionnaire Survey)

	Fathers % n = 505	Mothers % n = 493
I and II Professional and managerial	32	34
IIINM Clerical, etc.	15	31
IIIM Skilled manual	42	8
IV and V Semi-skilled and unskilled	10	27

Chapter 2

Table 2.1   Children's responses to vignette: Jane in the school playground

	Caring/ inclusive/ positive	Uncaring/ exclusive/ negative	Mixed	Other/no different	Don't know	N
Moral imperative – What should group do in principle?	53	2	4	–	–	59
Group's perceptions of Jane as outsider	7	31	17	2	2	59
What would group do in practice at child's school?	32	10	7	7	1	57
Effect on group's response of being teenagers	12	22	4	15	5	58

Table 2.2   Children's responses to vignette: two children in the shop

	Agree/yes	Disagree/ no	Ambivalent/ partial	Don't know	N
The shopkeeper should serve the children first	59	–	–	–	59
Children have similar experience of being bypassed by shopkeeper	41	13	–	–	54
Elderly lady should be served first	30	16	11	1	58
Adults should protect children	28	1	10	1	40

Table 2.3   Children's responses to vignette: Joe and his father's departure from the family home

	Yes/ positive/ better	No/ negative/ mixed	Other	Not sure	N
Children's views about whether Joe's father should leave	17	36	17	–	60
Children's assessment of Joe's feelings at the time of separation	–	60	–	–	60
If children consider Joe will feel better after 1 year	28	23	4	2	57
If children consider Joe should have a say concerning which parent he lives with	56	2	–	1	59

Table 2.4   'Should parents divorce?' by household type (Questionnaire Survey) (N = 895)

What should parents do?	One parent %	Two- parent %	Step parent %	Other %	All %
Parents should talk more to each other	40	47	37	25	44
Separate for a while and try living together again	30	26	30	50	28
Don't know	12	10	11	–	11
Divorce	8	4	10	19	5
Something else	7	7	8	–	7
Stay together even if unhappy	3	6	4	6	5

Significant difference $p < 0.02$.

Table 2.5   Children's responses: Seeta in the family business

	Agree/ positive	Agree conditionally	Disagree/ negative	Other	Don't know	N
If Seeta should help parents	12	36	8	–	–	58
If child would help	9	–	11	4	–	24
If gender makes a difference	11	1	44	–	–	56
If Seeta's parents' long hours affects family life	53	–	3	–	1	57

Chapter 7

Table 7.1   Children's contact with relatives outside the household *in the past week* by children's ethnic origin (Questionnaire Survey)

	Grandparents* % (N = 843)	Aunts/uncles* % (N = 843)	Cousins* % (N = 844)	Siblings* % (N = 764)	Other* % (N = 788)
Asian	34	63	59	9	36
Black	34	57	54	25	35
White	55	49	41	21	28
Other	50	53	48	25	21
All	46	54	48	20	31

* Significant difference $p < 0.05$.

Table 7.2   Who children report spending free time with by ethnic origin (Questionnaire Survey) ($N = 831$)

	Mainly with family %	Mainly with friends %	Partly family/ partly friends %	On own %
Asian	33	10	51	6
Black	26	24	47	4
White	24	20	52	4
Other	28	14	57	1
All	26	19	51	4

Significant difference $p < 0.04$.

Chapter 8

Table 8.1 Children's contribution in past week to 'self-care' and 'family-care' tasks without being asked by frequency (percentages in brackets are children's contribution, whether or not asked to do house work (Questionnaire Survey))

'Self-care' tasks	Every day %	Some days %	Not at all %	n
Make something to eat for yourself	37 (37)	51 (55)	12 (8)	788 (802)
Clear away own dirty dishes	24 (31)	48 (46)	28 (23)	791 (799)
Tidy/clean own room	25 (28)	58 (56)	17 (16)	797 (811)
Wash own sports kit	9 (8)	23 (24)	69 (68)	782 (799)
'Family-care' tasks				
Lay/clear the table	20 (26)	43 (49)	38 (25)	782 (797)
Wash up/fill or empty dish washer	17 (21)	39 (43)	44 (36)	777 (791)
Make something to eat for someone else	18 (18)	54 (60)	28 (22)	791 (803)
Vacuum or dust	16 (16)	49 (57)	35 (27)	786 (800)

Children in the study

N.B. For reasons of confidentiality, a few mothers who were working have been noted here as 'non-employed', and vice versa.

Children in two-parent families

Child's name	Ethnicity (white/black/South Asian)	Mother's occupation	Father's occupation
Harinder	South Asian	School special needs helper (f/t)	Plumber
Lujayn; Sunita (sister)	South Asian "	Non-employed "	Ambulance driver "
Kevin	White	Playgroup supervisor (p/t)	Driving instructor
Mustafa	South Asian	Shop assistant (p/t)	Van driver
Lee	White	School meals supervisor (f/t)	Labourer
Rohini	South Asian	Non-employed	Non-employed
Jahangir	South Asian	Computer operator (p/t)	Laboratory assistant
Latasha	Black	Cashier (p/t)	Trainee social worker
Ceri	White	Educational psychologist (f/t)	Systems analyst
Niaz	South Asian	Clothing cutter (f/t)	Delivery driver
Jake	Black	Dental nurse (f/t)	Packer
Bibi	South Asian	Social worker (f/t)	Solicitor
Hayfa	South Asian	Playgroup supervisor (p/t)	Student (accountancy)
Baldev	South Asian	Canteen assistant (f/t)	Electrician (s/e)

Children living with lone mothers

Child's name	Ethnicity (white/black/ South Asian)	Mother's occupation
Serena	Black	Care assistant, old people's home (f/t)
Willy	White	Barmaid (p/t)
Claudia	White/Black	Non-employed
Tara	South Asian	Non-employed
Rebecca	White	Homehelp (p/t)
Lenny	Black	Nursing auxilliary (f/t)
Leila	White/Black	Hospital administrator (p/t)
Salome	White	Non-employed
Sally	White	Non-employed
Mirza	South Asian	Non-employed
Inderpal	South Asian	Non-employed
Clark	Black	School meals supervisor (p/t)
Lucy	White/South Asian	Social worker (f/t)
Andrew	White	Playgroup supervisor (p/t)
Amos	Black	Non-employed
Leroy	Black	Non-employed
Zarina	South Asian	Bank clerk
Elliott	Black	Secretary (f/t)

Children in step father families

Child's name	Ethnicity (white/black/ South Asian)	Mother's occupation	Step father's occupation
Marsha	Black	Non-employed	Traffic warden
Amy	White	Playgroup helper/ Cleaner (p/t)	Housing officer
Daniela	White	Non-employed	Non-employed
Steve	White	Post-woman (f/t)	Machine tool operator
Scott	White	Non-employed	Carpet fitter
Tracy	White	Data processor (f/t)	Scaffolder
Barry	White	Cleaner (f/t)	Spray painter
Daniel	Black	Bank clerk (f/t)	Carpenter
Cliff	Black	Care assistant (f/t)	Telephone fitter
Chloe	Black	Dressmaker (f/t)	Ticket collector
Ben	White	Canteen assistant (p/t)	HGV driver
Emily	White	University lecturer (f/t)	Manager in NHS
Anna	White	Barmaid (p/t)	Toolmaker
Jasmine	White/South Asian	Non-employed	Postman
Jordan	White	Personnel officer (f/t)	Non-employed

Children living with foster carers*

Child's name	Ethnicity (white/black/ South Asian)	Male carer's occupation
Wayne	White	Transport worker
Gail Mandy } sisters	Black	Non-employed
David	White	Motor mechanic
Claire	White	Bus inspector
Jason	White	Non-employed
Melanie Liam } siblings	White	Ambulanceman
Debbie	White	Van driver
Jamie	Black	Non-employed
Robert	White	Computer programmer
Kayley	White	Care worker
Elaine	Black	Non-employed
Keith	White	Print machine operator
Adam	White	Dry-cleaner

*Most of the female carers in this group are full-time foster carers.

References

Ahmad, W. I. U. (1996) 'Family obligations and social change among Asian communities.' In Ahmad, W. I. U. and Atkin, K. (eds) *'Race' and Community Care*. Buckingham: Open University Press.

Alanen, L. (1998) 'Children and the family order: constraints and competitiveness.' In Hutchby, I. and Moran Ellis, J. (eds) *Children and Social Competence*. London: Falmer Press.

Amato, P. R. and Ochiltree, G. (1987) 'Interviewing children about their families: a note on data quality. *Journal of Marriage and the Family*, 49, 669–75.

Andenaes, A. (1996) 'Challenges and solutions for children with two homes in the Nordic countries.' In Brannen, J. and Edwards, R. *Perspectives on Parenting and Childhood: Looking back and moving forward*. London: South Bank University.

Andenaes, A. and Haavind, H. (1993) 'When parents are living apart: challenges and solutions for children in two homes. In Leira, A (ed.) *Family Sociology: Developing the field*, Report 93:5. Oslo: Institute for Social Research.

Aquilino, W. S. (1991) 'Family structure and home leaving: a further specification of the relationship. *Journal of Marriage and the Family*, 53, 999–1010.

Aries, P. (1962) *Centuries of Childhood: a social history of family life*. New York: Vintage.

Backett, K. (1982) *Mothers and Fathers: a study of the development and negotiation of parental behaviour*. London: Macmillan.

Benhabib, S. (1992) *Situating the Self*. Cambridge: Polity Press.

Berger, P. and Luckman, T. (1971) *The Social Construction of Reality: a treatise in the sociology of knowledge*. Harmondsworth: Penguin Books.

Berndt, T. L. (1986) 'Children's comments about their friendships.' In Perlmutter, M. (ed.) *Cognitive Perspectives on Children's Social and Behavioural Development*. Hillsdale (NJ): Lawrence Erlbaum.

Bernstein, B. (1975) *Class, Codes and Control: Vol. 3, Towards a theory of educational transmissions*. London: Routledge and Kegan Paul.

Berstein, B. (1996) *Pedagogy, Symbolic Control and Identity: theory, research critique*. London: Taylor and Francis.

Borland, M., Laybourn, A., Hill, M. and Brown, J. (1997) *Middle Childhood: the perspectives of children and parents*. London: Jessica Kingsley Publishers.

Brady, C. P., Bray, J. H. and Zeeb, L. (1986) 'Behaviour problems of clinic children: relation to parental marital status, age and sex of child.' *American Journal of Orthopsychiatry*, 56, 399–412.

Brannen, J. (1992) (ed.) *Mixing Methods: Qualitative and Quantitative Research*. Aldershot: Gower.

Brannen, J. (1993) 'The effects of research on participants: findings from a study of mothers and employment.' *The Sociological Review*, 41, 2, 328–46.

Brannen, J. (1995) 'Young people and their contribution to household work.' *Sociology*, 29, 2, 317–38.

Brannen, J. (1999) 'Caring for children.' In Walby, S. (1999) *New Agendas for Women*. Basingstoke: Macmillan.

Brannen, J., Dodd, K., Oakley, A. and Storey, P. (1994) *Young People, Health and Family Life*. Buckingham: Open University Press.

Brannen, J., Moss, P., Owen, C. and Wale, C. (1997) *Mothers, Fathers and Employment: Parents and the Labour Market in Britain 1984–1994*. Sheffield: Department for Education and Employment.

Brannen, J. and Storey, P. (1996) 'Child Health in Social Context: parental employment and the start of secondary school', *HEA Family Health Research Reports*. London: The Health Education Authority.

Cherlin, A. J., Furstenberg, F. F., Chase-Lonsdale, P. L., Kiernan, K. E., Robins, P. K., Morrison, D. R. and Teitler, J. O. (1991) 'Longitudinal studies of the effects of divorce on children in Great Britain and the United States.' *Science*, 252, 1386–9.

Chinouya-Mudari, M. and O'Brien, M. (1999) 'African Refugee Children and HIV/AIDS in London.' In Aggleton, P., Hart, G. and Davies P. (eds) *Families and Communities Responding to AIDS*. London: UCL Press.

Colton, M. (1989) 'Foster and residential children's perceptions of their social environments.' *British Journal of Social Work*, 19 (3), 217–33.

Dahlberg, G. (1996) 'Negotiating modern child rearing and family life in Sweden.' In Brannen, J. and Edwards, R. *Perspectives on Parenting and Childhood: looking back and moving forward*. London: South Bank University.

Davin, A. (1978) 'Imperialism and Motherhood.' *History Workshop Journal*, 5, 9–67.

Dawson, D. (1991) 'Family structure and children's health and well-being: data from the 1988 National Health Interview Survey on child health. *Journal of Marriage and the Family*, 53, 573–84.

Deven, F., Inglis, S., Moss, P. and Petrie, P. (1998) 'State of the art review on the reconciliation of work and family life for men and women and the quality of services.' *Research Report* RR44, London: Department for Education and Employment.

Dunn, J. (1988) *The Beginnings of Social Understanding*. Cambridge, MA: Harvard University Press.

Dunn, J. and McGuire, J. (1992) 'Sibling and peer relationships in childhood.' *Journal of Child Psychology and Psychiatry*, 33, 1, 67–105.

Edwards, R. and Alldred, P. (1999a) 'Children and young people's views of social research: the case of research on home–school relations.' *Childhood*, 6 (2), 261–81.

Edwards, R. and Alldred, P. (1999b) 'Home–school relations: children and young people negotiating familiarisation, institutionalisation and individualisation.' Paper presented in Leeds, July 1999.

Elliott, J. and Richards, M. (1991) 'Children and divorce: educational performance and behaviour before and after separation.' *International Journal of Law and the Family*, 5, 258.

Ferri, E. and Smith, E. (1998) *Step-parenting in the 1990s*. London: Family Policy Studies Centre.

Finch, J. (1989) *Family Obligations and Social Change*. Cambridge: Polity Press.

Finch, J. and Groves, D. (1983) (eds) *A Labour of Love: women, work and caring*. London: Routledge and Kegan Paul.

Finch, J. and Mason, J. (1993) *Negotiating Family Obligations*. London: Routledge.

Flewelling, F. L. and Bauman, K. E. (1990) 'Family structure as a predictor of initial substance use and sexual intercourse in early adolescence.' *Journal of Marriage and the Family*, 52, 171–81.

Frones, I. (1994) 'Dimensions of Childhood.' In Qvortrup, J. (ed.) *Childhood Matters: social theory, practice and politics*. Aldershot: Avebury.

Furstenberg, F. F. (1987) 'The New Extended Family: the experience of parents and children after remarriage.' In Pasley, K. and Ihinger-Tallman, M. (eds) *Remarriage and Step Parenting*. Guildford: New York.

Ghate, D. and Daniels, A. (1997) *Talking About My Generation: A Survey of 8–15 Year Olds Growing Up in the 1990s*. London: NSPCC.

Gilligan, C. (1982) *In a different voice*. London: Harvard University Press.

Goodnow, J. and Delaney, S. (1989) 'Children's household work: differentiating types of work and styles of assignment.' *Journal of Applied Developmental Psychology*, 10, 209–26.

Goodnow, J. (1991) 'The nature of responsibility: children's understanding of "your job".' *Child Development*, 62, 156–65.

Graham, H. (1991) 'The concept of caring in feminist research: the case of domestic service.' *Sociology*, 25, 1, 61–78.

Hallden, G. (1991) 'The child as "project" and the child as "being": parents' ideas as frames of reference.' *Children and Society*, 5, (4), 334–56.

Hartup, W. W. (1992) 'Friendships and their developmental significance.' In McGurk, H. (ed.) *Childhood Social Development*. Hove: Lawrence Erlbaum.

Haskey, J. (1994) 'Stepfamilies and stepchildren in Great Britain.' *Population Trends*, 76. OPCS/HMSO.

Hill, M. and Tisdall, K. (1997) *Children and Society*. London: Longman.

Hillman, M., Adams, J. and Whitelegg, J. (1991) *One False Move: a study of children's independent mobility*. London: Policy Studies.

Hockey, J. and James, A. (1993) *Growing Up and Growing Old*. London: Sage.

Hodges, J. (1996) 'The natural history of early nonattachment.' In Bernstein, B. and Brannen, J. (eds) *Children, Research and Policy*. London: Taylor and Francis.

Holtermann, S., Brannen, J., Moss. P. and Owen, C. (1999) *Lone Parents and* the Labour Market: results from the 1997 Labour Force Survey and Review of Research*. Report ESR23. Sheffield: Employment Service.

James, A. and Prout, A. (1996) 'Strategies and structures: towards a new perspective on children's experience of family life.' In Brannen, J. and O'Brien, M. (eds) *Children in Families: Research and Policy*. London: Falmer Press.

James, A. (1993) *Childhood Identities: social relationships and the self in children's experiences*. Edinburgh: Edinburgh University Press.

James, A. (1995) 'Methods of competence for a competent methodology?' Paper presented to Children and Social Competence conference, Surrey, July 1995.

James, A., Jenks, C. and Prout, A. (1998) *Theorising Childhood*. Cambridge: Polity Press.

James, A. and Prout, A. (1990) *Constructing and Reconstructing Childhood*. Brighton: Falmer Press.

Jamieson, L. (1987) 'Theories of family development and the experience of being brought up.' *Sociology*, 21, 591–607.

Kosonen, M. (1994) 'Maintaining sibling relationships – neglected dimension in child care practice.' *British Journal of Social Work*, 26, 809–22.

Kosonen, M. (1996) 'Siblings as providers of support and care during middle childhood: children's perceptions.' *Children and Society*, 10, 267–79.

Land, K. and Rose, H. (1985) 'Compulsory altruism for some or an altruistic society for all?' In Bean, P., Ferris, J. and Whynes, D. (eds) *In Defence of Welfare*. London: Tavistock.

Laybourn, A., Brown, J. and Hill, M. (1996) *Hurting on the Inside: Children, Families and Alcohol*. Aldershot: Avebury.

Levin, I. (1995) 'Children's Perceptions of Family.' In Brannen, J. and O'Brien, M. (eds) *Childhood and Parenthood*. London: Institute of Education.

Lewis, S., Smithson, J., Brannen, J., das Dores Guerreiro, M., Kugelberg, C., Nilsen, A., O'Connor, P. (1998) *Futures on Hold: Young Europeans talk about combining work and family*. Manchester: IOD Research Group.

Maclean, M. and Eekelaar, J. (1997) *The Parental Obligation: a study of parenthood across households*. Oxford: Hart Publishing.

Mason, J. (1996) 'Gender, care and sensibility in family and kin relationships.' In Holland, J. and Atkins, L. (eds) *Sex, Sensibility and the Gendered Body*. London: Macmillan.

Mauthner, M. (1997) 'Methodological aspects of collecting data from children: lessons from 3 research projects.' *Children and Society*, vol. 11, 16–28.

Mayall, B. (1994) 'Children in action at home and at school.' In Mayall, B. (ed.) *Children's Childhoods: observed and experienced*. London: Falmer Press.

Mednick, B. R., Baker, R. L. and Carothers, L. E. (1990) 'Patterns of family instability and crime: the association of timing of the family's disruption with subsequent adolescent and young adult criminality.' *Journal of Youth and Adolescence*, 19, 201–20.

Mitchell, A. (1985) *Children in the middle*. London: Tavistock.

Moore, M., Sixsmith, J. and Knowles, K. (1996) *Children's Reflections on Family Life*. London: Falmer Press.

Morgan, D. (1996) *Family Connections*. Cambridge: Polity Press.

Morrow, V. (1996) 'Rethinking childhood dependency: children's contributions to the domestic economy.' *Sociological Review*, 44, 1, 58–77.

Morrow, V. (1998) *Understanding Families: Children's Perspectives*. London: NCB.

Neale, B. and Smart, C. (1998) 'Agents or dependants? Struggling to listen to children in family law and family research.' *Working Paper 3*, University of Leeds: The Centre for Research on Family, Kinship and Childhood, Department of Sociology and Social Policy.

Neale, B., Wade, A. and Smart, C. (1998) ' "I just get on with it." Children's experiences of family life following parental separation or divorce.' *Working Paper 1*, University of Leeds: The Centre for Research on Family, Kinship and Childhood, Department of Sociology and Social Policy.

Newman, J. L., Roberts, L. R. and Syre, C. R. (1993) 'Concepts of family among children and adolescents: effect of cognitive level, gender and family structure.' *Developmental Psychology*, 29, 6, 951–62.

Nicholson, J. M., Fergusson, D. M. and Horwood, L. J. (1999) 'Effects of later adjustment of living in a step family during childhood and adolescence.' *Journal of Child Psychology and Psychiatry*, 40 (3), 405–16.

Oakley, A. (1996) 'Gender Matters: man the hunter.' In *Young people's social attitudes: having their say – the views of 12–19 year olds*. London: Barnardos.

O'Brien, M. (1995) 'Allocation of resources in households: children's perspectives.' *Sociological Review*, 43, 3, 501–17.

O'Brien, M., Aldred, P. and Jones, D. (1996) 'Children's Constructions of Family and Kinship.' In Brannen, J. and O'Brien, M. (eds) *Children in Families: Research and Policy*. London: Falmer.

O'Brien, M. and Jones, D. (1995) 'Young People's Attitudes to Fatherhood.' In Moss, P. (ed.) *Father Figures: Fathers in the Families of the 1990s*. Edinburgh: HMSO.

Ribbens, J. (1994) *Mothers and their Children: A Feminist Sociology of Childrearing*. London: Sage.

Richards, M. (1996) 'The socio-legal support for divorcing parents and their children.' In Bernstein, B. and Brannen, J. (eds) *Children, Research and Policy*. London: Taylor and Francis.

Riley, D. (1981) 'The free mothers': pronatalism in industry at the end of the last war in Britain.' *History Workshop Journal*, 11, 59–117.

Roche, J. (1996) 'The politics of children's rights.' In Brannen, J. and O'Brien, M. (eds) *Children in Families: Research and Policy*. London: Falmer Press.

Sevenhuijsen, S. (1993) Paradoxes of gender: ethical and epistemological perspectives on care in feminist political theory, *Acta Politica*, 2, 131–49.

Sevenhuijsen, S. (1998) 'Caring in the third way.' *Working paper 12*. Leeds: Centre for Research on Family, Kinship and Childhood.

Sibley, D. (1995) 'Families and domestic routines: constructing the boundaries in childhood.' In Pile, S. and Thrift, N. (eds) *Mapping the subject: geographies of cultural transformation*. London: Routledge.

Smart, C. and Neale, B. (1998) *Family Fragments?* Cambridge: Polity Press.

Social Trends, 28, London: The Stationery Office.

Song, M. (1996) ' "Helping out": children's labour participation in Chinese take-away businesses in Britain.' In Brannen, J. and O'Brien, M. (eds) *Children in Families: research and policy*. London: Falmer Press.

Thomas, C. (1993) 'De-constructing Concepts of Care.' *Sociology*, 27, 4, 649–69.

Thomas, N. and O'Kane, C. 'Experiences of decision making in middle childhood: the example of children "looked after" by local authorities.' *Childhood*, 6, 3, 369–87.

Triseliotis, J., Borland, M., Hill, M. and Lambert, L. (1995) *Teenagers and the Social Work Services*. London: HMSO.

Tronto, J. (1993) *Moral Boundaries: a political argument for an ethic of care*. London: Routledge.

Ungerson, C. (1990) (ed.) *Gender and Caring: Work and Welfare in Britain and Scandinavia*. Hemel Hempstead: Wheatsheaf.

Walkerdine, V. and Lucey, H. (1989) *Democracy in the Kitchen: regulating mothers and socialising daughters*. London: Virago.

Waerness, K. (1984a) 'The rationality of caring.' *Economic and Industrial Democracy*, 5, 185–211.

Waerness, K. (1984b) 'Caring as women's work in the welfare state.' In Holter, H. (ed.) *Patriarchy in a Welfare Society*. Oslo: Universitetsforlaget.

Walczak, Y. and Burns, S. (1984) *Divorce, the child's point of view*. London: Harper.

Wittner, J. (1980) 'Domestic labor as work discipline: the struggle over housework in foster homes.' In Berk, S. F. *Women and Household Labor*. Beverley Hills: Sage.

Wyness, M. (1999) Childhood, agency and education reform. *Childhood*, 6, 3, 353–68.

Index

Bold type refers to main treatment of a topic where several page references are given. Entries in italic type refer to tables.